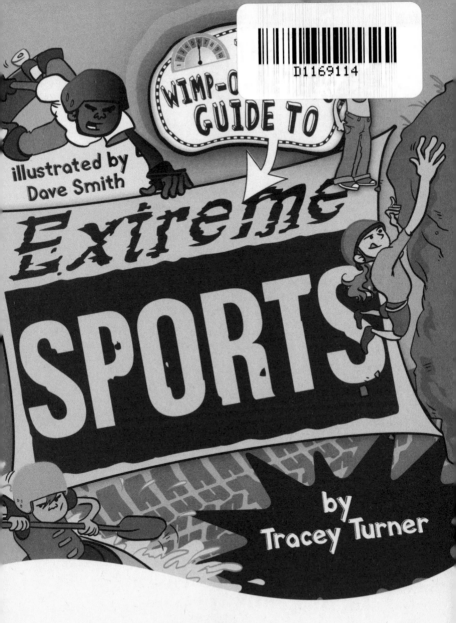

WIMP-O-METER
GUIDE TO

illustrated by
Dave Smith

Extreme

SPORTS

by
Tracey Turner

BARRON'S

First published as *The Wimp's Guide to Extreme Sports*
in 2013 by Franklin Watts, a division of
Hachette Children's Books, a Hachette UK company.

Text © Tracey Turner 2013
Illustrations by Dave Smith
© Franklin Watts 2013
Cover design by Cathryn Gilbert
Layout by Jonathan Hair

First edition for North America published in 2014
by Barron's Educational Series, Inc.

All inquiries should be addressed to:
Barron's Educational Series, Inc.
250 Wireless Boulevard
Hauppauge, New York 11788
www.barronseduc.com

ISBN: 978-1-4380-0399-3

Library of Congress Control Number: 2013943509

Date of Manufacture: January 2014
Manufactured by: B12V12G, Berryville, VA

Printed in the United States of America

9 8 7 6 5 4 3 2 1

*WARNING:
Extreme sports should
only be practiced under
expert supervision.

*The Publisher and Author accept no liability
for loss or injury sustained as a result of
reading this book. So you've been warned!

CONTENTS
• • • • • • • • • • • • • •

INTRODUCTION

There's nothing wrong with being a wimp. It makes perfect sense to be scared when, for example, you're plummeting down an almost vertical ski slope or dangling over a gaping abyss suspended by a piece of elastic.

There's a wimp inside all of us, and he or she is there for a very good reason— to stop us from doing dangerous stuff. Despite the obvious hazards of jumping off very tall things or sliding down slippery stuff, some people are determined to seek adrenaline-fueled adventure in the form of extreme sports. And there's a surprisingly wide variety of perilous stuff to do. . .

Prepare yourself, because we're about to take a white-knuckle ride through the world of extreme sports, dicing with danger and staring death straight in the eye. Though some of us might have to look through our fingers...

And just in case, maybe you should put on...

...a safety helmet...

...a life-jacket...

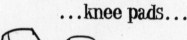

...a mouth guard...

...knee pads...

...and a safety harness.

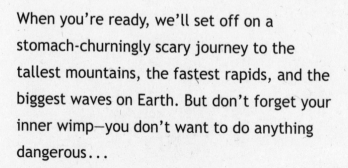

When you're ready, we'll set off on a stomach-churningly scary journey to the tallest mountains, the fastest rapids, and the biggest waves on Earth. But don't forget your inner wimp—you don't want to do anything dangerous...

EXTREME SPORTS: ON LAND

Dry land sounds like a pretty safe place to be— until you start hurtling down really steep parts of it at more than 150 mph, or performing impossible-looking tricks on bikes.

Extreme Bikes

Maybe you ride your bike to school. Perhaps, when you're feeling brave, you might cycle into the countryside, where you fearlessly ride along designated cycle paths. You have probably never considered speeding down steep slopes littered with jagged rocks and slippery mud banks, negotiating boulders and even wild animals...

BELIEVE IT OR NOT. . .
Mountain biker Robert Mennen was competing in the Cape Epic cross-country event in South Africa in 2013, when he encountered an unusual hazard: he was knocked off his bike by an antelope. The 40 mph crash broke the handlebars of Robert's bike and damaged his left collarbone, but fortunately both he and the antelope recovered.

He didn't see that coming!

Mountain Biking

This doesn't mean cycling down mountains—that would be really dangerous...

Oh, hang on a minute—actually it does mean cycling down mountains!

If you're brave enough, downhill cycling is one of the mountain bike events hard-as-nails riders can compete in, and they cycle down actual mountains as fast as they can.

Other mountain bike events include:

Cross-country (which is the most popular, and possibly the most grueling)

Dirt jumping (jumping over mounds of earth—but on your bike, which is a lot trickier)

Trials (mountain bike obstacle courses)

FACTS WIMPS NEED TO KNOW

DOWNHILL CYCLING
VITAL STATISTICS

• Races are against the clock, and courses usually take five minutes or less to complete— but it's an interesting five minutes.

• Some ski resorts double as downhill cycling courses in the summer. Courses include jumps and big drops.

• Mountain bikes designed for downhill racing have hydraulic disk brakes like the ones used in motorcycles and cars.

• Professional downhill bikes cost between $900 and $9,000.

• Bikes are made out of titanium.

Downhill cycling gear needs to be tough to protect the rider. In races, downhill cyclists reach speeds of more than 90 mph. **I hope they have good brakes!**

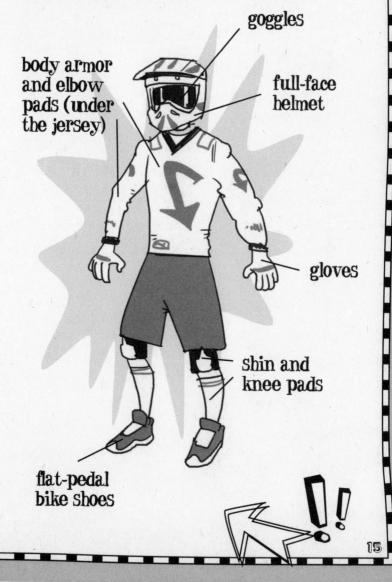

goggles

body armor and elbow pads (under the jersey)

full-face helmet

gloves

shin and knee pads

flat-pedal bike shoes

Extreme Bike Races

Could you ever, **in your wildest dreams**, be tough enough to compete in one of these tests of cycling endurance: La Ruta de los Conquistadores or the Race Across America?

LA RUTA DE LOS CONQUISTADORES

This is a mountain bike race across Costa Rica, in Central America. It follows the route of two of the sixteenth-century Spanish conquerors of Central and South America (the Conquistadors).

Sound easy enough? It's 224 miles long, from the west of the country to the east, and crosses the volcanic mountain chain that runs down the middle of Costa Rica—the peaks rise to more than 2 miles high.

Not put off yet? The race includes extremes of temperature—from tropical rain forests to freezing mountain passes—and competitors also have to deal with crossing rivers and active volcanoes.

La Ruta de los Conquistadores takes place every year in November over three days.

RACE ACROSS AMERICA

224 miles? Pah! Race Across America is more than ten times that—3,000 miles—from the west coast to the east coast.

Most bike races, such as the Tour de France, have stages. Each rider is timed for completing one stage, then they have a nice rest before beginning stage two the following day. But the Race Across America laughs in the face of such **namby-pamby** ideas.

• The clock runs non-stop, so competitors try to keep going as long as possible. There are rules about the amount of rest riders have to take, but there are no afternoon naps!

• Racers have a crew following them in a vehicle for safety reasons, and to provide food and water.

• Riders can race on their own or as part of a relay team. Solo riders cover between 250 and 340 miles per day.

Fastest Race Across America times:
Men—8 days, 9 hours and 47 mins.
Women—9 days, 4 hours and 2 mins.

FACTS WIMPS NEED TO KNOW ！！

FASTEST BIKES

There are a whole range of racing and mountain bike records:

- Flat surface (paced—towed by a specially designed motor vehicle)

- Flat surface (unpaced—not towed)

- Downhill on a volcano

- Downhill on snow

THE FASTEST SPEED EVER
RECORDED BY A BICYCLE ON
THE FLAT (UNPACED) IS . . .
A) 59 MPH
B) 71 MPH
C) 83 MPH
D) 242 MPH

Answer: C) The other speeds are a) top speed of an antelope, b) top speed of a cheetah, and d) the top speed of a plummeting peregrine falcon.

• Markus Stöckl from Austria holds the world record for the fastest bicycle speed downhill on snow*, at 130 mph.

• The Dutch cyclist Fred Rompelberg holds the flat surface (paced) world-record speed at 166.9 mph.

*On a factory-built bicycle

BMX

BMX is short for bicycle
motocross, because
it's the pedal-power
equivalent of motocross. There are five
different types of BMX: street, vert, park,
trail, and flatland. Each one has it's own
riding style and bike setup.

BMX has been an Olympic sport
since 2008. Riders compete on a
track at least 1,148 feet long.

The trickiest tricks include the "No Footer,"
where after a jump the rider kicks their feet
out to the side to make an "X" shape, and
combination tailwhips. For these, the rider
jumps and the whole frame of the bike rotates
underneath while the handlebars point forward!

BMX riders
are a worryingly
long way from the
ground when they perform
their tricks. The biggest ramp
used in competition—the X-Games
Big Air ramp—is 27 feet high, and riders
whizz up it and into the air high above it.

TERRIFYING TRUE TALE

Professional BMX rider Mike Aitken crashed his bike in 2008 while he was riding with his friends. He was just doing a trick he'd done lots of times before.

Mike was in a coma for three weeks and suffered a brain injury, a broken jaw, and a fractured eye socket, and he was paralyzed down his right side. **OUCH!** He had to learn how to walk again, and lots of other things. **And the good news?** Mike recovered! He's now riding, and even competing again.

Climbing

What on Earth possesses
people to go climbing
up mountains? Is it because:

   a) it's dangerous
   b) it's often extremely cold
   c) it's exciting
   d) it takes great skill

Answer: all of the above!

Most mountain climbers
have all that safety
equipment: ropes,
harnesses, carabiners,
etc. But there are some
people who insist on going
to extremes. You might
want to skip the next
section if you're afraid
of heights...
(Don't look down!)

BELIEVE IT OR NOT. . .
In 2010, Jordan Romero became the youngest person ever to climb Mount Everest, the world's highest mountain, when he was just 13 years old. In December 2011, aged 15, he climbed Mount Vinson in Antarctica to become the youngest person ever to climb the Seven Summits—the highest mountains on each of the seven continents.

FREE CLIMBING

Imagine yourself standing on a tiny ledge on a rock face, 1,970 feet from solid ground, with the wind whistling in your ears and no equipment to help you get up or down...

actually, don't.

It's far too scary!

Hey! That's my perch!

Free climbing is just like rock climbing, but without all the gear. Free climbers use only their hands and feet (they use ropes in case they fall, just not to help them climb). Free climbers aren't allowed to rest on ropes or pre-place any climbing gear to help them. There's a list of rules to make climbing as difficult for them as possible.

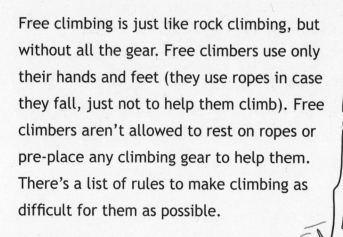

FREE SOLO CLIMBING (SOLOING)

This is even more extreme: climbers don't use any equipment at all—there's no safety rope in case they fall, and if they make a mistake it's often fatal. **They'd better not make any slipups then!**

BELIEVE IT OR NOT...

Alex Honnold is one of the world's best solo climbers. In 2008, he spent 2 hours and 50 minutes becoming the first person to climb the northwest face of Half Dome in Yosemite, California, which is 1,970 ft high. He climbed El Capitan, also in Yosemite, in just under six hours. It usually takes rock climbers at least two days to climb the same route.

Ice Climbing

If you're looking for more
excitement than climbing
boring old rock, you could
try ice climbing. The good news is that
you'll have harnesses and ropes and other
mountain climbing equipment. **Yay!**

The bad news is pretty obvious: you'll be
climbing up ice—frozen waterfalls, glaciers,
and icy mountains—so it'll be completely and
utterly freezing cold, and very slippery indeed.
There's also the risk of falling into a crevasse
or being buried under an avalanche.

TERRIFYING TRUE TALE

In 2012, David Warden was ice climbing on Britain's highest mountain, Ben Nevis. He and his climbing partner were scaling Zero Gully when they plummeted 1,312 feet down the mountain. Miraculously, David survived—though he was badly injured. He shouted for help and was airlifted to a hospital, where he made a full recovery. Sadly, his climbing partner didn't survive the fall.

Speed Skiing

Some people go to extreme lengths to get down mountains very fast indeed.

• Speed skiing is the fastest winter sport. Speed skier Simone Origone from Italy holds the world record at 156 mph (almost three times the speed limit on most highways).

Is he ready?

• Speed skiing courses are over 3,000 feet long and horrifyingly steep.

• The snow is absolutely smooth—the slightest bump could send a skier spinning off course.

• Skiers plummet down the course at such speed that the air hits them with the force of a hurricane.

• Equipment for speed skiing stops skiers being flattened by the force of the wind: it includes super-streamlined helmets, airtight latex suits, and triangular foam pads called fairings that attach to the backs of the legs.

• The fastest speed skiers accelerate as rapidly as a Formula One racing car.

• Skiing the course takes 15 seconds. Half of the course is for skiers to slow down and come to a stop.

MORE SPEEDY WINTER SPORTS

• **The luge**—the record for the luge is almost 87 mph. Riders lie on a flat sledge, just inches above the ground.

• **Speed skating**—these racers whizz along on ice skates at speeds of around 34 mph.

• **Ice racing**—cars and motorbikes are fitted with studded tires to race on frozen lakes.

A WIMP'S WORST NIGHTMARE

You gaze at the twisting, icy track in dismay. When you agreed to be part of a bobsled team of four, you hadn't realized the track was so steep, or so long. And it's slippery too. You've just been told that underneath that layer of ice is solid concrete, that bobsleds can reach speeds of more than 124 mph, and that a bobsled team was seriously injured on this track last week. "Ready?" calls your teammate. He shows you where to push. There's no going back now...

Suddenly you're pushing the bobsled with the others. You leap inside it when the pilot gives the signal.

Every bone in your body shakes as you go rattling down the track, faster and faster, at a death-defying speed that forces your body flat. As the bobsled turns almost onto its side, you're convinced it's out of control! **Aaarrrggh!**

BELIEVE IT OR NOT. . .

Georg Hackl, a luge gold-medalist, is also a champion wok racer: competitors race down bobsled runs on modified Chinese frying pans. (Chopsticks not required!)

Extreme Running

Lots of people like going for a run, but 26 miles? It's a bit much, by most people's standards, and yet marathons and half-marathons are becoming more popular. Marathons got their name because of the Battle of Marathon, fought in ancient Greece in 490 BCE.

I think I have a blister...

Before the battle, a messenger from Athens, called Pheidippides, ran to Sparta for help against the Persians. He ran 155 miles in two days, then ran another 25 miles from Marathon to Athens to announce the victory. Once he'd delivered the victory message, Pheidippides dropped dead, which perhaps isn't surprising.

HOW OLD WAS THE YOUNGEST
PERSON EVER
TO RUN A MARATHON?
A) FIVE
B) NINE
C) ELEVEN
D) SIXTEEN

Answer: A) Believe it or not, Jennifer Amyx was five years old when she ran her first marathon in 1975 in Johnstown, Philadelphia, and she did it in under five hours. Bucky Cox was also five, but a bit older than Jennifer, when he became the youngest male marathon runner in 1978. Things were different in the 1970s, and it's probably just as well—young children wouldn't be allowed to run in an official marathon now.

FACTS WIMPS NEED TO KNOW

EXTREME MARATHONS

Boggle your mind as you contemplate the runners for whom running a marathon is just a gentle warm-up... Every year a 155-mile race called the **Spartathlon** re-creates ancient Greek Pheidippides' run, except hopefully without the dropping dead part.

The North Pole Marathon is run on Arctic ice floes and is the only marathon not run on land. Runners endure freezing temperatures, with a wind chill of −13 degrees F. If you've run the North Pole Marathon, you could attempt to become a member of the North Pole Marathon Grand Slam Club by finishing a marathon on each one of the seven continents of the world.

The Marathon des Sables (the Marathon of the Sands) is an ultramarathon run across the Sahara Desert in Morocco over six days.

It's considered the hardest foot race on Earth. Runners have to carry their own food for the whole six days in a backpack, though the organizers generously provide water and tents for competitors to rest in at the end of each stage. The whole course is 158 miles long, and the longest stage is 52 miles. The extreme distance isn't helped by the baking heat, which can reach up to 122 degrees F.

BELIEVE IT OR NOT. . .

In 1983, a 544-mile race between Sydney and Melbourne in Australia was won by a 61-year-old sheep farmer named Cliff Young, even though he was running against top athletes from all over the world. The other athletes stopped each evening to sleep, before continuing the race the following day, but Cliff kept going, day and night. He gave away the prize money to five other runners.

TERRIFYING TRUE TALE

Italian policeman Mauro Prosperi was running in the 1994 Marathon des Sables when a sandstorm blew up. As the swirling sand blurred the landscape, he became completely disoriented. He wandered, lost and alone, for nine days.

Since he didn't have any water, he survived by drinking his own urine and eating snakes, scorpions, lizards, and bats (which he discovered when he took shelter in a deserted Muslim shrine).

Eventually, in a state of almost total collapse, he met a nomad family. He found out he had wandered more than 124 miles from the course and was now in a completely different country: Algeria. He recovered and has since finished the Marathon des Sables many times.

Triathlon

Not content with just running a ridiculously long way, some people have to show off by swimming and cycling as well, all in the same event.

You swim first, then cycle.

The triathlon is an Olympic sport consisting of a 1-mile swim, a 25-mile cycle, and a 6-mile run, but different competitions use different distances—and of course the Olympic distances aren't nearly enough for some people. Lots of triathlons are held each year, but some are extreme even by triathlon standards...

Ironman* Triathlon

The Ironman Triathlon takes place in Hawaii every year... The swim is just under $2\frac{1}{2}$  miles (it's in the sea, but no wetsuits are allowed—they are for wimps). The bike ride is 112 miles long (and it's hilly, with strong gusting winds). The run is the usual marathon length of 26 miles (and it's raced in very hot conditions). Frankly, we're disappointed—call yourselves ironmen? A mere $2\frac{1}{2}$-mile swim and an ordinary marathon?

Pah! Hang on, though...

*Not just for men; women can take part too!

Ultraman*

There's an even more grueling triathlon event, also held in Hawaii, with a proper run.

It's divided into three stages over three days. The first stage is a nice, refreshing 6-mile swim in the sea (yes, that's SIX miles), plus a 90-mile bike ride with steep climbs. The second stage is a 171-mile bike ride including more steep climbs (just in case you thought 90 miles was a bit tame). The third stage is a 52-mile marathon (twice the usual marathon distance). **That's a bit more like it!**

*Ultraman is open to women, too.

BELIEVE IT OR NOT...

You don't have to wait until you're an adult to compete in rock-hard triathlon events. Ironkids is for children aged 6 to 15. It's not quite as brutal as the grown-up Ironman competition: the senior group (aged 12 to 15) compete in a 900-foot swim, an 8-mile bike ride, and a 2-mile run.

I'm training for the Ironkids competition.

I'm training to be a wimp!

EXTREME WATER SPORTS

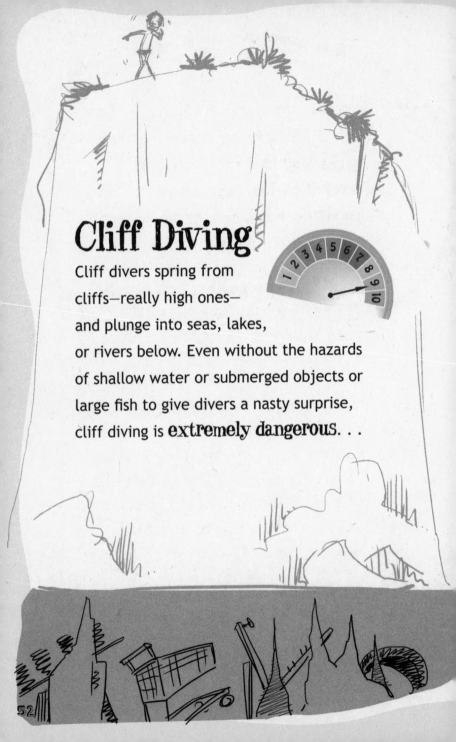

Cliff Diving

Cliff divers spring from
cliffs—really high ones—
and plunge into seas, lakes,
or rivers below. Even without the hazards
of shallow water or submerged objects or
large fish to give divers a nasty surprise,
cliff diving is **extremely dangerous**. . .

BELIEVE IT OR NOT...

Cliff diving first became a competition because of an 18th-century Hawaiian king. In 1770, Kahekili was famous for jumping off high cliffs and into the sea below, making hardly a splash. Kahekili insisted that his warriors did the same to prove they weren't wimps.

His successor, King Kamehameha I, went a step further and made cliff diving (rather than jumping) into a competition—at least according to legend. The world's most famous cliff diving site, Kaunolu, is in Hawaii.

FACTS WIMPS NEED TO KNOW !!

DANGEROUS CLIFF DIVING

In cliff-diving competitions, dives are from a maximum height of about 85 feet—that's like standing on top of an eight-story building. From that height, divers hit the water at up to 60 mph! Even if it's only water—hitting anything at 60 mph is very dangerous. Divers have to make sure they enter the water absolutely straight, with pointed toes or hands.

The impact of diving from a great height is enough to compress the spine, break bones, or give you a very nasty head injury. If the position of entry into the water isn't perfect, divers can be badly injured or even die. The safest way to dive from great heights is feet first, but professional divers dive head first and even perform somersaults or other tricks before making a streamlined entry into the water.

Cold water increases the stress on the body, and sea water is harder to dive into than fresh water because it's denser. The record for the world's highest dive is 172 feet, held by Dana Kunze. A higher dive—177 feet—was made by Oliver Favre, but because he was injured and had to be helped out of the water, his record doesn't stand.

Extreme Swimming

Extreme swimmers won't make do with a few lengths of the pool—even an Olympic-sized one. They insist on swimming vast distances that take days to complete, encountering watery perils such as jellyfish, sharks, strong currents, extreme cold, and huge waves.

Slow down, Martin. We can't keep up!

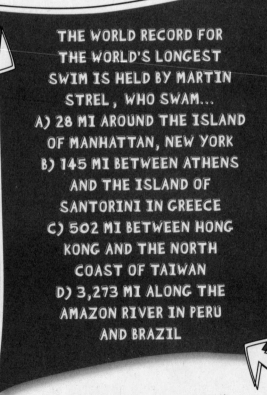

THE WORLD RECORD FOR THE WORLD'S LONGEST SWIM IS HELD BY MARTIN STREL, WHO SWAM...

A) 28 MI AROUND THE ISLAND OF MANHATTAN, NEW YORK

B) 145 MI BETWEEN ATHENS AND THE ISLAND OF SANTORINI IN GREECE

C) 502 MI BETWEEN HONG KONG AND THE NORTH COAST OF TAIWAN

D) 3,273 MI ALONG THE AMAZON RIVER IN PERU AND BRAZIL

Answer: D) Of course! Martin has also swum the Yangtze River (2,487 miles), the Mississippi River (2,414 miles), and the Danube (1,780 miles).

MARATHON SWIMS

The English Channel: The first person to swim the Channel, a distance of 21 miles, was Matthew Webb in 1875. Since then, around 1,200 people have swum the Channel—the youngest was 11-year-old Thomas Gregory, and the oldest was 70-year-old George Burnstad.

Um...

Competitors keep out the cold by smearing themselves in goose fat, Vaseline, or, in Matthew Webb's case, porpoise oil.

The Cook Strait: This marathon swim between New Zealand's North and South Islands isn't as far as the Channel—it's 14 miles—but the waters are known for strong and unpredictable currents.

The Catalina Channel: This swim, between California and Santa Catalina Island, is 20 miles wide and known for its sharks—but you're still far more at risk from exhaustion, dehydration, the cold, and jellyfish. **So not to worry.**

Extreme Boats

Getting out of the
water and into a boat
seems like a very good
idea. Then again . . .

WHITE-WATER KAYAKING

If you enjoy paddling a boat along a
churning mass of white water punctuated
with jagged rocks, with only a few
millimeters of fiberglass to protect
you, white-water kayaking is for you.

There are six grades of difficulty: the first is just moving water with a few ripples in it, which sounds as though it could be attempted by even the most fearful wimp. But grade six is not for the fainthearted: it means severe rapids and comes with the worrying warning **"danger to life or limb."**

ATLANTIC ROWING

If you've ever rowed on your local pond and found it quite difficult, you probably don't want to compete in the Atlantic Rowing Race. Competitors row 2,900 miles across the Atlantic Ocean, from the Canary Islands to the West Indies, in a journey that lasts more than six weeks (the fastest-ever crossing took 36 days).

Some are in teams of two or four, while others attempt the crossing alone. They face enormous waves, driving rain and wind, plus the risks of exhaustion, dehydration, or drowning if the boat sinks or competitors fall overboard.

Surfing

THE PERILS OF SURFING

Think twice before you grab a body board
and paddle out to the breakers... The most
obvious hazards are the waves. Don't attempt
really big ones unless you're experienced.
A big wave can send you plummeting down
50 feet as it breaks, not leaving you much
time to get to the surface and take a breath
before the next wave hits you.

- The pressure change can burst eardrums.

- Waves can fling you into reefs, rocks, or the sea bed, causing serious injury or even death.

- Surfboards often give surfers a hard smack, and the fin at the back of the board can cut flesh.

- Surfers use a leash to attach themselves to their boards, but the leash can become entangled in reefs or seaweed and hold the surfer underwater.

- Surfers can be caught out by rip currents. Don't swim against a rip current, which could exhaust you—swim parallel with the beach until you're free of the current, then swim back to shore.

- Sea creatures! Sharks, stingrays, jellyfish . . . for more information on scary sea life, see *The Wimp-O-Meter's Guide to Killer Animals.*

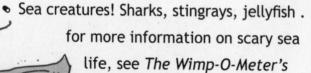

EXTREME SPORTS IN MIDAIR

If you're a true wimp, you're probably afraid of heights. So it might be best to read this next section with one hand covering your eyes, while holding on to a heavy piece of furniture with the other.

Skydiving

This extreme sport involves leaping out of a plane, helicopter, or even the basket of a balloon, with a parachute—**for fun**. The really "fun" part, at least according to serious skydivers, is right before the parachute goes up, when skydivers are falling toward the ground, thousands of feet up in the air. **(Seriously, what's wrong with these people?)** Once the parachute is opened, skydivers slow down and can control direction and speed using steering lines.

Hello! Looks like someone's dropping in for lunch...

WARNING
TIGERS

Some skydivers are determined to make falling out of a plane even more interesting...

Formations—groups of four, eight, sixteen, or even bigger teams—grab hold of one another as they fall, sometimes forming patterns or standing on one another's shoulders. The most people in a formation skydive involved 400 skydivers in Thailand in 2006.

Naked Skydiving—Um ... Enough said.

squawk!

Skysurfing—skydiving with a surfboard or snowboard. It's like you're riding the air! Kind of.

Skydiving with a bike—the bike has to be ditched before the skydiver lands, so add "being flattened by a skydiving bicycle" to your list of things to worry about.

Plane-to-plane skydiving—yes, that means jumping out of a plane, freefalling, and—somehow—climbing into a different plane! The list of reasons never to attempt this is very long.

WHICH OF THESE DIDN'T
REALLY HAPPEN?
A) SKYDIVING IN AN
INFLATABLE BOAT WHILE
SOLVING A RUBIK'S CUBE
B) SKYDIVING WITHOUT
A PARACHUTE
C) SKYDIVING IN A CAR
D) SKYDIVING WITH JET
SKIS AND KAYAKS

Answer: Actually, they all really happened. Travis Pastrana
jumped out of a plane without a parachute, but two of his
friends parachuted with him and he landed safely in tandem
with one of them. Your list of "things that could fall out of the
sky and flatten you," just got longer.

Wingsuit Flying

Wingsuits are special suits with webbing on the arms and legs to make the wearer feel just like a bird. Well, a bird that has to take off from a very high cliff or jump out of a plane in order to gain enough height. And a bird that has to wear a parachute—you can't slow down to a safe landing speed with only a wingsuit.

Look, Mom! It's Superman. Look, Mom, look! It really is. Mom!

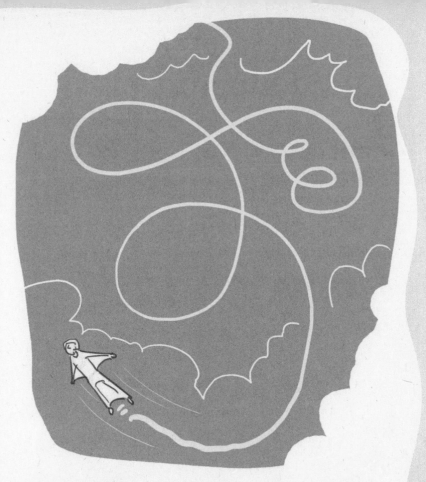

You can fly almost horizontally with a wingsuit and even perform aerial acrobatics. The suit slows you down so that you fall much more slowly than if you were skydiving. The average skydiver plummets at around 120 mph, while the average wingsuit flyer plummets at around 56 mph.

BASE Jumping

Have you ever wanted to launch yourself off a very tall building or bridge, shouting "Geronimo!" as  you nose-dive toward the ground? Thought not. But apparently plenty of people do, hence the sport of BASE jumping. In case you're wondering why BASE always has capital letters, it's because it stands for Building, Antenna (tall towers), Span (bridges), and Earth (cliffs)—the four things BASE jumpers leap from.

Geronimo!

DANGER!

Obviously, BASE jumping is dangerous—**duh!** It's even **more dangerous** than skydiving because BASE jumpers:

• have less control over their position and can go into a spin,

• have less time to open their parachute,

• can be blown back against the object they leapt from by high, swirling winds,

• have a small landing area.

BELIEVE IT OR NOT. . .

In one of the riskiest BASE jumps ever, Anders Lau Nielsen and Chad Henderson both rode mountain bikes off a 3,280-foot cliff in Norway in 2012. They were fine, but the bikes went to pieces...

Bungee Jumping

A WIMP'S WORST NIGHTMARE

You knew you shouldn't have taken that dare. You look over the side of the Macau Tower and feel the blood drain from your face. Below you, the Zhu Jiang river glitters in the sun, a dizzying 764 feet down. Someone is strapping you into your harness. You look at the clips and safety equipment. What if something goes wrong? You start to feel sick. "Come on," says someone, cheerily, "it's time to jump!" You gulp and look down—the ground far, far below seems to spin. You feel a pressure on your back, and suddenly you're plummeting through the air. **"Aaaarrgggh!"** you scream, as your stomach lurches violently...

BELIEVE IT OR NOT...
The people of Pentecost Island in Vanuatu, in the South Pacific, still perform the earliest form of bungee jumping in an annual ritual. They climb a 98-foot-high wooden tower and leap off it with vines attached to their ankles. A New Zealander named A.J. Hackett watched the ritual and came up with the idea of bungee jumping as a result.

FACTS WIMPS NEED TO KNOW

BUNGEE JUMPING

• Bungee jumping means leaping off a fixed structure while attached to it by a length of elasticized rope. It began in the 1980s and, for some reason, became very popular.

• The highest bungee jump is at the Macau Tower in China. It's 764 feet high, and jumpers plummet at up to 125 mph. There's a 4–5 second free fall, followed by a series of nauseating bounces as the elasticized rope springs you up and down before it comes to a rest. There have been serious injuries and deaths as a result of bungee jumping.

• Some of the biggest accidents have occurred because of equipment failure. Erin Langworthy, an Australian woman, fell 364 feet into crocodile-infested waters when her bungee cord snapped.

• There have been several cases where the cord used was too long for the drop.

• People have suffered problems with their eyesight because of the sudden change of pressure as you drop and bounce back again very quickly, in addition to whiplash injuries due to the extreme jolt.

• You're less likely to be injured if you relax. So chill out—it's not as if you're about to jump off a tall building or something . . . **oh.**

IN THE FILM *GOLDENEYE*,
WHAT STUNT DOES JAMES BOND
PERFORM AT THE VERZASCA
DAM IN SWITZERLAND?
A) HE RAPPELS DOWN IT
B) HE BASE JUMPS FROM IT
C) HE BUNGEE JUMPS FROM IT
D) HE DIVES FROM IT INTO
THE WATER

Answer: C) The dam is 722 feet high, and, if you want, you can bungee jump from it between April and October every year.

Is the stuntman ready?

How far down is it?

81

Slacklining and Highlining

You've probably heard of tightrope walking, where people who should really know  better balance on a cable above the ground, using a pole for balance. Slacklining is similar, but instead of a tight cable there's a slack nylon line that bounces like a trampoline as you walk along it.

You're probably thinking it sounds extremely sensible. Maybe you can't wait to give it a try. Actually, it is fairly safe as long as you're not very far from the ground. Most slackliners string their lines between two trees close to the ground, or above water, so that the landing's nice and soft if they fall off (if a little wet). But of course, there are people who have to take their slacklines up higher...

FACTS WIMPS NEED TO KNOW

HIGHLINING—THE STOMACH-CHURNING FACTS

Walking on a slackline high up is called highlining—and the lines can be very, very high. Highliners walk across their lines hundreds of feet up—for example, the Lost Arrow Spire in Yosemite National Park in California—its summit is 6,929 feet.

Extreme highliners insist on wobbling around on slacklines hundreds of feet above ground without using any kind of safety line or harness. It's known as free solo highlining, and it's not recommended.

BELIEVE IT OR NOT . . .

One of the world's best slackliners,
American Faith Dickey, holds world
records for women's highline,
highline free solo, and longline—
where the slackline is so long that
every small movement makes the
line bounce around like a horizontal
bungee. One of her most death-
defying stunts was walking a line

tied between two trucks . . . that were hurtling—at high speed and in a strong wind—toward two parallel tunnels. Faith had to walk across the thin line, battling to stay upright against the wind, before the trucks entered the tunnels and the line snapped on the dividing wall. She only just made it!

Last Word

You've been very brave. You've teetered on the brink of the world's highest peaks and risked being smashed against rocks. You've brushed up against the perils of extreme sports. **Now you can relax.** No one's going to force you to climb up a frozen waterfall or run 155 miles in the searing heat of the Sahara Desert. Actually, there are plenty of far more scary things for a wimp to worry about...

Come and give your nana a nice big kissy...

Your Wimp Rating

Answer these questions with **"yes"** or **"no."**
How many do you answer
"yes" to? Add up the number
to generate your very own
wimp rating on page 91—go
on, how tough are you **really?**

1. You're at the beach when someone says you should go out on a board to catch some waves—hey, it's only water after all. You say. . .

2. Martin Strel invites you for a quick swim. You say. . .

3. A friend has just been given a wingsuit for her birthday and offers to let you test it. You say. . .

4. You win a competition to join Faith Dickey on her latest record attempt. You say. . .

5. You think La Ruta de los Conquistadores is a gentle bicycle ride. You say. . .

7. A friend has pulled out of the Atlantic Rowing Race with an injury. Do you take his place?

8. You'd be happy to enter an Ultraman event.

9. The X-Games Big Air ramp is for babies on tricycles.

10. You'd be happy to jump off a bridge with only a piece of elastic tied to your legs.

Three questions: you're a novice wimp—you're on a sloping trail to wimp excellence.

Four questions: you're a wannabe wimp—banish those extreme sports thoughts!

Five questions: you're a splash away from wannabe status.

How many questions did you answer "yes" to?

Six questions: you're marathon mad for extreme sports.

Seven questions: you speed ski through life.

Zero questions: you're the ultimate wimp—superb! You have truly embraced your inner wimp.

One question: you're a mega wimp—a perfect example of extreme wimpiness. Well done!

Two questions: you're a champion wimp—give yourself a gentle pat on the back!

WIMP-O-METER

Eight questions: you swoop through sports challenges with a wingsuit.

Nine questions: you're high-wired as a highliner in the Himalayas.

Ten questions: too tough! You're not even a weany bit wimp-like—but you are slightly nuts! You'll have to dig deep to find your inner wimp.

Glossary

abyss an extremely deep hole or gap between rocks

adrenaline a hormone (chemical) produced by the body when you are frightened, angry, or excited

compress squeeze

crevasse a deep crack in an ice sheet or glacier

current in the sea, a body of water moving in a particular direction

dehydration extreme thirst

designated official named (footpath, in this case)

grueling requiring hard work

hydraulic disc brakes these use brake fluid to operate

karabiner a metal safety clip used on climbing ropes

mountain chain a connected group of mountains

mountain pass a route over a mountain

nomad someone who does not live in one place but moves from place to place to find fresh grazing for animals

rapids fast-flowing section of a river

titanium an extremely strong, light metal

vertical straight down

vine climbing plant

wet suit close-fitting item of clothing made of rubber and worn by swimmers to keep them dry/warm

whiplash injury to the neck caused by a sudden jerk

Index

Belt Three

John Ayliff lives in Vancouver, Canada. He honed his writing skills while working in the computer games industry, and still sometimes calls his protagonist the 'player character' by mistake. Outside of writing, his hobbies include tabletop roleplaying games and going to the opera. He can be found on Twitter @johnayliff and online at his website: http://johnayliff.com/

Belt Three

JOHN AYLIFF

HARPER
Voyager

Harper*Voyager*
An imprint of HarperCollins*Publishers* Ltd
1 London Bridge Street
London SE1 9GF

www.harpervoyagerbooks.co.uk

This Paperback Original 2015

First published in Great Britain in ebook format by
HarperCollins*Publishers* 2015

A catalogue record for this book
is available from the British Library

ISBN: 978-0-00-812046-7

Set in Sabon by Born Group using Atomik ePublisher from Easypress

Chapter One

The ship was a spindly two-ring clipper, tacking against orbit as it dropped sunward through the main shipping lanes of Belt Three. Jonas magnified the image to fill the bridge screen, so that the insect-like body of the clipper stood out against the golden plane of its sail. The ship was battered, asymmetrical, its grav-rings and spine lost beneath a crust of repairs. There was a marking on the side of its cargo bay, a feathered spiral of white on blue, presumably the logo of some minor shipping company. Apart from its heading, it looked like any of the other ageing tramp freighters that plied the orbits of the inhabited belts.

'Ayla, is that course reading correct?' Jonas asked.

The pilot jumped in her seat. 'What was that, sir?'

Ayla often became so lost in her connection with the ship that she stopped paying attention to her physical surroundings, but she normally hid it better than that. Jonas made a mental note to give her some time off when they reached port. The stress of the evacuation was getting to all of them.

'That ship,' Jonas said, indicating the screen. 'It looks like it's heading for our rock. Can you get its transponder data?'

Ayla's eyes defocused for a moment as she checked the *Coriolis Dancer's* sensors. 'Yes, sir, the course reading is correct. It's the *Remembrance of Clouds*, a private trader registered out of New Calais.'

Jonas frowned. '*Clouds*? Odd name for a ship.'

Ayla consulted her implant again. 'That's not its original name. The transponder has been hacked. With more time I could tell what the original name was.'

'No, don't worry about it,' Jonas said. A hacked transponder was a warning sign, but if the ship really was heading into a Worldbreaker Red Zone, time was the last thing it had.

He looked back to the local belt chart. His abandoned uranium mining outpost, LN-411, was a day's orbit behind the *Dancer*, deep inside the conical Red Zone that marked the probable course of the Worldbreaker. Warning glyphs flagged that the rock was forty-five hours from Black Line. The trajectories of dozens of ships traced curved lines across the screen, abandoning rocks in the Red Zone and fleeing towards distant cities.

There were the usual couple of Scriber Immolation ships heading back into the Red Zone, cheap eggshells filled with suicidal cultists on their final pilgrimage. Jonas stabbed a control to filter them out of the image. With the Scribers gone, the only ship moving into the Red Zone was the *Remembrance of Clouds*.

Something was wrong here, and if it might affect the *Dancer's* safety then Jonas wanted to know what it was sooner rather than later.

'Hail the *Remembrance of Clouds*.' Ayla spoke quietly into the air, letting her implant pick up the words. '*Remembrance of Clouds*, this is the Reinhardt Industries mining hauler *Coriolis Dancer*. Please acknowledge.'

A woman's face appeared on the screen immediately, as if she had been waiting for the hail. She looked perhaps thirty, square-jawed, with a mass of unkempt blonde hair and a web of pale scars across one side of her face like an impact crack on glass. Jonas could make out a blue-and-white circular symbol behind her, the same one that he had seen on the side of her ship. She looked at him with an unfriendly smirk, not speaking.

He ignored the woman's expression and put on a business-like smile. 'This is Captain Gabriel Reinhardt on the Reinhardt Industries mining hauler *Coriolis Dancer*.'

'Captain Keldra '82-Pandora, *Remembrance of Clouds*.' Her voice had the coarse accent of a Belt Three tank-born.

'Captain Keldra, it looks like you're heading for the LN-411 asteroid. Are you aware that rock is in a Worldbreaker Red Zone? All the mining stations have been evacuated, so if you're going there to trade . . . ' Jonas left the sentence hanging. The woman's smile was unnerving, and she had shown no surprise at the mention of the Worldbreaker.

'I'm not heading for LN-411 right now,' Keldra said. The transmission shut off.

Ayla swivelled in her seat to face Jonas, looking on the verge of panic. 'Captain, the ship's altering course. They're not heading for LN-411. It looks like . . . '

'They're heading for us,' said Jonas.

'Yes.'

He cursed under his breath. 'Pirates.'

Ayla's eyes widened. 'Pirates?'

'Full burn. Evasive manoeuvres.'

Ayla closed her eyes for a moment, and Jonas felt the deep rumble and the shift in gravity as the hauler's ponderous engines fired.

'I can try, but we're overloaded, and there's nowhere to run to, even if we went deeper into the Red Zone,' she said.

'No, stay out of the Red Zone.'

Ayla nodded, relieved. She was no Scriber. Even with pirates bearing down, no normal person would willingly head into the path of a Worldbreaker.

Jonas swung out of his chair and headed for the door. 'You have the bridge. I'll be back soon.'

From the outside, the *Coriolis Dancer* resembled a fat metal mushroom. A single grav-ring ran around the outside of a domed cargo bay, with the fuel tank and chemical reaction drive protruding below the bay like a stalk. Jonas kept the grav-ring spun up at a quarter gee to match the home gravity of most of the miners. Normally on a homeward run the cargo bay would be packed with canisters of uranium to sell at the nearest city, but today it was crammed with the mining and hab equipment they'd salvaged from their hurried evacuation of LN-411, with their last haul of uranium nestling forlornly in the centre.

Jonas's two dozen mining servitors stood in a row along the ring's orbital corridor. He tried not to meet their blank stares as he ran past. As Gabriel had, Jonas made sure only to use legal servitors – condemned criminals, or tank-borns who had been unable to pay off their cloning debt – but he knew there was a thriving black market in the mind-wiped victims of pirate raids. That would be how Ayla and the rest of his crew would end up if the *Remembrance* caught them, and Jonas as well, if Keldra learned his secret.

Most of the free-willed personnel were crammed into the crew lounge, almost the only room on the ship not filled with hastily rescued mining equipment. There were six

Worker-caste mining supervisors, and a couple of Engineer-caste members of the *Dancer's* regular crew. They looked up from game pads as Jonas opened the door. He found Matton, the huge red-bearded mining foreman, and gestured for him to come out into the corridor.

Matton waited until they were in the corridor and the door was shut before he spoke. 'We felt the engines fire.'

'Ayla's putting us on an evasive course,' Jonas said. 'Pirates.'

Matton had worked for years to build up his physical strength, but he still moved with the grace of someone who'd been raised in quarter gravity. Now he closed his eyes for a moment and took a breath, and Jonas could tell he was suppressing an urge to punch something.

'Damn scavengers, picking us off at a time like this. Well, we had a good run while it lasted. Do you know what to do?'

'I want you to jettison the cargo. Empty the bay.'

Matton sighed. 'You know that's not what I meant.'

'It might make us light enough to outrun them.'

'Wouldn't work. What kind of ship is it?'

'It's a two-ring clipper. Salamander class, I think.'

'No, it wouldn't work. The Salamander has some of the best engines outside of a Solar Authority cruiser. If they're looking to rob us they'll be flying with an empty cargo bay. We don't have the acceleration to evade them.'

'It's still worth a try. What if we strip out everything non-essential? Empty the grav-ring. We just need engines and life support.'

'That would take hours. The pirates would be on us before we were done.'

Jonas frantically tried to think. 'We've got a servitor combat programme, haven't we?'

'A basic one, yes, but we've no weapons. The servitors couldn't repel a pirate boarding party.'

'No, of course not, but they could be a diversion. If we tie the pirates up in a fight, the rest of us can escape in the shuttle, and if we jettison some junk at the same time then they might not notice us.'

Matton shook his head. 'They would notice us, and we'd be lucky if they stopped to pick us up rather than shooting us out of space. Sir, you've got to surrender. Pirates don't hurt true-borns. They'll ransom you to your family – that's how it works. You can't save us, but you can save yourself.'

'I've got to try something. Give me a programming spike.'

Matton drew the device from the pocket of his overalls and handed it to Jonas. 'It's up to you, sir, but it's a bad idea. I should get back in there and tell the men what's happening.'

'Tell them I'll get them out of this,' Jonas said. 'I don't just want to ransom myself. I'll find a way to save all of us.'

'Sir, you can't, so don't try. I'm not going to go in there and give those people false hope.'

'Matton—'

'Sir, you're more important than us,' Matton said gently. 'We're just tank-borns. Clones. You're a true-born. Look for a way to save yourself.'

'You know I don't think I'm better than you.'

'Don't let the men hear you say that.' Matton put his hand on the lounge door, and then paused. 'It's been an honour working with you, sir.'

Jonas nodded sadly. 'And for me.'

He went up to the nearest servitor and raised the programming spike to the back of its neck, then lowered it again. Matton was right: a straightforward fight would be no good, even as a diversion. He had to think of something else.

6

When Jonas got back to the bridge, the *Remembrance of Clouds* had furled its sail into a bud and was firing up its reaction drive. Ayla had put the *Dancer* on course for a cluster of small rocks where they might be able to hide, but the pirate ship was closing too quickly. The pilot looked up from her concentration as he entered.

'I'm sorry, sir.'

'It's all right,' he said. 'How long?'

'Just a couple of minutes.'

Without the glare of reflected sunlight from the sail, the *Dancer's* scope was able to resolve more details on the *Remembrance of Clouds*. Some of what Jonas had taken to be repair jobs were actually weapons: he could see dozens of small missile turrets sprouting all over the ship, and something larger, like a launch tube made of industrial piping, built into the nose complex.

His mining outpost on LN-411 had deterred pirates using surface-mounted cannons, but most of the cities with which he traded did not allow armed civilian vessels to approach them, so the *Coriolis Dancer* itself was unarmed. Normally, the *Dancer* would only travel to a city when the orbits brought it and LN-411 close enough for it to cross without danger, or when it could join a convoy with an armed escort ship. But a Worldbreaker evacuation meant a breakdown in the normal routine of inter-city commerce. At any time there were hundreds of Worldbreakers starward of the veil. When one of them passed through an inhabited section of one of the belts, the Red Zone of its probable course became thick with unarmed ships making long spins to whatever unthreatened outposts they could reach: rich pickings for any pirate ships nearby. Worldbreakers and pirates both struck rarely enough that true-born ship owners accepted the risk; and since pirates would normally ransom true-borns back to their families, the risk to them was purely financial. It was Jonas and his crew's bad luck that this pirate had focused on them.

'Hail them again,' Jonas said.

Ayla put the call through. 'They're not responding.'

'Keep trying.'

He sat back in his control chair and tried to form an image of Keldra in his mind. She had no reason to keep him waiting. It was possible she was tied up by some unrelated task, but more likely she was deliberately keeping him waiting, he decided. Perhaps she liked the feeling of power.

'Are we sure they're pirates?' asked Ayla hopefully. 'That symbol they're using . . . I thought pirates used skulls.'

'They usually do.' Jonas pulled up a magnified image of the logo on the pirate ship's cargo bay. The spiral was only the skeleton of a more complex pattern: the blue circle was criss-crossed with white streaks and swirls, looking irregular and feather-edged as if they had been hand-painted. He stared for a few seconds before he realized what it depicted. 'Clouds. That's a picture of the Earth.'

'Oh,' Ayla said. 'I didn't know what it looked like. I suppose you'd know.'

'I suppose.'

'I'm getting a response through now.'

Keldra's expression was smug and cruel; she knew she had already won. 'Captain Gabriel Reinhardt. I see your ship's changed course. I hope your pilot isn't taking matters into her own hands.'

Jonas made himself smile. 'Captain Keldra, as you can see, the Worldbreaker has forced us to travel through dangerous territory with no escort. I'm prepared to offer you a substantial fee in exchange for your protection.'

'I'm not interested in being bought off. I want your cargo and your crew.'

'There must be some deal we can reach. This doesn't have to end with my crew mind-wiped.'

Keldra looked at him with disgust. 'You want to *negotiate*? Spineless true-born scum, think you can talk your way out of every problem.'

'They're locking weapons,' Ayla said.

'We have no basis to negotiate,' Keldra continued. 'You have nothing I want that won't be mine in a few moments anyway.'

'I'll destroy the ship,' Jonas said suddenly.

'What?' Keldra froze, and fixed Jonas in a piercing gaze.

'You heard me.' He had made the threat without thinking, but now he couldn't take it back. 'If you try to dock, I'll overload the reactor.'

'You won't,' Keldra said, but Jonas could tell she wasn't sure.

'Ayla!' he shouted. 'Remove reactor safeties!'

Shocked, Ayla hesitated, but then she closed her eyes for a few seconds and warning icons appeared all over Jonas's console.

Keldra seemed to study him for a moment, not quite hiding her uncertainty, then her mouth curled into a wicked smile. 'So do it. I'm not turning back.' The transmission shut off.

Ayla turned back to Jonas, her eyes wide with panic. 'Gabriel, don't do this.'

The *Remembrance of Clouds* had matched orbit with the *Dancer* and was closing in to dock. Jonas's heart sank; he wasn't sure he could go through with his threat. 'I can't let her turn you and the others into servitors,' he said.

'Sir, we're dead anyway,' Ayla pleaded. 'Let her ransom you to your family. You're the important one. You . . . you knew what Earth looked like.'

On his console's lidar display, the *Remembrance of Clouds* was drawing alongside. Jonas's finger hovered above the control that would overload the reactor, but he found himself unable to press it. Ayla was right: she and the crew were dead, one way or another. Gabriel wouldn't have wanted Jonas to die like this. There had to be a way out.

He couldn't beat the ship, but perhaps he could beat the person. He knew Keldra was emotional; he was sure that her anger had been genuine and not an act. She seemed to have enjoyed gloating, so he knew she was cruel. Perhaps he could use that.

He had an idea. Jonas had years of experience with servitor programming, from his time as an Administrator. Keldra didn't know that, so she wouldn't expect him to know some of the tricks he did. The servitor combat programme wouldn't be any use while the ship was being boarded, but if he could save it for the right moment . . .

A shudder ran through the ship as the pirate's docking lines locked on. The pirates would cut through the *Dancer's* cargo bay door and enter the ring through the cargo airlock.

He walked over to Ayla's chair. 'Ayla, hold still.'

She looked up, startled but obedient. Jonas put a hand on her shoulder and held the programming spike to the back of her neck, just below the base of her skull. Her eyes glazed over as the spike momentarily took control of her pilot implant. He tapped in his Administrator override code and then loaded the combat programme into the implant's free space. 'Prepare to enter dormant mode,' he said, speaking to the combat programme through Ayla's ears. 'Verbal re-activation, my voice, password . . . ' He searched for a word. 'Oberon.'

The implant blinked Ayla's eyes twice, acknowledging its new instructions.

'Short-term memory wipe. One minute.' If this was to work, it was better that Ayla didn't know. 'Enter dormant mode now.'

She swayed as the implant released control. Jonas kept his hand on her shoulder to steady her.

'Are you all right?'

'What happened?'

'I think you blacked out for a moment.'

'I'm sorry, sir.'

He held the pilot's gaze. 'You have nothing to be sorry for.' He nearly told her that it was his fault, but then stopped himself: she would respond that it wasn't, and he would be fishing for her forgiveness for what he was about to do. These were her last moments as a free-willed human being and he had no right to make them about him. Instead, he said, 'you were the best pilot I've worked with, and it's been an honour flying with you.'

There were tears in her eyes, but she managed to smile.

There was a noise outside the door. It sounded like the pirates had reached it, and were preparing to blow the lock. There was no point resisting now. Jonas pressed the door release.

A pirate walked in, a large man dressed in an armoured vacuum suit. A servitor; he walked with a robotic gait, and his face inside the visor was expressionless. He scanned the room with a pistol and then fired quick bursts at Jonas and Ayla.

Jonas's muscles seized up painfully, rooting him to the spot. A nerve gun, set for paralysis. He could move his eyes and

11

facial muscles a little, but nothing else. The servitor lowered the gun and gave a hand signal to someone in the corridor.

Captain Keldra strode into the room, followed by a second servitor. She was tall, and from the way she was built Jonas guessed she had been raised in at least half gravity, probably more. She wore a yellow armoured vacuum suit, but her helmet was clipped to her belt, leaving her head arrogantly unprotected. She looked around the room critically, then pointed at Ayla.

'Spike her.'

Jonas could see the helpless panic in Ayla's eyes as the first servitor produced an enslavement spike and walked up to her. The servitor held the spike to the back of her neck and there was an unpleasant organic sound as it injected a servitor implant. Her eyes moved wildly for a moment, and she twitched, muscle spasms fighting against the paralysis, as the servitor implant systematically destroyed her higher brain functions and installed its own tendrils in their place. The pirate servitor touched her with an anti-paralyzer but she remained motionless, her mind gone.

Keldra pointed at Jonas. 'Search him for weapons, and cuff him.'

The first servitor kept Jonas covered with a nerve gun while the second patted him down for weapons, put a pair of cuffs on his wrists, and then released him from the paralysis. Keldra watched smugly.

'Make sure your ransom is worth more than the trouble you give me,' she said.

Jonas nodded silently. He intended to cause her a great deal of trouble – and she'd be getting no ransom, in any case – but for now he had to bide his time.

Keldra's nerve gun dug into his back as she marched him around the orbital corridor. Any last-ditch resistance the crew had put up was over, and pirates were already beginning to strip equipment from the walls. The pirates were all servitors; he couldn't see any free-willed humans among Keldra's crew.

They passed a group of newly mind-wiped mining foremen putting on vacuum suits in preparation for the transfer to the other ship. Keldra prodded Ayla to join them. Now was the moment. Jonas waited a calculated second, and then rushed forward as dramatically as he could.

'Ayla! Where are you taking her?'

Keldra grabbed his arm and brought him round to face her. 'Oh, was she yours?' she asked. 'Was she special?' The cruel smirk was back on her face, as he had hoped. 'Don't worry. I'm sure I can find a buyer for a pretty young thing like that.'

She let out a little snorting laugh and undid his cuffs as a servitor pushed a patched and blood-stained vacuum suit into his hands. Jonas kept his eyes on Ayla for as long as he could while he donned the suit, trying to look desperate and dejected. He had to let Keldra think she could use Ayla to hurt him. From the smug look on the pirate's face, he thought he had succeeded.

They climbed a ladder to the centre of the cargo bay, their weight dropping off until they were in microgravity. Across the gap, the *Remembrance of Clouds* kept station with the *Dancer*, its two grav-rings casting spokes of shadow across its cargo bay. The *Dancer's* bay was emptying as Keldra's servitors sent cargo containers along the lines to the pirate ship. She put the cuffs back on Jonas and then clipped them to a personnel transfer line. As it hauled them along, they passed a pair of servitors manoeuvring uranium ore canisters across the gap.

'You should have fought,' Keldra said, suddenly.

13

'What?' Jonas said.

She pressed the nerve gun against his back. The shock couldn't penetrate the vacuum suit, but the pointed tip of the weapon pressed in painfully. 'You ran,' she said. 'You people always run. You should have fought.'

Chapter Two

The prison cell was a converted cargo container a few metres wide. There were three light strips in the ceiling, but only one of them worked, so the room was filled with an eye-straining half-light. A hard-angled metal bed was bolted to the floor, and in the corner was the sealed box of a chemical toilet.

Jonas got up slowly, still nauseous from the nerve gun paralysis, and rubbed his wrists where the cuffs had dug in. He felt heavy: he estimated the ring's gravity was close to one gee, much more than he would have expected on a pirate ship. There was a little barred window in the cell door, through which he could see a brightly lit corridor and a security camera bolted to the opposite wall. He pressed his face to the bars to see as far as he could into the corridor, but he couldn't see any guards, or any other sign of life. The only sound was the faint rattle and gurgle of the ship's systems.

He lay down on the bed. After what he guessed was an hour the vibration changed in tone, and the room seemed to tip sideways as a gentle new acceleration dragged him towards the wall. The *Remembrance of Clouds* was unfurling its sail and pulling away from whatever it had left of the *Coriolis Dancer*.

Sometime later he heard footsteps in the corridor. A slot at the bottom of the door opened and a tray of food slid in. He waited, but the footsteps did not depart. When he sat up on the bed he saw a face, dark against the window.

'You should have fought,' Keldra said.

He didn't move. He had expected her to come to gloat, although he hadn't expected her so soon. He glowered up at the door for a moment but said nothing. He wanted her to be angry at him, and for now the best way to achieve that would be to ignore her.

'Eat!' she commanded.

'What have you done with Ayla?' he asked.

Keldra let out a snorting laugh. 'Eat!'

'If you want obedience, why don't you spike me?'

'Don't tempt me. I bet your family would pay something just for your body.'

Jonas went to the tray and picked it up. Keldra's face was close to the bars. He examined her, keeping his face controlled.

'If you spiked me, you'd have no one to talk to,' he said. 'We're the only free-willed people on the ship.' A subtle movement of her eyes told him he was right.

He sat down and began to eat. It was the tasteless, nutritious slop that servitors were fed. He grimaced, deliberately, as if he were used to only the finest true-born cuisine.

'You should have fought.' Keldra banged on the door, making him jump. 'Look at me!'

He lay the spoon across the bowl and sat up haughtily. 'You have no right to keep a true-born like this.'

That set her off. 'You think you're better than the rest of us. You're not. You're just a spoiled ruling class.'

'You're just a clone. My ancestors walked on Earth.'

16

Keldra thumped the door again, making the cell rattle. 'You know nothing about Earth! I'm closer to Earth than any true-born. I'm a genetic duplicate of someone who lived on Earth.'

'You're a clone. What's your name, clone? Your full name?'

'To hell with you.'

'You don't have a name. You have a serial number. You were *made*.'

Keldra was leaning close to the bars, as if she were the one locked up. She seemed like a caged animal that might tear the door open at any moment. Making her angry was almost too easy. Had she come down here looking for a shouting match?

'I'll tell you my name,' she said. 'Keldra 2482-Pandora-33842, Engineer.'

Assuming it was true, that made Keldra 28-years-old. He hadn't heard of Pandora, but there were a lot of minor Belt Three cities he didn't know.

'I am Gabriel Dominic Ellis Reinhardt,' he said, slowly emphasizing each name. 'I can trace my family tree back to people named Reinhardt and Ellis who lived on Earth. You have no such continuity. You have a serial number, *clone*.'

'You've got a past but no future. You're letting the human race die.'

'True-borns are the only ones that matter.'

'You're letting them win!' Keldra shouted. 'In a few hundred years the Worldbreakers will have destroyed everything. There'll be nowhere for us to live.'

'There's nothing we can do. You can't beat the Worldbreakers. We're living at the end of the human race.'

Keldra banged on the cell door again. 'You should have fought!' She disappeared from the bars and her footsteps echoed away along the corridor.

'Don't hurt Ayla!' Jonas shouted after her. 'I want her back!'

A few hours later the lights abruptly went off. Jonas lay on the bed and tried to sleep. The cell was cold but stuffy, the air not circulating properly. The faint sound he could hear resolved itself into a dozen different ship systems: rattles, hums, rhythmic thuds, and a trickle of water that sounded as though it came from just beyond the wall. There was a gentle, regular swaying sensation, as if the grav-rings were not quite properly aligned.

He still didn't know if he had judged Keldra's personality correctly. She seemed so volatile that he couldn't be sure she wouldn't forget about the ransom and slave-spike him in a fit of anger.

Six years ago he'd promised to do something worthwhile with Gabriel Reinhardt's name. He had set out to prove that he could run a successful business while treating his tank-born employees decently, or at least better than the exploitation that was the norm. Not exactly a grand dream, now he thought about it, but even there he had failed. Gabriel Reinhardt's uranium-mining business had survived but had not prospered. Jonas had found himself living day-to-day, plans to do more pushed to the back of his mind. Now the double blow of Worldbreaker and pirate had ended even that, his employees were dead, and there was no goal left for him but to escape and survive.

At least he had a chance of doing that. Keldra was volatile, but if he trod carefully his plan should still work. Soon he would be free, and then he could think about what to do next.

Jonas had guessed right. When another tray rattled through the slot the next morning, the face at the bars was the expressionless servitor that had been Ayla. Jonas ran up to the door. Keldra stood behind the servitor, smirking, a nerve gun in her hand.

Servitor-Ayla remained at the door after delivering the tray, giving Jonas a chance to look at her. Her face was bruised, one eye half-closed from the swelling, and he could smell blood from where Keldra had beaten her. He reminded himself that Ayla's personality had died the moment Keldra had slave-spiked her, so she was no longer suffering, but that didn't make the bruises any easier to look at. She had been a brilliant young woman with so much potential, but the only place his society had found for her was as a living control system for a mining hauler. Worse, she had accepted that place, humbly buying into the belief that true-borns were her natural superiors and her role was to serve them. Jonas had tried to tell her that he wasn't better than her, but she hadn't listened. Now his decisions had led to her personality death and the mutilation of her still-living body. At least it would soon be over and, if his plan worked, she would be avenged.

He leaned close to the bars, and let the emotion he was feeling show on his face. He had to give Keldra this triumph to make her feel secure. He glanced left and right. Keldra and Servitor-Ayla were alone in the corridor.

Keldra let out a little laugh. 'You know, there are some theories that consciousness survives a mind-wipe. It has no control, but it can perceive what's happening. Your Ayla could know exactly what I've been doing to her.'

Jonas pressed his face against the bars, and whispered.

'Oberon.'

Servitor-Ayla blinked twice. Her original pilot implant, now running his combat programme, had a deep connection to her brain, and quickly wrested control of her body from the more recent slave implant. He stepped back from the door, and Servitor-Ayla's eyes followed him. He nodded in Keldra's direction.

'Neutralize her.'

Keldra started to react, but not quickly enough. Servitor-Ayla spun around fluidly and landed a kick squarely in her stomach. As Keldra reeled, Servitor-Ayla neatly struck her hand, sending the nerve gun clattering across the corridor. Keldra swung at the servitor, but clumsily. Servitor-Ayla placed one more sharp blow to Keldra's neck and the pirate collapsed against the wall.

Jonas grinned, triumphant.

'Get this door open.'

He saw how the door locked when Keldra had put him in: there was nothing electronic, just a big manual lever that released the bolts. The unarmed combat programme should be able to follow his instruction.

Servitor-Ayla ducked out of sight. A second later the door swung open.

Keldra was moving sluggishly, winded but not unconscious. Jonas grabbed the nerve gun from where it had fallen, clicked the slider up to 'kill', and levelled it at the pirate. There was no fear in her eyes, only anger, as if she were daring him to kill her.

He closed the trigger and held it closed as Keldra convulsed, muscle spasms making her limbs flail in unnatural directions. He kept the trigger closed until she lay still. She wasn't breathing. The nerve gun should have stopped her heart.

Jonas felt sick. The hand that held the nerve gun shook uncontrollably, and the corridor seemed to spin around him. He closed his eyes and tried to control his breathing, but when he opened them the body was still there. He should have felt pleasure at having avenged Ayla and the others, and won his chance at freedom, but all he felt were nausea and guilt. He had never killed anyone before, and now he knew he was capable of it.

He looked away from the body and managed to stop shaking and think clearly. He could reassess his moral compass later, once he knew he was safe. He looked up and down the corridor, trying to orient himself with what little he knew of a Salamander's layout. If he reached the bridge he should be able to take control of the ship and put it on course for a friendly city. The bridge would be in the first grav-ring, and he was fairly sure he was in the second. If he headed around the ring he should come to a transport hub, eventually. He gestured Servitor-Ayla to follow him.

The bulkhead door at the end of the corridor was open. Beyond was a dim storage area, large enough that the far end was hidden behind the grav-ring's ceiling horizon. The corridor ran between transparent partitions, on the other side of which deactivated servitors knelt in neat rows like Scriber cultists at prayer. Jonas recognized some of them as his mining servitors and the former crew of the *Dancer*; a few of them wore bruises where they had tried to resist capture. Their down-turned faces were corpse-like in the bluish light.

They were some way along the corridor when Jonas saw movement. A ripple of sharp twitches passed along the rows of servitors as their implants activated them. They began rising to their feet, each making the same smooth, compact movements. Doors in the partitions slid aside.

Jonas looked around in panic. Someone was in control and trying to stop him. He must have read Keldra incorrectly when he had guessed that she was the only free-willed person on the ship. He looked for controls to the partition doors, but none were visible. The servitors were on their feet now. The ends of the corridor were beyond the grav-ring ceiling horizon in both directions, so he didn't know which end was closest. He broke into a run, towards the far end of the corridor, away from the prison cell.

The partition doors were fully open now. A servitor stepped into his path, massive hands outstretched. He had been a mining servitor, and was still wearing the Reinhardt Industries uniform. Jonas raised the nerve gun and fired. The servitor convulsed and fell, but two more were already stepping out into the corridor behind him. Their movements were unco-ordinated: it looked as though they had only a basic non-combat programme. He fired wild bursts along the corridor and shouldered past the servitors as they fell.

The bulkhead door to the next corridor section was in sight now. Jonas kept firing, pushing past bodies, and fighting off clumsy, grasping hands. The door was locked, but there was a manual override behind an emergency panel. He pushed down on the lever, putting all his weight behind it. The door resisted for a moment, then sprang open, revealing a grey corridor mercifully free of servitors.

Servitor-Ayla was a few metres behind Jonas, the combat programme fighting its way through the other servitors easily, delivering swift chops precisely to their nerve points. He fired into the throng, clearing a path for her, until she was in reach, and then grabbed her by the wrist and pulled her through. He shut the door and engaged the emergency hard lock. A minute later there was a series of thuds as the servitors banged inef-fectually on the door. He rested his head on the steel wall and paused for a moment, fighting to get his breathing under control.

He had reached the ring's transit hub. The door to the transit module tube was closed, and lighted icons indicated that the modules were elsewhere in the ship. Whoever was in charge of the servitors would no doubt prevent him from recalling one. His plan for taking control of the ship had already failed. He needed a way out.

Each ring should have its own set of escape shuttles, and they were normally close to the ring's transit hub. After a few moments Jonas found the door he needed.

The shuttle bay was cramped, with vacuum suit racks and tool lockers running along its walls. In the floor were four circular airlock hatches. Between them, through thick, foggy windows, the coffin-like shapes of the shuttles were visible, clamped in their recesses in the outer hull.

Like the doors, shuttle control had a local override, a fail-safe so that the crew could evacuate in the case of a ship-wide malfunction. There was even a local belt display based on the shuttle bay's own lidar. At the moment it showed a binary pair of rocks, the smaller of which had a habitation beacon. Jonas grinned. If he could reach that outpost he would be home free.

An intercom on the control board crackled to life.

'That's as far as you get, true-born.' The voice was breath-less and uneven, but it was Keldra's. She sounded as if she was running.

Jonas leaned in to the intercom. 'How did you survive?'

'This ship won't let me die.'

He stabbed the controls to prep one of the shuttles for launch. 'I've got shuttle control. You can't stop me leaving.'

'I've got fire control. If you launch one of those shuttles I'll blow it out of space.'

He hesitated. 'You wouldn't. You want me alive for ransom.'

'You think I make empty threats?'

A chime sounded to signal that launch prep was done, and a hatch hissed open. Jonas stared at the cramped, cocoon-like space beyond. With the system running on local override, there was no way to launch a shuttle except from inside it.

Servitor-Ayla was standing behind him, obedient and alert, the combat programme scanning the room for threats to its master. Her face was expressionless; the woman behind it was already dead.

'Servitor,' Jonas said slowly, 'go into that shuttle and use the launch control.'

Servitor-Ayla paused, and, for a moment, Jonas thought that the command to launch a shuttle had been too complex for the combat programme, but then she walked forward and climbed through the hatch. Jonas watched through the floor window as the clamps released and the shuttle fell away from the hull, drifting to one side as the Coriolis effect took it away from the shuttle bay. Ayla was visible momentarily through the tiny filtered window, before the thrusters fired and the shuttle dwindled to a point.

A missile streaked across the window. The shuttle exploded into a million glittering shards.

Jonas punched the side of the control panel in frustration. Now there was nowhere he could run. Involuntarily, he thought back to what Keldra had said about consciousness surviving a mind-wipe. He knew it wasn't true, but if it was, then letting her destroy Ayla's body had been the most merciful thing.

The door from the corridor opened. Jonas turned just in time to see Keldra powering across the floor towards him. Before he could move she grabbed his throat and slammed him against the wall.

'You don't steal from a thief.'

He wriggled in her grip. She pulled upwards, choking him and nearly lifting him off his feet. A pair of burly servitors entered behind her and trained their nerve guns on him.

'You don't steal from a thief,' she repeated. 'You steal from a business owner, they have insurance, they have law enforcement. They have their true-born *family* to help them out. A thief doesn't have all that.' Her grip tightened, making his eyes water. 'You steal from a thief and they'll hunt you down and kill you as a warning to everyone else, because you *don't* steal from a *thief*. You don't steal from *me*.' She released him and he doubled over, gasping. 'Why didn't you wait? I could ransom you to your family. That's the way this normally goes.'

Jonas lay against the wall, feeling his throat. He could taste blood in his mouth. The game was up; she had already shown she was prepared to kill him rather than let him escape. He might as well tell the truth for once.

'I'm not a true-born,' he croaked.

Keldra delivered a swift kick to his ribs. 'What's your name, *clone?*'

'Jonas 2477-Athens-20219, Administrator.'

She kicked him again, less hard this time. 'Bastard. I lost a good shuttle because of you.' She looked down at him, calculating. 'What happened? How'd you get where you are?'

'Gabriel Reinhardt was a Scriber. He Immolated six years ago. The Belt Three branch of Reinhardt Industries should have passed to his next of kin, but . . . '

'You took over.' She smiled slyly. Was that admiration Jonas saw on her face, or did she just like the thought of a true-born family being screwed over?

'I was his personal assistant, so I had access to nearly everything,' he said. 'I fired all the staff who knew his face,

25

and rebuilt the business. His family's up in Belt Four. He didn't talk to them much, and they never knew he was a Scriber.'

'But if I ransomed you to them, they'd know you weren't him. Hah.' Keldra was still looking thoughtful, as if sizing him up for something. 'You'd still have been living like that if that Worldbreaker hadn't shown up. You must hate the Worldbreakers.'

'Hate the Worldbreakers?' Jonas looked up, incredulous, trying to work out if she was serious. 'I hate you, you damn pirate! There's no point hating the Worldbreakers. They're just *there*. There's nothing we can do about them.'

Keldra grabbed the front of his shirt and pulled him to his feet, her eyes flaring with a resurgence of anger. 'No point. Nothing we can do,' she mimicked acidly. She thrust his face into the local belt display. 'Do you know what that rock is?'

The local belt display showed two bodies near the *Remembrance of Clouds*. One of them was flagged as having a habitation beacon, but the display did not show any more information; the other was dark, visible only as a lidar trace. A pair of rocks orbiting a common centre, one of which was inhabited: any number of outposts in the belts matched that description.

'What? No. It could be anywhere.'

'It's LN-411.'

'But LN-411's a lone rock, it doesn't have . . . oh God.' An awful chill ran through his body, quite different from the mundane fear of enslavement by a pirate. The other rock was the Worldbreaker.

Chapter Three

Keldra put the cuffs on Jonas's wrists and marched him to the transit hub, once again jamming the nerve gun into his back. The transit module could take half a dozen people, but she dismissed her servitors and entered with Jonas alone. He noticed a slave-spike among the tools hanging from her belt as she strapped herself into the acceleration harness opposite him. He had no idea why she didn't use it.

He felt the gravity drop away as the module travelled up to the ship's spine, then return as it moved outwards to the first ring. There were no servitors waiting when the door opened, and Jonas saw none as Keldra prodded him along a corridor to the bridge.

Jonas had seen a Salamander's bridge before so he could tell that this one was heavily modified. All but one of the crew terminals had been ripped out, making the room seem larger than it normally would, and it was dominated by the holo-screen taking up the front wall. Right now the screen showed an external view centred on the red-brown dot of LN-411.

In the centre of the room was what Jonas could only think of as a nest. A chaotic arrangement of screens and control boards formed a half-circle around a battered captain's chair, whose padding leaked through splits unevenly patched with black tape. The control boards were stained, and every empty surface held a foil food tray or empty stim pill packet.

The ceiling was painted dark blue with streaks and splotches of pale grey. He thought, for a moment, that it was an abstract pattern, before he realized what it depicted: clouds. The sky of old Earth, or at least Keldra's guess of how it would have looked. The paintwork was rough, with great scrawled brush strokes, not like the neat work of a servitor painting programme. Jonas was sure that she had painted it herself.

Keldra glanced at one of the screens on her control nest. 'We're just in time.'

The view on the bridge screen zoomed in. The familiar crags of LN-411 loomed large, dotted with the docking scaffolds and solar panel arrays of Jonas's abandoned mining operation. Beside the rock floated the fragile-looking white ovoid of a Scriber Immolation ship. Keldra hadn't touched the controls. Her full name had indicated she was Engineer-caste, but she must be controlling the ship using a pilot implant.

Beyond LN-411 another object was visible, much larger than the rock but totally black. Its shape was hard to make out against the stars, but Jonas knew what it was. A regular dodecahedron, a little more than fifty kilometres across, each face a flat plane composed of an exotic material that absorbed almost all radiation, leaving it utterly black and cold. He felt a chill run through him. He had seen recordings, but he had never been this close to a Worldbreaker before.

Keldra had climbed into her nest and was leaning forward in the chair, a grin of anticipation on her face.

'You like to watch them eat?' Jonas asked. 'That's sick.'

Keldra didn't react to the insult. Whatever was going through her head was more important to her than being angry with him.

'Any moment now,' she said.

A spot of pale green light appeared in the middle of the dark mass and spread into a thin five-pointed star, whose arms began to thicken. One of the Worldbreaker's faces had split into five triangular petals that were opening outwards, and the light was shining from inside, creating a tenuous beam in the rock dust surrounding LN-411. The beam began to sparkle as bits of the rock broke off and streamed into the Worldbreaker's flickering pentagonal maw. Jonas watched the Scriber ship as it drifted into the beam and vanished in a puff of orange flame.

After about ten seconds the near surface of the rock glowed green and then crumbled inwards, the solar panels shattering. The Worldbreaker beam had worked its way through, obliterating in moments the installations that Jonas's workers had taken months to carve out of the rock. The last few fragments fell into the Worldbreaker's mouth and disappeared, and the light shut off. Dimly, Jonas could see the five petals starting to close.

'Now watch this.' Keldra raised her hand with two fingers extended, miming a gun, and pointed it at the Worldbreaker. 'Pow!' She fired, swinging her arm expansively.

A white rocket trail flared on the bridge screen and receded, gathering speed towards the Worldbreaker. Through the glare, Jonas could just make out the missile itself: ugly and asymmetrical, looking as though it had been made out of scavenged parts. The shell looked like one of the Reinhardt Industries uranium ore canisters.

Jonas frowned. The sight of a uranium symbol on a missile reminded him of something from Planetary Age history. 'Is that a nuclear missile?'

Keldra shot him a momentary approving look. She seemed excited. 'I told you. You should have fought!'

The missile dwindled to a white point that curved into the Worldbreaker's mouth. The petals were still closing slowly. Jonas's heart pounded. What if the Worldbreaker turned its beam on them? But Worldbreakers never reacted to people. Keldra was staring at the screen, teeth bared like some prehistoric hunter, waiting for the moment . . .

There was a bloom of white light from inside the throat, and then the Worldbreaker cracked open. Massive pieces of debris spun away, and from the centre, a cloud of glowing green gas spilled out and began to fade. Keldra punched the air.

'Yes!'

Jonas stared in disbelief. 'You killed it.'

'I've killed six of them now.' She glanced between Jonas and the screen and spoke rapidly, her words tumbling over one another in her excitement. 'There's a window, after the beam shuts off but before the mouth closes. Normal weapons weren't enough, so I found out how to build a nuke. I've got my own enrichment plant here on the ship.'

'You killed it,' Jonas said again. The green cloud had faded away now. The Worldbreaker and LN-411 were both gone, their remains visible only as a flickering blackness where the debris passed in front of the stars. Jonas watched in silence as it dispersed.

Keldra tapped at a couple of her control boards and the ship began to turn, aligning itself to a new course. Still radiating triumph, she swung herself out of the control nest and grabbed the enslavement spike from her belt.

30

'All right, show's over.'

Jonas sighed, and let his shoulders droop, relaxed. He'd been resigned to this since he'd seen Ayla's shuttle explode. 'At least I got to see a Worldbreaker die.'

She put a hand on Jonas's shoulder and pressed the spike to the back of his neck, where his skull met his spine. He felt a sharp pain as the implant spike broke the skin, then dizziness, then his vision blurred and he blacked out.

Keldra's face swam back into focus. Jonas flexed his fingers and found that they responded. He blinked, trying to clear his head. 'You didn't wipe me,' he said.

'The implant's in dormant mode. I just need to say the word and you're wiped.'

He rubbed his wrists. The cuffs were gone.

'There are some other triggers too,' Keldra continued. 'If you try to hurt me, even indirectly, it'll knock you out. If you're off the ship for more than twenty-four hours without my say so, it'll kill you.'

'Sounds pretty foolproof,' he said. With his mind still foggy he couldn't think of a way around the restrictions, and those were just the restrictions Keldra was telling him about. 'Why?' he asked.

'You nearly killed me. I've got a system in place to monitor my vitals, so servitors came and revived me. But you nearly *beat* me. That means you've got skills I can use.'

He nodded slowly. That was true, but he didn't think it was the real reason. 'And you want someone to talk to,' he said.

That threw her. She glared at him, but said nothing.

'You want someone to talk to, and you want someone to *watch*. Don't you? Killing that Worldbreaker was sweeter because someone saw you do it.'

She glanced up at the painted clouds. 'They stole from you as well.' She put her hand on the nerve gun at her hip, and a sideways jerk of her head directed him to the door.

Keldra took Jonas around the ring to the crew living area. They went through a lounge, where a threadbare couch faced a big wall-screen, and a dining room with a doorway through which a cluttered kitchen was visible. The next corridor had eight cabin doors leading off it, and they looked like part of the original ship design, not later modifications. Being pilot as well as captain was meant to burn people out with the overload of responsibilities, but he thought Keldra must be doing the jobs of half a dozen other people, as well.

She bundled him into one of the cabins. 'I'll be back for you later.' She shut the door, and he heard the mechanism click as the hard lock engaged.

The cabin was not much larger than the prison cell, but it had more comforts. There was a padded bunk built into the wall, and a water-conserving shower. There was a desk terminal, but it didn't respond when Jonas pressed its power button. He checked under the desk and found that the terminal had been gutted, the parts no doubt finding their way into Keldra's nest or some other modification project elsewhere in the ship.

He sat at the useless desk and idly fingered the back of his neck where Keldra had injected the implant. He thought he could feel something, numbness, or an irregularity of the skin, but he knew it was his imagination. An implant injection wound was undetectable.

He had to find some way to escape from her, and now it meant escaping from the implant's control as well. He wondered briefly if some of the implant programming she mentioned had been a bluff, but dismissed the idea. He knew enough implant engineering to know that everything Keldra had said was possible, and he didn't think that she was one to bluff, not for any length of time. It wasn't that she was honest, but he didn't think she was subtle, either.

He needed to escape from her, and, more than that, he wanted to *defeat* her, to avenge the deaths of his crew. He tried to channel that anger, to make something useful of it, to formulate a plan, but he couldn't concentrate. All he could think of was the sight of the Scriber ship vanishing into the green beam, and the Worldbreaker cracking apart.

An hour later the door lock clicked and Keldra opened it without knocking. When Jonas got up, she threw a bundle into his arms. Frayed blue servitor overalls, with the logo of some minor freight company on the shoulder.

He tossed the clothes onto the bed. 'You want me to get changed now?'

'No. Come with me.'

He followed her into the corridor as she stalked off. 'You can't win, you know,' he called after her.

'What?'

'You can't beat the Worldbreakers. I did some calculations. From what my ship was carrying, you couldn't have enriched enough weapons-grade uranium for a warhead that size. I don't know if you got it all from mining ships or bought it on the black market, but that missile must have burned through your loot from a dozen kills.' Keldra didn't say anything, but she wasn't good at bluffing; Jonas could tell he was right. 'You can't even attack until they've finished eating, so you couldn't defend a city from one. You've killed six Worldbreakers. Do you know how many there are?'

33

'That's not the point.'

'There are tens of thousands, and for all we know they're making more of themselves, down beneath the veil. Even if every city used all its resources to build nukes to fight them, they would still keep coming. This isn't a war you can win. This isn't a war at all, and if it ever was then the Worldbreakers won it a long time ago.'

Keldra grabbed the front of his shirt and pushed him into the wall, just as she had in the shuttle bay. 'You don't talk to me like that.'

Jonas looked into her eyes, not blinking, not even raising his voice. 'You killed my crew and God knows how many other people. You can wipe me, or I'll talk to you howso-ever I like.'

'They should have fought.'

'They didn't fight because they couldn't win, and they knew that. Do you really think you're justified in murdering people because they won't join in with your futile gesture of defiance?'

'I don't care what you think of me.'

'I think you do. Otherwise why do you want me around?'

'Shut up and follow me. I'll give you the tour.'

Chapter Four

Olzan strapped himself into the transit module and gestured for the new recruit to join him. 'I'll give you the tour.'

The girl hesitated, still in the docking airlock. She had a rectangular face and a frizz of blonde hair, tied back but with a few strands floating out at odd angles. She'd come dressed in an engineering jumpsuit and had an overnight bag floating over her shoulder, just as Olzan had asked. She held herself a little awkwardly, keeping her body stiff rather than letting it float naturally. Olzan knew she'd been a worker in the city's spine, so she'd have microgravity experience; he guessed her awkwardness was due to nerves. When she entered the module and strapped herself into a seat she did so competently enough.

Olzan put on a cocky smile and rolled into his normal half-ironic introductory speech as the transit module started to move.

'Welcome to the *Thousand Names*. Most reliable ship in the Cygnus Group, maybe in the whole of Belt Three. She's 20 years old, built in the Cassiopeia shipyard, though we've made a few tweaks of our own since then. The cargo bay holds 10,000 tonnes, and we run the grav-rings at a breezy

0.67 gee. Owner's a guy named Wendell Taylor Glass, but he leaves us to pick our own routes and cargoes.' The transit module settled in to the forward ring's transit hub, and the door opened. Vazoya was leaning against the far wall, arms folded. Her facial tattoos were neon-blue today. 'We go where the solar wind takes us, my friend,' Olzan concluded with a flourish, as he and Keldra disembarked. 'It's a life of freedom and adventure.'

Vazoya glared critically at the module's occupants. 'You're full of crap, Olzan.'

He beamed. 'And this is my charming first mate. How are things, Vazoya?'

Vazoya ignored him. 'Keldra, right? Don't believe a word our captain says. Ship's a junk heap barely holding together. Owner's a scumbag who'd kill us all if he found a way to make money out of it.'

'Vazoya, my dear! You could be a little more positive while we have a new recruit on board.'

'She'll come with us. You'll come with us, won't you, Keldra? Anything beats rotting on Pandora.'

Keldra's voice was guarded; she looked deeply uncomfortable with being on a strange ship. 'I'm not sure yet.'

'I saw your engineering test scores. You're coming with us.'

Olzan ignored his first mate and strode off along the central corridor with Keldra half-jogging after him. 'And this is the forward ring, where we keep the crew quarters, kitchen, recreation area, medical bay, and most importantly …' he swung the door wide, 'the bridge! How's it going, Brenn?'

Brenn looked up from the pilot console blearily, as if Olzan had pulled him out of a daydream. 'We're fuelled up and the cargo's stowed. Our window for the spin to Xanadu lasts another twelve hours. We can set sail as soon as the new recruit's on board.'

'New recruit's here, Brenn.'

'Oh! Hello.' Brenn looked startled, even though Keldra had been in the doorway for several seconds. He could sense everything that happened to the ship, but a lot of the time he only seemed half-aware of his own surroundings. But he was a good kid, and Olzan had never met a pilot who was quite all there in the head.

'That's nearly everyone,' said Olzan. 'Just got to introduce you to our engineer.'

Keldra had moved into the bridge and was peering at the captain's console, or maybe at the hash of wiring beneath it. It looked as though her interest in ship engineering had overcome her nervousness, and from the way she was looking at the wiring, Olzan could easily believe she was the genius engineer her scores showed. She looked up at him with a puzzled expression.

'There's just the four of you? How do you manage without a full crew?'

Olzan grinned. 'We're just that good. Anyway, it's five of us now we've found you.'

'Still not sure I'm joining,' she said.

Olzan ignored her. 'Tarraso will be in the other ring. Come on.'

The second ring housed storage for grav-dependent cargo, the ship's own stores, and Tarraso's workshops. Olzan could hear the sound of his tinkering as soon as the transit module opened. He followed the sound, with Keldra still in tow.

Tarraso had one of the air scrubbers laid out on a workbench. The scrubber had stopped working a week ago, coughing graphite across the corridor, but Pandora's markets didn't have a replacement for a price they could afford. Olzan had cursed his bad luck and told Tarraso to extend its lifespan as much as he could. Despite the messy nature of the work, the room was spotlessly clean, with a dozen tools laid out on a side table and everything else tucked away in neatly hand-labelled cupboards. Tarraso didn't look up as Olzan and Keldra entered.

'Tarraso,' said Olzan. 'This is Keldra. She's our new second engineer.'

Tarraso acknowledged Olzan with a tiny nod, but finished the adjustment he was making and carefully laid down his tool before turning around. He looked Keldra up and down, his expression just the same as if he were inspecting some flawed and dirty piece of machinery.

'No,' he said.

Olzan moved closer to his old friend and spoke more softly. 'We've been through this. We're half-falling apart here.' He gestured to the other damaged ship components resting in a line against the wall. 'You need another pair of hands.'

Tarraso wiped his hands on a cloth and walked up to Keldra. 'You ever been assistant engineer on a Salamander before?'

'No,' she said. It was a simple statement, devoid of emotion.

'Ever served on a freighter?'

'No.'

'Ever even flown inter-city?'

'No.'

Tarraso turned his gaze to Olzan. 'No,' he said. He went back to his work.

Olzan gave Keldra a frustrated look. 'Come on, sell yourself some more!' To Tarraso he said, 'Keldra's worked in city habitat maintenance, and you saw her test scores. We're not going to find a better assistant in the cluster.'

'I'm engineer here. I don't need an assistant.'

'I'm the captain, and I'm telling you, you do.'

Tarraso fumed, but relented. He turned his critical gaze onto Keldra again.

'You. Look at this air scrubber. What would you do to fix it?'

She peered into the dusty guts of the machine. Her hand floated above it, almost but not quite touching the components.

'Get the whole module replaced,' she said after a few seconds. 'It's well past the end of its life. You can fix individual problems but the whole thing's going to keep failing in different ways.'

Tarraso snorted. 'We're not living in a perfect world, girl.'

Keldra looked as if she was about to say something, but then stopped. She seemed surprised, offended even. It was the first time she'd shown a definite emotion since she came aboard.

'We can't replace the module,' Olzan prompted. 'What do you do?'

She examined the machine again, this time bending down to peer at its innards and feeling some of them with her fingertips. When she straightened up her face and hands bore thin smears of graphite dust and oil.

'Take out these catalyst fins,' she said, pointing. 'Run the module at three-fifths capacity. You'll get a few more months out of it. You can afford to run life support below capacity since you don't have a full crew.'

Olzan glanced at the workings of the machine – he barely understood them – and then at Tarraso. 'Would it work?'

'Yeah, it would work,' Tarraso said grudgingly. He turned to Keldra, looking now as if he was assessing a broken machine's value as a source of spare parts. 'You do what I say, all right? You give your opinion when I ask for it, and only then. Your main job's going to be cleaning up. There's a lot of that, and you're going to take the time to do it right. Understand?'

'I've got some other ships interested in me,' Keldra said. 'I need to think about it. I'll let you know.'

'No, you're coming with us,' Olzan said. He subvocalized the command that would put his implant in touch with the bridge. 'Brenn, release docking clamps. Get us under way.'

'You can't do that!' That anger was the second emotion Olzan had seen Keldra show. 'I haven't signed anything. I was here for an interview.'

Tarraso laughed. 'Hah. Girl from a perfect world.'

'Sorry, kid. We can't risk losing someone with your skills. You'll get your cut, don't worry, but you're not getting off. You've just joined the noble ranks of inter-city traders.'

Keldra looked as though she was about to argue, but then seemed to think better of it. She stood sullenly, saying nothing.

'Come on. I'll show you to your quarters.'

'Jonas! What are you doing?'

His head swam, as if he were being shaken awake from a dream. It took him a few seconds to become aware of his surroundings. He was still in the corridor of the first ring on the *Remembrance of Clouds*. Keldra was yelling at him, but he ignored her, closed his eyes again, and tried to work out what was going on.

That had been a memory playback. The implant Keldra had put into him must have been an admin implant with memory-recording functionality, belonging to this Captain Olzan. Keldra might well be the genius engineer that Olzan had believed her to be, but according to the memory her training was in habitat engineering. That would transfer easily enough to other ship systems, but less well to the arcane mix of electronics, software engineering, and neurobiology required to hack an implant. Keldra must have made a mistake when she turned the implant into a control device, causing it to push one of Olzan's recorded memories into his head, unbidden.

'What happened?' Keldra demanded. 'Talk to me!'

Jonas thought for a short while before answering. It looked as though only a few seconds had passed in the real world. Memory-playback implants didn't play back experiences in real time; they just inserted the memory image of having just experienced the scene, adding minutes or hours of subjective time that the brain couldn't tell from the real thing. If Keldra didn't know that Jonas's implant was malfunctioning, he didn't need to tell her.

'I blacked out for a moment. I'm tired.'

Keldra seemed to believe him. She gave him an unsympathetic sneer. 'You can sleep when we're done with the tour. Try to keep up.'

The tour confirmed what Jonas had suspected: the *Remembrance of Clouds* was the same ship as the *Thousand Names*, the ship from Olzan's memory. Keldra had modified it, added the armaments he'd seen earlier, and done a decent job of repairing several years of wear, but underneath it was still the same ageing tramp freighter, held together by duct tape and bloody-mindedness.

The tour Olzan had given Keldra had been about meeting the crew. There was no free-willed crew on the ship, but Jonas suspected that, even if there had been, they would have been a side-point, at best, on Keldra's tour. She took him through the ship section by section, from nose to tail, pointing out her modifications and explaining its technical specifications in more detail than he understood. He couldn't see much use in giving such a detailed tour to a non-engineer, especially an untrustworthy prisoner, but he suspected that it wasn't entirely for his benefit. Now that she'd decided to keep him around, it seemed that she was enjoying having someone to talk at. A few times, when pointing out some particularly clever modification, she forgot to be aggressive and Jonas detected some honest pride entering her voice.

The tour began in the ship's nose, a bulbous structure consisting of the forward observation blister, the docking airlock and umbilicals, and the extendible gantry that housed the sail bud. Right now the sail was unfurled, and the kilo-metres-wide plane of ultra-thin nanomaterial dwarfed the rest of the ship. The sail was perfectly flat, possessing an eerie mathematical beauty, as if it were an intruder into normal space from a universe of pure geometry. From inside the observation blister Jonas could see his gold-tinted reflection looking down at him, at the nose of a vertiginous duplicate of the *Remembrance of Clouds*.

From a distance, a sail clipper looked like an insect, or a jewel, suspended from its sail by hundreds of gossamer nanotech threads. The sail was Earth-tech, of course; a forgotten technology, invented in the last flush of learning of the Planetary Age. The belt-dwellers could produce it in semi-automated factories, and even maintain it in a rote way, but could never have invented it.

Behind the nose were the two grav-rings, rotating in oppo-site directions for stability. Keldra ran them faster than Olzan had, fast enough to provide one gee of centrifugal pseudo-gravity. Jonas wondered why, before he remembered where the ancient measurement had come from: one gee had been the surface gravity of Earth.

Looking down from the blister he could see the inner surface of the first ring as it rotated around him. The repairs were more extensive than they had looked from the *Coriolis Dancer*; he could see a great swathe of the ring where the surface had been replaced with mismatched sheets of scrap metal.

Keldra dragged Jonas around the orbital corridors of each ring, showing him each room. Besides modifying the bridge to suit her one-person control, it looked as if she had changed little from Jonas's second-hand memory of the *Thousand Names*. She had also painted murals on various walls and ceilings: images of the Earth from space, or scenes of its surface as she imagined it to have looked, in big, messy brush-strokes of green and blue. Every image included the white scrawls of clouds across the sky.

It looked as if Keldra had made more changes to the second ring. The engineering workshops were still there, but the rest of the ring was packed with servitors and all the support machinery needed to sustain so many of them, as well as the prison cells where Jonas had been kept. Now that the ship was underway the servitors shambled through a simple daily routine, feeding and exercising themselves. A few performed maintenance tasks, replacing worn-out pipes or cleaning the graphite from the air scrubbers. Besides generally being physically fit, there was no pattern to the servitors' appearance, and Keldra hadn't given them the uniforms or liveries that most servitor-owners used.

The door of one of the store rooms in the second ring was locked with a heavy bar, linked to an iris-recognition lock screwed to the wall next to it. It looked as though the lock had been installed recently, while Keldra had left Jonas locked in his cabin. She hauled him up to the door, seemingly just to point it out.

'That's off-limits,' she said. 'If I catch you so much as looking at that door, you're wiped. Understand?'

'I've already seen your stolen goods and illegal servitors. What could be worse than . . . oww!'

Keldra jabbed the nerve gun into his side and sent a shock running through his body. 'It's off-limits. Do you understand?'

'All right! I understand.'

Aft of the grav-rings was the cargo bay. Keldra didn't take Jonas into it, but she showed it to him through the grimy windows of the docking control room that looked out on the interior of the bay, turning on the floodlights to bathe the brightly-coloured shipping containers in a sterile white light. Like the *Dancer's*, the bay was non-rotating and without air, little more than a radiation shield wrapped around a volume of vacuum, with the ship's spine running down the centre. Half of the outer surface was a door that could open to space, and it was on this that Keldra had painted the huge Earth-and-clouds mural that Jonas had seen on the *Coriolis Dancer's* bridge screen.

Beyond the cargo bay were the main heat radiation fins, although, Keldra explained proudly, most of the ship's surface could act as a radiation system in an emergency. Behind the fins was the reaction drive and its fuel tanks. Despite its size, this was a secondary drive, intended for close city approaches where a sail couldn't be used, and as a backup, in case the sail failed. It could provide more acceleration than the sail, but not for long before the fuel tanks were exhausted.

To Jonas's relief, Keldra didn't take him into the unpressurized maintenance crawl-spaces that ran through it, but she described it to him in the loading control room. Most of the technical details washed past him, but he didn't think she was showing off, as such, she just wasn't used to translating her Engineer-caste language for the benefit of a layperson.

Keldra didn't go into detail about the ship's weapons, but Jonas didn't think there was more to them than he'd seen. The main armaments were a dozen missile turrets, spaced around the ship's hull to provide a near-complete firing sphere, but unable to concentrate much fire on any one target. There were also the Worldbreaker-killing nukes, but each one was a massive investment of time and money, and he didn't think she would want to use one except against a Worldbreaker. The small missile turrets might be used to shoot down incoming missiles, but the *Remembrance* had almost no armour. It could hold unescorted mining haulers to ransom, but it wouldn't last long against a city patrol boat, still less a Solar Authority cruiser.

After the tour they rode the transit module back to the first ring. Keldra fell silent, but she looked at him as if expecting him to say something.

Jonas decided to fill the silence. 'So, where are we going?'

'Columbia. The civil war there means lots of unprotected refugee ships. We need to start building another nuke.'

'How noble.'

'Fuck you.'

He licked his lips, thinking back to Olzan's memory. Keldra was emotionally vulnerable, open to manipulation, he was sure; he just had to find the right key. It was worth a try.

'You know, when you told me about your crusade against the Worldbreakers, I thought you were an idealist. I thought you believed in a perfect world.' He pronounced the last two words deliberately, hoping that they'd strike a nerve.

Keldra's face went pale. She broke eye contact and turned away.

'You're right that we ought to fight the Worldbreakers,' he went on. 'We've given up, collectively, as a species. We all just climb over one another to get to the top of the heap, while the Worldbreakers make the heap smaller and smaller. There ought to be more people living in a perfect world.'

The words made her flinch. Jonas suppressed the urge to smile as he moved in for the kill.

'What you're doing isn't fighting back, and you know it. You're nothing but a common pirate with an obsession. You should find an effective way to strike against the Worldbreakers, and if you can't do that you should find a way to live without killing people.'

The transit module had come to rest in the first ring.

'Tour's over,' Keldra spat as she unclipped herself. 'You know where your cabin is.' She pushed Jonas out of the module and then closed its doors and departed for the second ring.

A few moments later, as he closed the door of his cabin, he felt the gentle drifting sensation of the ship rotating to reposition its sail. Keldra had changed course.

Chapter Five

Jonas sat at the desk in his cabin and pushed the lid of the useless terminal down until it was flush with the desktop. He flexed his fingers like a pianist about to play. His hands were steady, but he could feel the nervousness in his chest. It was just possible that what he was about to do would trigger Keldra's implant and kill him.

'Open virtual office,' he said.

Nothing happened.

It had been too much to hope that Olzan had left his implant on the default settings. Most administrators with implants set the commands to something more personal. There was no point in making them obscure – no one could use the implant but the person in whose brain it was implanted – but if Olzan had set the command to something idiosyncratic then Jonas might never be able to guess it.

'Access admin functions,' he said. That had been his command when he had been Gabriel's administrator back on Oberon. Still nothing. 'Virtual office, open. Open office. Open desktop. Admin functions. Admin office.'

It took Jonas a few minutes to get through all the command combinations he could think of. If Keldra had a bug in his quarters then she'd know what he was trying to do, but he didn't think she did: implanting him had been a spur-of-the-moment decision, and since then he'd been either in his quarters or with her the whole time, so there was no time in which she could have planted anything.

No luck with any phrase that he tried. If the trigger was an obscure voice command then he might never find it, but it was possible that it was something non-verbal.

He clapped his hands together and then pulled them apart, as if conjuring the virtual desktop out of the air. Nothing. He tried clapping twice in quick succession. Three times. Four, five, six. Any more than that and it felt too unwieldy to be convenient. He didn't think Olzan would have wanted to start applauding the air whenever he wanted to work.

Perhaps clicking his fingers would be more Olzan's style. He tried once. Twice. Three times—

Icons exploded into the air in front of him, whirling around for a moment as they tried to anchor themselves in space, before settling onto the surface of the desk like ghostly ornaments. In the centre of the desk was a rectangular pad with the implant's general status report.

2510-AUG-14
Last login: 2503-FEB-03
Warning: Possible implant damage. Diagnostic needed.
0 unread messages.

Jonas waved his hand through the icon representing the implant's saved memories. A list of memories scrolled onto the middle of the desk, each identified by a time/location stamp. There were a few dozen, covering the years from 2498 to 2503.

Jonas scanned down the list and found Olzan's memory of giving Keldra the tour. It was dated 2502-NOV-01. There were half a dozen memories after that point, the last one recorded on the same date as Olzan's last login to the virtual office. If there was something he could use against Keldra, it would most likely be in one of those later memories, recorded while she had been on board.

The next memory after Keldra's tour had a timestamp of 2502-DEC-14. Jonas attempted to play it.

Implant malfunction. Playback unavailable.

Of course. That would have been too easy. He guessed the implant malfunction was deliberate hacking on Keldra's part. Implants were Earth-tech, their workings only partially understood. It might be that disabling the memory playback was easier than deleting the stored memories themselves.

He tried a few other memories. All the memories after Keldra's tour were similarly locked.

He tried the memory of Keldra's tour. He knew the implant could play that one . . .

Implant malfunction. Playback unavailable.

Jonas smiled. It seemed that Keldra's hacking was imperfect. If the right trigger phrase had got around the block for that memory, then it was possible that different triggers – phrases, images, or sensations – would allow him to play back other memories.

He had to hope there was something in one of those memories that would help him to manipulate Keldra. The implant meant that he couldn't overpower her, or slip away into a city; but if he played her right, she would deactivate the implant and let him go.

Finding the triggers for the other recordings would take time, if it was possible at all, but he had the entire journey to Columbia – or wherever the *Remembrance* was headed now – in order to try.

The woman stood close, her face filling the recording servitor's view. She pushed a strand of long black hair from her face and smiled, nervously, as if not quite comfortable with recording a message through an expressionless servitor.

Jonas looked out through the servitor's eyes. He felt a ghostly sense of dissociation from inhabiting the servitor's body, but he retained his sense of identity: the servitor had no identity of its own to override his. This was a memory that Olzan had received as a message, rather than one he had recorded himself.

He had been thinking of Gabriel, he realized. That was what must have triggered the memory. He and Gabriel had used servitors to record messages for one another when they had been apart. As well as being able to record all five senses, a servitor recording had the advantage that it didn't leave a trace on the city datanet: no one could read it without physical access to the servitor on whose implant it was recorded; the perfect means to carry on a clandestine love affair.

Jonas had treasured the messages Gabriel had sent him over the few years they had known one another. Awkward and endearing, gradually becoming more intimate as their professional relationship changed into friendship and then something more. He had intended to keep them after he'd had his admin implant removed in order to pass as a true-born, but the black market surgeon he'd used had damaged it beyond repair. Now all he had were his natural memories of Gabriel, and those were too painful for him to think of often.

'Olzan, I've got news,' the woman said. She had a mellifluous Belt Three true-born accent, the type of voice that Jonas had spent the last six years affecting. 'I talked to father again, about us. He's not angry any more. He says he would have liked me to marry a true-born, but he wants me to be happy as well. He's . . . ' She looked away for a moment. 'He's not a bad person, Olzan. He just wants what's best for the family. Next time you're here, you should talk to him some more.' The woman paused, as if waiting for Olzan to reply, but of course, the servitor said nothing. 'Listen, he says a new job has come up,' she continued. 'Something a bit different from what you normally do, something important. I don't know what it is. He'll send the details. But he said that, if you do it, he'll pay for the treatment, so we can get married.' She moved closer, put a hand on the servitor's shoulder. Jonas found its lack of response unnerving. 'You'll be part of the family, Olzan. We can have children, and they'll be true-borns. Just one more job and we can be together.'

She leaned in and kissed the servitor, a long, slow kiss, and the message ended, leaving Jonas alone in his dark cabin.

The next day, Jonas found Keldra in her control nest on the bridge. The room was dark, and projected onto the bridge screen was a full-system chart: five concentric rings showing the five inhabited belts. A tangle of curving red lines marked the estimated courses of the hundreds of Worldbreakers currently starward of the veil, as they swept through the belts on great destructive arcs. In the centre was a solid ring of red, the hazy image of the thousands more Worldbreakers within the veil performing their mysterious industries in close orbit around the sun.

Yellow blobs picked out the two hundred or so remaining human cities. There were no name labels, and on a map this scale Jonas couldn't tell which city was which. One city down in Belt Two was close to the red line of a Worldbreaker, and was picked out with a warning symbol. If that Worldbreaker changed course towards the city, it would have to be evacuated.

There was one other symbol that Jonas didn't recognize, a blue star, in the void between Belts Two and Three.

As soon as Keldra noticed Jonas she made a hand movement and the blue star vanished. She was holding a foil tray of instant breakfast, something like powdered eggs, and a stained coffee cup perched on the edge of her control nest.

'So, where are we going, Captain?' he asked.

She swallowed her mouthful. 'Columbia. I told you.'

'You're not much of a liar, Keldra. I felt us change course.'

She looked for a moment as if she were about to deny it, but then seemed to change her mind. She made a hand movement and a line appeared on the screen, showing the *Remembrance's* new course. 'We're stopping off at Santesteban first. I want to sell the stuff I got from your ship. Pick up some supplies.' She gave him a patronizing smile. 'I don't suppose it's your kind of place.'

Santesteban was one of the independent cities that thrived off of piracy. It allowed armed civilian ships to dock, and it didn't have law-enforcement treaties with other cities, so pirates could use it as a safe haven as long as they didn't interfere with the city's own interests.

Jonas studied the chart. Now that he knew which dot was Santesteban, he thought he could identify Columbia from his memory of belt orbits. Going to Santesteban first would be a significant detour, too large just for the sake of offloading loot and buying supplies. Keldra's story was clearly a lie, but for now he decided not to push her for an answer. 'So what do I do here?' he asked. 'I'm Administrator-caste, but there's no one for me to administer. I can't help much with the engineering.'

'You get communications,' Keldra said. 'You're a lying, manipulative bastard. From now on you get to lie and manipulate for me. That's when we get to Santesteban, though. In the meantime there's some grunt work you can get on with.' She pointed across the room, and a terminal to one side lit up and purred. It hadn't been there yesterday; it looked like Keldra had installed it for him.

He sat down and examined the terminal. It was set up as a communications console, but actual access to the communications laser was locked out for the moment. If he waited until she ordered him to transmit something he might be able to get out a coded message at the same time, although he wasn't sure to whom. Perhaps the Solar Authority would help him if he could keep up his Gabriel Reinhardt act.

He flipped through the terminal's other settings. Cargo space allocation, servitor duty rosters, damage monitoring. Dozens of tasks that needed a human eye from time to time, but not a very talented one. There was no access to anything critical, of course, and even if he did find some way to use cargo space allocation against Keldra, she would know about it instantly.

'I'll give you access to the comms laser when you need it,' Keldra said. 'For now, there's a list of tasks in the console. Get to work.'

Keldra kept the ship on a twenty-four-hour cycle, with the corridor lights dimming for twelve hours each day. Another sign of the pirate's obsession with Earth, Jonas assumed. Despite the cycle, Keldra herself kept an irregular schedule. He sometimes heard her moving about in the corridor in the middle of the night, and there was no pattern to the times he would find the foil tray from an instant meal lying on the dining room table. He preferred to keep a regular sleep pattern, and after a couple of days he had synced himself with the ship's day-night cycle, but he never knew when she would buzz the intercom and summon him to help with some repair or maintenance task.

Keldra had put in place an impressive network of automated routines to make her small army of servitors work with the mechanical systems to keep the ship in good repair and respond to minor incidents. Watching the servitors in action, the *Remembrance* seemed more like an organism than a machine, with the servitors as individual cells and Keldra in her nest as the brain. Even so, no amount of automation could completely make up for the lack of a free-willed crew. Keldra spent most of her time just maintaining the ship, coping with the daily minor emergencies caused by its age and its many modifications. The workshop that had been Tarraso's was now cluttered with untidy heaps of machinery, waiting for Keldra to either repair them or strip them down for parts. Jonas's mechanical skills were modest, but she put him to work anyway; there were many jobs that benefited from a second free-willed pair of hands.

When she didn't need him for some ship maintenance task, Keldra barely spoke to Jonas. Sometimes she would walk into the dining room while he was eating and look at him in confusion, as if she had forgotten he was on the ship, before giving him a disapproving glare and walking off. At other times she would stride haughtily by, not making eye contact, as if she thought she could hurt his feelings by ignoring him. But she trusted him – or rather, trusted the threat of her implant – enough that she no longer carried the nerve gun.

Jonas spent his free time roaming the ship, looking for ghosts.

Olzan sat at the head of the dining room table as the rest of the crew filtered in and took their seats. Tarraso and Keldra were both speckled with machine oil from whatever task he had called them away from; Tarraso arrived a few moments after Keldra, since he insisted on thoroughly washing his hands no matter how urgent the summons. Brenn was there immediately in person, although perhaps not mentally. Vazoya arrived last and didn't sit down, instead hovering in the kitchen doorway with a cup of her bitter black coffee in her hand.

'I've just got new orders from Mr Glass,' Olzan said, once everyone was seated. He tried to say it casually, to head off any hostility from the crew. This wasn't something that would be easy to break to them. 'We're to abandon the Alexandria run and make for Konrad's Hope.'

Vazoya made a sour face. 'What about our cargo?'

'We dump the cargo to reduce our mass. We're to get to Konrad's Hope quickly.'

'That's bullshit. Wendell Glass doesn't know what the hell he's doing. We should go to Alex first. Whatever's in Konrad's Hope can wait.'

'No it can't,' Olzan said. He cleared his throat, not sure of the best way to break the real reason to them. He'd been nervous too when he'd heard it. 'There's something else. Konrad's Hope—'

'There's a Worldbreaker,' Keldra said.

Everyone stared at her. She had barely spoken since Olzan had press-ganged her onto the ship. She was sitting at the end of the table, leaning back in her chair, placing her a little way away from the rest of the group. She had her arms folded and her expression was hard to read; she seemed angry, but not at anyone in the room.

'There's a Worldbreaker,' Olzan said, breaking the silence. 'It changed course twenty-eight hours ago, so Konrad's Hope is in the danger zone.'

Tarraso was staring at Keldra. 'How the hell do you know that? We didn't know we were going to Konrad's Hope until just now.'

'Keldra monitors the Worldbreakers,' Brenn said helpfully. 'She likes to know where they all are.' He was the only one who didn't seem affected by the news. If something wasn't happening to the ship right now, Olzan thought, it wasn't quite real to him.

'Who the hell does that?' Tarraso said. 'That's . . . morbid.'

Keldra shrugged.

Vazoya took a sip of her coffee and smiled thoughtfully at Olzan over the top of the cup. 'So we're part of an evac run? I didn't think Wendell wanted us to do those.'

'This is an exception.'

'Are we going in for anyone specific, or seeing who'll pay?'

'Neither.' This was the other part of the news that the crew might take badly, especially Vazoya. 'We're not picking up passengers. Mr Glass has some items he wants us to acquire.'

'Items? Bullshit.'

'What items?' Tarraso asked.

Olzan quickly consulted the message in his implant. 'Planetary Age artefacts. It's a collection belonging to Anastasia Zhu. She's already evacuated, but she's leaving her collection. We're going to, ah, rescue it.'

'Bullshit!' Vazoya slammed her cup in the middle of the table, spattering hot liquid onto the surface and making

Brenn blink. 'You don't rescue objects. If we're on an evac run then we should rescue people. I'm fine with us making a profit out of it. We can't take everyone, so taking whoever can pay is as good a way of choosing as any. But you don't visit a city in a Worldbreaker Red Zone unless you're going to come away with your ship crammed with people.'

Olzan shook his head sympathetically. 'Orders from Mr Glass. We take the artefacts. We can take some evacuees if there's room after that.'

'Bullshit.'

'He's right,' Keldra said.

Vazoya looked at her in disgust. 'Keldra, what the fuck?'

'Mr Glass is right. They're Planetary Age artefacts. There are only so many left and when they're gone, they're gone. They're important, people are just . . . ' she shrugged, 'people.'

Vazoya leapt across the table at her, scattering foil plates and sending the coffee cup spinning onto the floor. Olzan grabbed her around the waist and held her back as she struggled to reach the other woman. Keldra had sprung up, ready to return the blows.

'Pack it in, both of you,' Olzan shouted. 'This isn't up for discussion. We do the job Mr Glass pays us to do.'

'Tell Mr Glass he can go fuck himself,' Vazoya said, directing her anger towards Olzan now, or rather towards the implant they all knew sat at the base of Olzan's skull. 'I know you'll watch this recording. You can go fuck yourself. I've had enough of this outfit. I'm getting off at the next rock.' She stormed off down the corridor towards her quarters. Olzan let her go. She'd be back. She needed to vent, but she'd follow orders.

Brenn hesitated and then went out after Vazoya. Tarraso shrugged.

'Ah, what's it matter anyway? All be the same when the last rock's gone.'

'Doesn't have to be.' Keldra seemed to be talking to herself.

'What was that?' asked Olzan.

'We should fight them. Don't have to let them win.'

Tarraso laughed. It wasn't a sarcastic or mocking laugh. He had genuinely found Keldra's comment funny. 'Can't fight the Worldbreakers,' he said as he left.

Keldra didn't respond. She stayed seated, staring at the table.

Olzan watched her for a moment and then walked back to his cabin. 'All right,' he said under his breath, for the recording. 'We're on our way.'

'What are the Worldbreakers?'

Jonas looked up from his terminal as Keldra strode onto the bridge. With a click of her fingers she summoned an image of a Worldbreaker onto the screen. It was a simple diagram, a black dodecahedron with its edges picked out in green wireframe. One of its twelve faces had five lines meeting in the centre where the Worldbreaker's mouth could open, and from that face a faint wireframe extended inwards, sketchily showing what little was known of the Worldbreaker's internal anatomy.

He stopped work and closed down his bridge terminal. He had a feeling this would take a while. 'No one knows,' he said.

'Wrong.' Keldra walked past her control nest, and stood in front of the screen like a schoolteacher giving a lecture. She stared critically at Jonas, as if expecting another response.

'People say different things about them,' he said. 'Scribers believe that they're angels, sent to usher us into Paradise.'

'They're wrong. They're idiots.'

58

Jonas remembered the earnestness on Gabriel's face, shining through the smoke from his incense burner as he'd talked about his beliefs. 'They might be wrong, but they're not stupid,' he said carefully, not letting any emotion show.

'The Scribers are idiots,' Keldra repeated, as if she had just cut through all the complexities of their beliefs and settled the matter. 'What else do people say?'

Jonas decided there was no point in arguing about Gabriel's honour now. He pushed Gabriel's memory out of his mind and tried to recall the other religions' beliefs about the Worldbreakers. 'The Arkites say they're a second Flood.' He had only a vague idea what the first Flood was meant to have been; he had trouble visualizing enough water to cover the surface of a planet. 'Once the belts are gone, God will make the planets re-form and people can start again.'

'Hah. Any day now, I'm sure.'

'The Eternalist groups believe that they're part of the natural order,' Jonas said. 'The planets are made and un-made on an endless cycle. The True Belters say that there never were any planets – they're a myth – and the Worldbreakers and the belts have always been there. Some people say they're a natural phenomenon and it's nothing to do with God, if there even is a god.'

'Wrong, wrong, wrong,' Keldra said. 'What do you believe?'

He shrugged. 'I don't believe anything.'

'You believe whatever works best for your persona, I bet.'

'Sometimes,' he said. He let a little of his annoyance show. 'Are you going to get to a point? If you're so sure everyone is wrong, I assume that means you've got it all figured out.'

'They're not angels, or demons, or gods,' Keldra said. 'But they're not natural either. They're machines.'

He gave her a disdainful look. 'Machines. Built by people?'

'Built by *aliens*.'

'Machines built by aliens.'

'It's not so far-fetched. It's obvious, if you look at the data rather than listen to the babbling of the churches.'

'Really.'

'I'm not even the first one to have this idea. It was the scientific consensus, back in the first century after the Worldbreakers came. Back when there were still universities and researchers.' Her voice dripped venom. 'The information's out there, on the city datanets, if you know where to look. But no one does look. They'd rather believe in angels and gods.'

'So what is this information?'

Keldra clicked her fingers again. The Worldbreaker disappeared from the screen, replaced by a belt chart, concentric circles around the yellow orb of the sun. But instead of the normal five belts, there were nine, and instead of the normal hazy toroids, all but one of the belts was a fine line with a single circle standing out on it like the jewel on a necklace.

'This is the solar system before the Worldbreakers arrived,' she said. 'Four inner rocky planets, the primordial belt, four outer gas planets. Plus other minor bodies; this is a simplification.' She snapped her fingers and a line appeared on the edge of the chart, arrowing in from interstellar space. 'That is the first sighting of the Worldbreaker Cluster. It arrived from another star system. It didn't just appear.'

'That doesn't mean anything,' Jonas said. 'Angels could come from another star system.'

'Shut up,' Keldra said. 'You don't need angels to explain the Worldbreakers. Look at what they do.' She waved at the screen and the circles began spinning, fast-forwarding through time. The Worldbreaker Cluster moved in towards the planets and then split into countless red lines, like the tendrils of a microgravity adjusted plant. In Jonas's day, each Worldbreaker travelled alone, independent of the others, but the ones on the screen moved in swarms, hundreds or thousands strong. The largest swarm went straight down towards the sun. Others swerved towards the jewel-like dots on the belt lines: the planets.

One by one, as the Worldbreaker swarms reached them, the planets winked out.

'They need two things,' Keldra said. 'Raw material and energy. Energy they get from the sun. That's why they get so close to it. Raw material they get from the planets. They blew them up, and then they started scooping up the debris.'

'What do they need it for?'

'To keep running. They're self-sustaining; they make more of themselves. My point is, they're not *magic*. They're technological artefacts. Machines.'

'They don't look like any machines I've seen,' Jonas said.

'That's because they weren't made by *us*. They're much more advanced, maybe by millions of years.' She brought back the Worldbreaker diagram. 'I think they've learned to manipulate gravity somehow. They use that for both their weapon and their reactionless drive. I don't know how it works, but I don't think it breaks any physical laws. They can't create something out of nothing; they still need energy and raw materials.'

'All right. Supposing that's true, why would anyone want to build these machines?'

'To destroy us,' Keldra said. The image on the screen changed again, this time filling with stars scattered through three-dimensional space. 'Someone else out there must have spotted us. We were broadcasting from Earth for hundreds of years before the Worldbreakers arrived; maybe they heard us. Or maybe it was longer ago, and they just spotted a planet with life on it in our system. I think they saw us as a threat. As competition. They wanted to wipe us out before we became too powerful.'

'Or maybe they had a reason we can't imagine,' Jonas said.

'However alien your mindset, kill or be killed will always apply.'

'Maybe.'

'Maybe. Maybe. What do you think?'

He shrugged. 'You've got the implant in my head. I'll think whatever you tell me to think.'

She glared at him but didn't seem to have anything to say to that. Behind her, the stars on the screen vanished.

'Why did you tell me all this, Keldra?' he asked.

'I want you to know what we're up against,' she said. 'This is the enemy: the Worldbreakers and whoever made them. This is what we're fighting.'

'You don't need me to know anything about that,' Jonas said. 'It won't make me help you run this ship more efficiently. You're not telling me what we're doing in Santesteban, which might be more useful.'

Her sarcastic laugh was weaker than usual. 'You'll find out when we get there.'

'You told me your theories about the Worldbreakers because you wanted an audience. You've been working on these theories on your own for years, and now you want the validation of someone saying they agree with you. Well, you won't get it from me, not while I'm your slave. While you've got the implant in my head, I'll believe whatever you tell me to believe.' He tilted his head forward and pulled the back of his shirt collar down with one hand, exposing the back of his neck. 'Deactivate your triggers and then I can tell you what I really think.'

Keldra stood scowling at him for a moment, as if she were considering it, but then strode back out of the bridge. 'Get back to work.'

A few hours out from Santesteban, Keldra walked into Jonas's cabin and tossed another bundle of clothes at him: a grey business suit from his wardrobe on the *Coriolis Dancer*, along with some jewellery suitable for a formal true-born gathering. 'You wear that tomorrow.'

'You're letting me off the ship at Santesteban, then?'

'You're a true-born business owner,' Keldra said. 'You ran the LN-411 mining operation. When the Worldbreaker showed up you packed up and ran like the coward you are.'

'Should have fought, yeah. We've been through this.'

'Shut up. You didn't have your hauler ship with you when the Worldbreaker arrived. It was off making a delivery. You only had your private escape shuttle, so you had to abandon most of your operation. You had space to take your free-willed employees and the most valuable bits of equipment. The hab system core, some other things. Here's a list.'

Jonas glanced at the data pad she handed to him. Miscellaneous bits of technology, the valuable and portable stuff: it was what he would have chosen to save if her story were true. 'Okay,' he said. 'Where's this going?'

'During the journey, you decided you didn't want to pay your employees, so you slave-spiked them all. They struggled, and the shuttle took some damage.'

'Is that something you think I'd do?'

'Yes, it is. But that doesn't matter. It has to be part of the story.' She snapped her fingers and a belt chart appeared on the pad in Jonas's hand, with a line picking out his imaginary course. 'You got as far as the Kellman trading post. Kellman didn't have the parts to repair the shuttle, so you sold it for scrap. You couldn't sell the servitors there because they were illegal; no paperwork. So you bought passage on the *Remembrance of Clouds*, a perfectly innocent freighter, which was heading to Santesteban. If you look at the ship's logs you'll find it was at Kellman at the right time.'

'I'm sure I will. So what's the plan? I take it you're not letting me go with some servitors and a hab core.'

'You're going to meet the owner of the city.' Another click of Keldra's fingers, and a man's face appeared on the pad. He looked somewhere in his fifties, completely hairless, with flabby, unhealthy looking features. 'You can get in to see him because you're a true-born and you have things that he'll want. You're going to him because you want to offload the servitors: you don't have the black market connections to sell them, but you know that he won't care that they're illegal. The reason he'll talk to you is because of the hab core. Santesteban's life support is in a poor state because the owner doesn't like paying full price for anything. Your used hab core is exactly the sort of deal he'd want, but it's legally yours so you're not in so much of a hurry to get rid of it, as you are the servitors. You could take it to another city if you thought you could get a better deal.'

Jonas paused as he took all this in. 'So what's the job? I'm guessing we're pulling off some kind of con. What do I do when I get in?'

'You sell the servitors. You sell the hab core if you can get a good price. Then you spend a few hours hobnobbing with true-borns, drinking champagne out of real glass glasses, or whatever. Then you come back here. If you try to leave . . . ' She tapped the back of her neck.

'Come on, Keldra. You need me for something more than just getting better prices for your stolen goods. Tell me the plan and maybe I can help.'

'When did you think I started trusting you? I've told you all you need to know.'

'All right.' As she turned to leave he called after her. 'Who's the mark, anyway? I mean, the city owner. What's his name?'

'Wendell Taylor Glass.'

Chapter Six

Santesteban was a dark grey lozenge thirty kilometres long, once a droplet of iron that had spilled out of a planet's molten core, now swarming with the signs of habitation. The city's first owner had spun the rock up around its long axis, and its surface was studded with solar panels, heat sinks, and high-grav starscrapers. One end of the lozenge tapered to a point that formed the base of the counter-rotating docking spindle, and a dozen ships nuzzled against their docking pylons amidst tangles of boarding tunnels and fuel lines. Rickety looking freighters and light cruisers, some of them sporting visible weapon emplacements and the skull-and-gun motifs of pirates, floated next to the glittering playthings of the true-born elite.

Keldra furled the sail a safe distance from the city and made the final approach using thrusters, while Jonas exchanged messages with the weary voice of traffic control. Assigned a pylon, the *Remembrance of Clouds* began the careful process of docking.

Jonas made his way to the docking airlock at the tip of the *Remembrance's* spine. Floating with his arm hooked through a handhold, he could feel the gentle shudders running through the walls as the ship made contact with the spindle. A dozen servitors, the mind-wiped husks of his mining foremen from LN-411, hung around the wall behind him, their microgravity movement programmes keeping them inhumanly still. Keldra had shaved their heads and dressed them in orange coveralls. Strapped to the back of one was the life support core, a bulky mass of machinery that would have taken two strong men to lift under gravity. It took a few moments for Jonas to realize that the servitor carrying the core had been Matton. His face was skull-like with his beard gone.

I'll find a way to save all of us, Jonas had told Matton as the *Remembrance of Clouds* bore down on them, while Matton had told Jonas that he could only save himself. In the end, Matton had won the argument and lost his life. Jonas still couldn't think of anything he could have done to save his crew, but the feeling that he'd failed them persisted.

On the airlock's monitors he could see servitors in city issue vacuum suits working to attach fuel and power lines to the *Remembrance's* ports. A light went green, indicating that the airlock connection was in place. Jonas cycled through the airlock and then floated along the white tunnel of the pylon into Santesteban's docking spindle.

After weeks cooped up on the *Remembrance of Clouds* with only Keldra for company, Jonas felt a catch in his breath as he emerged into the huge space filled with noise, colour, and people. The interior of the spindle was a polished steel wall broken by the hatches to docking pylons. Automatic transfer lines ran along the surface, their varying speeds distinguished by colourful patterns. Jonas climbed hand-over-hand across increasingly fast lines until he was on a true-born-only express line towards the city. The servitors followed him faithfully, but he made sure not to do more than glance at them: a self-assured true-born didn't acknowledge his servitors in public.

The express line took him past an open pylon gate where an inter-city liner's passengers were disembarking. The few experienced microgravity travellers were already on transfer lines, but most of the people were struggling to keep their drifting suitcases in check. Tank-borns, all of them, in utilitarian jumpsuits. Despite their drab appearance, all of these tank-borns must have done very well for themselves if they could afford passage on an inter-city liner. Many of the stragglers would be immigrants taking the only inter-city voyage of their lives.

It wouldn't be proper for a true-born to make eye contact with passing tank-borns, but Jonas watched the travellers enviously from the corner of his eye. He wished he could lose himself in the throng and set up a new life on Santesteban. With the last of Gabriel's assets gone he'd have to drop the name in order to avoid contact with his family. He'd drop the true-born pretence; Gabriel's Immolation would finally be complete. The idea felt like a betrayal, both of Gabriel's memory and that of his crew, but it might be the only way to survive.

But that was impossible, in any case. The implant sat at the top of his spine like a bomb waiting to go off if he didn't get back to the *Remembrance* on time. There was a chance Keldra was bluffing, but he didn't think it was likely.

A free-floating attendant with a puffer belt spotted Jonas and moved over to meet him as he reached the end of the line. She was tall, with slender limbs and a bulbous, shaved cranium. It looked as though she had been raised in microgravity, part of a tank-born subculture that could never live in their own city's high-grav areas or travel on a high-acceleration ship. She folded her long body briefly in a microgravity bow, and then extended a datapad towards him. 'Your passport, sir?' Her voice was politely apologetic, as if ashamed to submit a true-born to such a humiliating process.

Jonas reined in his emotions to present a self-confident face, and touched his forged passport to the datapad then held it up for the attendant to inspect. She consulted the pad and nodded. 'Gabriel Reinhardt, *Remembrance of Clouds*?'

'That's right.'

'Reason for your visit?'

'Business. I'm here to see Wendell Taylor Glass. He's expecting me.' Jonas had sent a message before they had docked, putting himself on Glass's schedule.

The attendant made a note on the pad. 'There's a taxi waiting for you, sir. Enjoy your stay in Santesteban. Is there anything I can do for you?'

'Please have my servitors and cargo taken to a secure storage area.'

The attendant glanced at the servitors that were lined up behind Jonas. 'We can put them in a store room here in the spindle for 800 credits an hour. Is that . . . ?'

Jonas waved dismissively, as if the mere mention of such a small amount of money was distasteful to him.

'Very good, sir.' The attendant handed Jonas a wafer-pad storage ticket. He directed the servitors to follow her, and then skimmed her one-credit tip from the spending money he had convinced Keldra to give him. The attendant opened a door to let him through a rotation transfer hub and into the city proper. He saw her puffing away at the head of the line of servitors.

On the other side of the rotation transfer hub was a slowly spinning cylindrical concourse with walls of bare iron. It was swarming with people, many of them spidery low-grav tank-borns, moving around elegantly using puffer belts, or swimming through the air with membranous wings built into their jumpsuits. There was a steady stream of travellers struggling against the inertia of their luggage, and loitering freighter crews hooked into crannies in the wall. Jonas didn't make eye contact with anyone. When true-borns passed through places like this they did so quickly, on their way to somewhere more luxurious.

He navigated the handholds to the rail-taxi rank and found the cab with *Gabriel Reinhardt* flashing across its side.

'Diamond spindle,' he said as he strapped himself in. The driver acknowledged and the cab set off into a tunnel.

Wendell Taylor Glass didn't live on Santesteban proper, Keldra had told him, but on a luxury ringship, the *Haze of the Ecliptic*, orbiting a few dozen kilometres from the city. The only way he allowed visitors to reach him was via the diamond spindle, a private shuttle dock on the opposite end of the city from the spaceport. Most city owners lived apart from their subjects, but few did so as thoroughly as Glass.

The cab followed a tunnel that led away from the rock's rotation axis, and after a few moments there was enough gravity for it to feel as if they were moving down a gentle slope. Once they had reached about one-third of a gee, they emerged into a habitation cavern, the cab running across a network of rails suspended beneath the ceiling. The floor was hundreds of metres down, and he could see it curving up on either side of him. From below, he knew, the taxis passing overhead looked like angels on a wire.

This first cavern appeared to be an entertainment district. Steel buildings were arrayed across the rust-coloured floor; any pattern to their layout had been lost by years of ad hoc modifications and repairs. The permanent structures were encrusted with a shanty town made from discarded building materials and cargo containers. Garish neon signs rose up out of the mass, advertising various entertainments to spaceship crews just docked after long voyages. A thin film of rock dust covered everything, standing out starkly in the glare of the cavern's ceiling lights.

The car passed through a gap in the thin wall of iron that separated the cavern from the next one. This cavern was centred around a marketplace thronging with people. Most looked like natives to this low gravity area, tall and gangly and walking with long bounding strides, but there was a healthy presence of squat full-gravity figures as well, and even a few of the microgravity people lolling in wheelchairs. Every so often the crowd would part to make way for the rickshaw or palanquin of a visiting true-born.

Along one side of the market was a Scriber kitchen, where a long line of tank-borns shuffled forward to receive bowls of soup from white-robed monks. Some of the people in the queue wore white themselves, or had shaved their heads, signs of the first stages of initiation into the Scriber religion. A pair of Arkite preachers stood half way along the line. From the way they were gesticulating, Jonas guessed that their sermon must include vivid descriptions of hell, but they didn't seem to be dissuading anyone from coming forward.

The next cavern was a birthing village. Jonas didn't want to look down, but he couldn't help it. He'd spent the first twelve years of his life in a village like this. The villages in Athens had been orderly, all rectangles and right angles, with cool steel walls that were kept meticulously clean. This one was more chaotic, the steel partitions seemingly placed randomly, and the pervasive red dust covering everything.

The principles were the same, though, as they were on every city in the belts.

The wide spaces between the partitions were filled with groups of children. Some sat in circles around teachers, each squatting on the ground with a school-pad on his or her knee. Others were on breaks, chasing one another through corridors and dormitories. They all wore identical grey coveralls, distinguished only by the patterns of the red dust stains.

The children took their studies seriously. The classes were quiet, orderly, and a lot of the older children were using their break time to study further, sitting alone, with spare pads. Jonas remembered the sense of fear and urgency that overcame each age group as the final aptitude tests grew closer. Based on your final assessment score, you would be assigned your specialization and your initial role in the city. If you didn't make at least the Worker-grade, if there was nothing in your free-willed mind that the city deemed useful, it was a spike to the back of the head and servitordom.

Rising above the maze of partitions were the rows of cloning towers, the machines that fed this human production line. Each unit was self-contained, a few dozen tanks around a central pillar. They were all identical, as were the ones in every city in the belts. Another forgotten technology, like the solar sails. They had been designed on Earth, by the last generation before the Worldbreakers, and they were largely self-replicating, each one able to produce the parts for another unit, and instructions to help semi-skilled workers assemble it. Each tower contained the genetic codes of around two billion human beings, a large fraction of the doomed final population of the Earth. You fed them power and organic material, and they would produce new human beings, each baby a genetic duplicate of someone who had lived in that last generation.

Gabriel had explained the history of the cloning towers to Jonas. The idea had been to preserve genetic diversity and rebuild population numbers faster than the remnant of humanity could. But in their haste the designers had made a mistake. The clones suffered from genetic abnormalities, most of them harmless, but one of them devastating. Clones were sterile: without expensive genetic modification, they could never reproduce. But the towers kept working, churning out generation after generation of genetic duplicates.

At least, that was the official story, the one that Jonas had been taught in his birthing village and had never had reason to doubt. Gabriel had told him another version, one that some true-borns believed but that most tank-borns never got a chance to hear. The mistake that had led to clone sterility might have been deliberate, and even if it wasn't, the later failure to correct it certainly was. The original, official plan was for the cloning towers to function for a few generations, until there was enough genetic diversity for a strong population, and then for natural reproduction to take over. But the first generations of true-borns living after the disaster, those who might have had the power to correct the mistake, had not seen it in their interest to do so. With a population of naturally reproducing humans they would have had competitors for wealth and power. With the sterile clones they had a slave class, each of whom began life in debt to their creator and who could not pass wealth on to the next generation.

Gabriel had hated the system, both for condemning most of the population to lives of drudgery and for imposing on his own class the sacred duty of continuing the family line. They had dreamed together of better, more equal worlds. But, 300 years later, the system was too entrenched for any individual to change it.

The car entered another tunnel, and emerged at another rail-taxi rank at the floor of a smaller cavern. It looked as though this was the entrance to Mr Glass's diamond spindle. It was square and neatly carved, and the opposite wall was a complex façade of blue glass and chrome-steel columns, brightly illuminated by hidden lights. Beyond a double layer of glass doors, a staircase wound up and out of sight. No doubt the tank-born citizens from the habitation caverns would be turned away if they tried to enter the spindle, but they would come away with the engineered impression of the entrance to some exotic dream-world.

A valet in powder-blue livery opened the taxi door. The guards' smiles were polite but less deferential than that of the docking attendant had been, and they held large crowd-control nerve rifles. Jonas brushed a bit of imaginary dust from his shoulder and tried to inject confidence into his stride. Projecting a sense that he belonged in true-born gatherings had become second nature to him, but requesting a meeting with a city owner was still daunting, and the unfelt presence of Keldra's implant added an extra layer of nervousness.

'Gabriel Reinhardt of Reinhardt Industries. Mr Glass is expecting me.'

The guard gave a respectful nod that was not quite a bow, and held out another datapad to read his passport. 'Yes, sir, your arrival was noted,' he said, once the pad had confirmed Jonas's forged identity. 'Mr Glass will be able to see you today. There is a shuttle waiting.'

The guard summoned an attendant, who ushered Jonas up the steps and through a lavish waiting area centred around an ornamental fountain. He showed him through an airlock to a waiting shuttle, and strapped him in to one of half a dozen acceleration couches before leaving him alone.

The shuttle tipped back and trundled up the sloping tunnel to the city's rotation axis. Jonas felt the gravity ebb away, and then he was pushed back into his seat as the shuttle accelerated down the launch tube and out into space. The walls vanished, replaced by the dizzying three-dimensional vista of ships and minor rocks that surrounded the city. The shuttle's passenger cabin was a transparent bubble protruding above the cockpit, so Jonas could see all around the ship. Looking back, the diamond spindle was a tiny white spike on the face of the asteroid, just a set of shuttle launch tubes and mooring lines for a pair of private yachts.

Ahead was Wendell Taylor Glass's private luxury ringship, the *Haze of the Ecliptic*. Apart from a small hub containing the ion drive and other essential systems, the entire ship was a single grav-ring, angled so that sunlight would shine through the translucent panels that made up the ring's inner surface. It looked like some kind of jewel; even the exterior surface was polished to a shine, and the panels glinted one by one as the ring rotated in the light.

The shuttle docked, and another liveried attendant helped Jonas into a transit module that took him down to the ring floor. The interior was a single chamber filling the whole width of the ring and stretching around as far as he could see. It was made up as an ornamental garden. The transparent ceiling was tinted a dark purple, turning the sun into a washed-out disc and rendering the bulk of Santesteban almost invisible. The floor was a spongy lawn, with a tiled path weaving through the centre of it and disappearing under the ceiling horizon in both directions. Plants were arranged around in neat beds, lit by varicoloured spotlights. Most of them were engineered into unnatural shapes, twisted bonsai-like trees, or abstract topiary carvings. Among the plants, on spotlighted pedestals, female dancers in blue body-paint gyrated to the soft music that played in the background.

Dotted around the twilit garden were ornate little buildings of white and pink stone, in a garish array of architectural styles. Stepping out of the transit module, Jonas saw that the transit hub was disguised as a marble pagoda, its stepped roof rising up to touch the ring's ceiling.

Another attendant led Jonas around the path towards one of the architectural follies. The dancers ignored them, expressionlessly repeating the same movements, precise but devoid of emotion. Jonas tried not to do more than glance at them. They were as much ornaments as the plants and the architectural follies, and it would be uncouth to pay them too much attention. He hoped that they were servitors rather than free-willed dancers with muscle-override implants; he didn't like to imagine that there was human intelligence behind those blank eyes.

The attendant led him to a circular arena, like a miniature Coliseum, its stone walls artistically crumbled. He went up the steps to the viewing area. A man and a woman sat on a cushioned bench, a little way apart, watching as a pair of gladiators circled one another in the ring, crackling raised shock-knives. The watchers didn't appear to have noticed Jonas arrive.

He stepped forward. 'Excuse me, I'm looking for Mr Glass.'

The man looked around. He wore a dark suit and had neat blond hair that looked silver in the purple light. 'It seems our host likes to keep his guests waiting, I'm afraid. Captain Lance Hussein Cooper, Solar Authority.' He handed Jonas a business card. It was a fancy Earth-tech communicator card, featureless, except for the captain's name and the five concentric circles of the Solar Authority flag.

Jonas took the card, shook the man's hand, and sat down. Close to, he saw that the man's suit was a Solar Authority dress uniform, with captain's stripes on its wide sleeves and the Authority's five concentric circles picked out in gold thread on the shoulders.

'Gabriel Reinhardt, Reinhardt Industries. It's a pleasure to meet you. You don't often see Solar Authority officers this far from Fides.'

'Perhaps not. But the Solar Authority has jurisdiction over all of the belts.'

Jonas smiled disarmingly. 'Of course.'

The woman had glanced briefly at Jonas when he arrived, but now turned back to the gladiators. Studying her face, Jonas felt a surge of second-hand recognition. She was eight years older, but this was Emily Taylor Glass, Olzan's true-born lover. She was staring at the gladiators, not taking her eyes off them as she took a colourful sweet from a bowl beside her and raised it slowly to her mouth. She had the silver mesh of a memduction helmet over her dark hair. Her face was gaunt and expressionless, her eyes sunken. Something about her suggested to Jonas that she had neither laughed nor cried for a long time.

'Reinhardt,' Cooper said, rolling the word over his tongue as if tasting a fine wine. 'That used to be a Belt Four family, didn't it?'

'It mostly still is,' Jonas said. 'I moved down here for business.'

'Ah, like our host. It seems we're all gradually drifting down to Belt Three. Returning home, you might say.' He took a sip of his drink. His eyes were defocused slightly, but beneath that Jonas could sense a controlled alertness, as if he was letting himself relax for now but would spring back into action in a moment. He wasn't wearing a memduction helmet, although there was a row of helmets on stands in front of the spectator bench.

Cooper noticed Jonas looking at the helmet. 'We have sensation laid on,' he said. 'Either gladiator, or even both, which I believe our lady Emily is experiencing. I don't, myself, but I have no objection if you want to partake.'

'I think I'll pass,' Jonas said. 'It's a little intense for my tastes.'

One of the gladiators lunged at the other, swinging her shock-knife in a desperate arc. The other gladiator danced back, but not quickly enough. The shock-knife scored a bright red line across his chest. He retaliated, but he was overweight and slower. They resumed their cautious circling, two roughly equal combat servitors facing off. The combat programmes in their implants would be examining every muscle movement, seething with possible outcomes. Emily Taylor Glass stared at them, unblinking.

Cooper looked thoughtfully at Jonas for a moment. 'Tell me, are you related to a Sophia Reinhardt Cooper?'

Jonas tried to recall his assumed family tree. He had memorized it, all the way back to the last generation on Earth, but he hadn't needed to use the information for years. 'She was my great-aunt,' he said at last.

Cooper smiled with the look of someone who could bring his entire family tree into his mind at any time, and was now drawing mental lines on it to link him to Jonas. 'Then we are related by marriage,' he said, apparently satisfied by the new picture.

Jonas returned the smile. 'It's a small universe.'

'And smaller all the time. Ah, it looks like our host is here.'

Jonas looked around. A man was coming up the steps to the viewing area. He wore a gaudy kimono draped with gold jewellery, on top of which, his bald head seemed to perch like an egg. Jonas stood and put on a nervous expression, as if impressed by his host's expensive tastes. Cooper was standing as well, but not bothering to hide his distaste.

'My guests!' exclaimed Wendell Taylor Glass. 'I'm so sorry to have kept you waiting.'

'That's quite all right,' said Jonas, moving forward to shake Glass's hand. 'Naturally, you must be busy.'

'Taylor Glass,' said Lance Hussein Cooper. 'My grandmother was a Taylor. A distinguished family.'

'Oh, then we are cousins!' said Glass, shaking Cooper's hand vigorously. 'You are part of the family!'

Cooper's expression was cool and dismissive. 'Nearly everyone's part of an extended family these days. At least, those of us who have kept the bloodline pure.'

'Oh, very nearly pure,' Glass said, squirming just slightly under Cooper's gaze. 'Of course, I can't deny I have a little tank-born blood, just a little, a long way back. But that can't be helped now, I mean, I can't be held responsible for what my ancestors . . . ' He trailed off, withering under Cooper's gaze. 'I would never allow another tank-born into the family line,' he said.

Jonas glanced at Emily. A hint of a frown seemed to cross her face for a moment, but it might have been his imagination. She stared at the gladiators, ignoring the men talking behind her. The male gladiator had sustained another wound and was moving more slowly, but the female was still circling rather than moving in for the kill.

'I've always been very interested in Earth, as well, you know,' Wendell Glass said. 'Keeping the old knowledge alive, the old arts, all that. You must see my collection.'

'Maybe later,' Cooper said.

'Of course.' Wendell Glass sat and peered down into the ring. 'It looks like I'm in time for the end of the match. How delightful. Do finish it quickly, my dear Emily, and then we can get down to business.'

Emily looked up at her father with sunken eyes, and then leaned over the little control panel built into the stone balcony in front of her. Her finger hovered over two buttons for a moment before stabbing down on one of them. The male gladiator froze, his implant shutting off the combat programme and paralyzing him. The female moved in step by step, her combat programme no doubt running through scenarios of feints and bluffs. She grabbed the man, plunged her knife in, and cut downwards, scoring a deep wound from the bottom of his ribcage down to his pelvis. When she pulled the knife back, her hand was dripping blood.

Rather than releasing her dying opponent, the female gladiator put an arm around him and lugged him over to the viewing area. They disappeared from Jonas's sight for a moment, but then a whirring mechanized platform raised them up so that their heads appeared over the balcony. The male's head lolled sideways, drooling, eyes closed. The female stared straight ahead, looking even deader.

Emily Taylor Glass had slipped on a pair of silver gloves linked by thick wires to her memduction helmet. She leaned forward and put one hand on the head of each of the gladiators. Lights flickered on the gloves and on the helmet, and Emily's eyes moved as if in a dream-filled sleep. The gloves would be pulling recent memories from the gladiators' implants and she would be reliving the fight from each gladiator's point of view, simultaneously experiencing the motions of victory and the agony of the shock-knife slicing through flesh and the damaged body failing. The briefest flicker of a smile passed across her face. Done with the gladiators, Emily pushed them aside. They stood patiently, the woman supporting her dying opponent.

Wendell Taylor Glass had put on a memduction helmet and gloves. He grabbed the gladiators' heads and made a sucking sound, as if taking the memories like snuff. Jonas noticed that only the glove on the victor's head activated. When he was done, he gestured to the helmets on stands in front of Jonas and Captain Cooper. 'You're not going to partake?'

'I don't use any neural technology,' Cooper said coldly.

'Ah, er, of course,' Wendell stammered. 'You, perhaps, Mr Reinhardt?'

Jonas shook his head. 'A little strong for my tastes.' He was relieved he wasn't the only one declining.

'Of course. My daughter does have a penchant for rather, ah, intense memory experiences, don't you, my dear?'

Emily sullenly ignored him. With another few button presses she lowered the platform, and summoned another pair of servitors to take the defeated gladiator's body away.

'Now, to business.' Glass took off his memduction helmet and clicked his fingers to summon a servitor with a glass of dark red wine. After taking a sip of the drink his composure seemed to return, and he beamed playfully as he looked between Jonas and the Captain. 'I was expecting one guest this evening, but it seems I have two! To what do I owe the pleasure of your company, Mr Reinhardt?'

'I have some items for sale I thought might interest you. Some servitors and a hab system core.' Jonas produced the wafer-pad storage ticket and activated its live feed. It showed a grainy black-and-white image of the servitors floating around the hab system core in one of the docking spindle's storage bays.

'Interesting,' Glass said, barely glancing at the pad. 'A pleasant opportunity. I'm afraid I will have to ask you to wait. I have very important business with Captain Cooper that I want to settle as soon as possible. Please, help yourself to a drink. You could take a pleasure servitor, or perhaps some more gladiatorial games . . . '

'You should deal with Mr Reinhardt first,' Cooper said. It sounded more like an order than a suggestion. 'Our business may take some time.'

'I, er, of course,' Glass said. He took another gulp of his wine and then wiped his head with a silk handkerchief. Captain Cooper sat back, watching the exchange.

'Tell me about this hab module,' Glass said.

Jonas reeled off the module's technical specifications, with only the amount of creative omission that would be expected when making a sale. 'It's two years old; I bought it first-hand on Oberon. I used it as the main hab system of a mining outpost.'

'Ah, and what became of this mining outpost, to put the module on the market so suddenly?'

'I had to evacuate because of a Worldbreaker,' Jonas said, trying to keep his voice nonchalant.

'Ah, how terrible.'

'You have my commiserations,' Cooper said formally.

'Yes, quite, and mine as well,' Glass said.

Jonas smiled as if the loss of LN-411 had been nothing more than a minor financial inconvenience, pushing his memories of the frantic evacuation and the subsequent battle with Keldra to the back of his mind. 'That's just how life is,' he said.

'Such is life, such is life, indeed,' Glass said. 'I certainly think I can give you something for the hab module, to help a fellow true-born back on his feet.' He glanced at Cooper as he spoke, but the captain's face didn't betray a reaction. 'What of these servitors? A hab system core is always useful, of course, but as you can see, I have no shortage of bodies.'

Jonas hesitated, conscious of Cooper in the corner of his vision. The story of illegal servitors might not play so well with a Solar Authority captain as it would with Wendell Taylor Glass, but he didn't think Cooper was one to care, as long as the victims were tank-borns. He smiled conspiratorially. 'These are more than just bodies. They have servitor implants on top of learned mining-supervision skills with years of free-willed experience. I was told that this wouldn't be a problem here.'

Glass glanced at Cooper before answering, seemingly going through the same thought process that Jonas had. 'Oh, no, I don't think that should be a problem,' he said, and then laughed, a high-pitched, nervous sound that Jonas found intensely grating. He laughed politely along with him. Cooper smiled and took another sip of his drink. It looked as though he had no objections.

'I believe I will buy your servitors, and your hab system core, Mr Reinhardt,' Glass said. 'I will have my engineers inspect the system before agreeing to a final price, but provisionally—'

There was a brilliant flash of light from outside the canopy, for a moment, outshining the sun and casting jagged purple shadows from the mock ruins of the arena. Then they were plunged into darkness, all the lights dead, leaving only the pale sun to highlight the true-borns in silhouette. From somewhere around the ring came the ululating whine of an alarm.

Glass looked around in panic. 'What was that?'

'EMP,' Captain Cooper said. He was composed, barely moving, although there was a note of puzzlement in his voice. 'That was a big explosion, though. That wasn't a regular EMP device.'

Keldra, Jonas thought. Another use for a nuclear bomb was to create an electromagnetic pulse, and it would be a perfect use for the scraps of nuclear material left over from the *Dancer*. Most electronic warfare used less exotic means, but if you had a ship-board nuke-making plant anyway . . .

'We're under attack!' Glass screamed. 'Quickly! I have a safe room. Come with me.'

Some emergency lighting came on, enough for them to follow Glass as he blundered down the steps and through the foliage. As he ran he shouted into a pocket communicator. 'Colonel Henrick! *What* is going *on?*' Jonas couldn't hear the colonel's response.

They came to one of the follies, a white stone hut picked out by rings of emergency lights. There was a security door delicately hidden in the façade. Glass left a sweaty mark on the palm-reader and then hurried down a set of steps.

They cycled through an airlock and emerged into a room like a security vault, windowless, the walls visibly reinforced. Glass's fondness for darkness and highlights was visible here as well: most of the room's light came from white spotlights shining down from the ceiling onto miscellaneous objects arrayed in wide rows. Some were large enough to stand on their own, but most were tiny, suspended in almost invisible glass frames on the top of black display stands.

Glass collapsed against the wall as the inner airlock door closed.

'We'll be safe in here. This segment is self-contained. Escape module. Captain Cooper, you've got to help me! Gouveia's attacking already!'

Cooper was listening to his own pocket communicator. 'No hostile ships,' he said, flipping it shut. 'The pulse came from a free-floating missile disguised as a piece of debris. We don't know who fired it.'

'Of course, it's Gouveia! You said she wouldn't be able to attack for six weeks!'

'Perhaps I was wrong,' Cooper said dismissively, as if the thought of his being wrong had never occurred to him before, but now that he had, it wasn't very interesting. 'There's a shuttle on its way to take me back to the *Iron Dragon*. I'll review the tactical situation when I'm there.'

'You've got to help me,' Glass said again. He wiped sweat from his bald head and then waved a hand vaguely, indicating the objects on plinths. 'Anyway, this is my collection,' he babbled. 'These are all Planetary Age artefacts. I keep them down here, in the safe room – it's very important to keep them safe – Planetary Age artefacts.'

Jonas glanced around at the artefacts. Most were pieces of machinery, damaged or corroded so that their purposes were no longer obvious. There were also fragments of clothing, art objects, papers. There was even a mummified human corpse, wearing a dark blue uniform vaguely reminiscent of Cooper's, with similar captain's stripes on the sleeves.

Jonas wandered over to one of the display stands. The artefact seemed to be a self-contained module: it had power and data sockets that could link it to a larger system, but it looked as though it had its own power supply as well. Part of its surface showed scorch marks, but apart from that it was intact, and it had been polished to so much of a shine that Jonas could almost believe it was new. Astonishingly, it seemed to be active: there was a set of tiny lights set into a groove on its side, one of which was glowing red. There was writing in one of the grooves: *EAS-S4 Seagull*.

'I do apologize for the inconvenience, Mr Reinhardt,' Glass babbled, half to himself. 'I can assure you, this, ah, this does not happen often.' He let out a nervous titter. 'Mr Reinhardt?'

'That's quite all right,' Jonas tried to say, but no words came. He tried to turn around, but his muscles weren't responding to him. The Planetary Age artefact remained locked in the centre of his vision. He couldn't move.

Chapter Seven

The Worldbreaker was hours away, but Konrad's Hope was already coming apart. Most of the starscrapers were dark, and the surface bore scars where solar panels and heat sinks had been stripped away. The end of the docking spindle was a twisted, molten ruin, no doubt damaged during the evacuation riots. The true-borns and their favoured servants would have gone first, followed by any tank-borns who could scare up the cost of an evac ship berth. With the last evac ships gone, maybe fifty thousand tank-borns would be in the city, with nothing to do but wait for the end.

The space around the city was clear of the normal controlled traffic chaos. The industrial orbitals would have been nudged into orbits towards other cities, and even the smallest tugs and shuttles would be carrying refugees in desperate escape attempts. The only bodies orbiting the city now were smaller rocks and the debris from the shattered spindle.

'*Thousand Names*, this is the Konrad's Hope evacuation committee. We've gathered the high-priority evacuation cases in one location. Send your shuttle to these coordinates . . . '

'*Thousand Names*, my name is Jananna Smith. I'm the only true-born left. I've got a lot of wealth tied up in other cities – take me away from here and I'll see that you're rewarded—'

'*Thousand Names*, please, there's a birthing village full of children still here. They don't even know what's happening. For God's sake, you'll have room for them, please—'

The breathless voices sounded in the background of the *Thousand Names's* bridge, coming across what had once been the city's traffic control channels. Everyone with the means to detect them would hope that they were a late-coming evac ship, and everyone with access to a transmitter was bargaining for passage.

'*Thousand Names*, this is Sister Greyda of the Konrad's Hope Scriber chapel. We're delighted you've chosen to join us—'

'Brenn, turn that shit off.' Olzan's voice came out more strained than he had expected.

Brenn looked a little startled, but the voices shut off. Vazoya squeezed his hand and muttered something reassuring, but Olzan knew whom she was really trying to reassure.

Without the chatter, the silence was oppressive. Olzan replaced the live view on the screen with a city map, and began running through the plan again, to take his mind off the approach as much as anything else. 'The collection is housed in a hangar near the bottom of that starscraper,' he said, pointing. 'We'll take a shuttle in. Docking with a rotating 'scraper will be tricky but Vaz can do it.'

'Of course, I can do it.' Vazoya's normal arrogance seemed forced now.

'The power's out in that 'scraper so it should be empty, but we might get company when folks see the shuttle docking. Most likely the elevators will be down so they won't reach us too quickly.

'There's one exhibit in particular that Mr Glass wants. It's called the *Seagull*, and it's the centrepiece of Zhu's collection. I don't know what it is, but Mr Glass said we'll know it when we see it. It's vacuum-safe, so we can just open the hangar doors and push it out, then the *Names* can pick it up. We get in and out as quick as we can. I don't want any encounters with the inhabitants.' He didn't want the crew to see them: it would make them real, make it harder to leave them to die. He didn't want to see them himself, for the same reason.

'Understood,' said Keldra from the back of the room. Olzan shot her a look. No one had asked her.

The city spun above Olzan's head, the shadows of the starscrapers processing like raking fingers across the grey surface. He could feel the gravity change as Vazoya teased the shuttle into a powered orbit that matched the city's spin. There was a shift in perception, and then he was sitting in a steady one gravity, with the city stationary above him, both of them in the middle of a rotating sphere of stars. Vazoya was gently manoeuvring the shuttle *up*, towards the hanging mass of Anastasia Zhu's starscraper.

Olzan was crammed next to Keldra in the shuttle's tiny cargo section, both of them dressed in stuffy vacuum suits. If she had such an interest in Planetary Age artefacts, Olzan had decided, then they might as well put that to use. Brenn and Tarraso were still on board the *Thousand Names*, keeping it in a wide orbit of the city, ready to pick up the artefact and then make a rapid escape once the shuttle was back on board.

Vazoya moved the shuttle up to the side of the starscraper. Olzan could see the blue-white reflections of their thruster flames in the windows. One wide gap between the windows resolved into the door to the hangar housing Anastasia Zhu's collection.

Vazoya stabilized the shuttle next to the small personnel airlock at the edge of the hangar door. A magnetic grapnel line shot across the gap and latched onto the starscraper's metal wall, and then the shuttle's hatch swung open. The external airlock wasn't built to take this type of shuttle, and hovering too close to the wall would be dangerous. They would have to cross the gap in vacuum suits.

Keldra's face was pale behind her visor. She hadn't said much on the shuttle flight, despite her constant talk of the Earth artefact while they were still on the *Names*. It was vertigo, Olzan realized with amusement. With the rotational pseudogravity in place, they were suspended over an infinite drop filled with shooting stars. Keldra had been a habitat engineer, working in her city's spine, well away from the outer skin. For someone not used to these manoeuvres the experience could be terrifying.

Olzan wasn't in much of a mood to spare Keldra's feelings. 'All right, Engineer, get that door open. Your precious artefact's in there.' Keldra hesitated. For a moment Olzan thought she wasn't going to move. 'Go on. We'll retrieve you if you fall.'

'Might not be worth the fuel,' came Vazoya's voice from the cockpit.

Keldra scowled, stood up, and clipped her suit to the wobbling grapnel line. She swung out into the gap and climbed hand-over-hand to the personnel airlock, moving confidently now that she had started. She reached the ledge beneath the airlock door and began fumbling with the door control.

'It's not going to open,' she said after a minute.

'What's the matter with it?' Olzan asked.

'The lock's physically jammed. We might be able to open it from the inside.'

'We can blast it,' Vazoya said. 'Get the charges. The decompression might even push the thing out for us; problem solved.'

'No!' Keldra snapped. 'It could be damaged.'

'Then we can give Mr Glass the damn pieces and tell him that's how we found it. Olzan, let's get the hell out of here.'

'Mr Glass won't be pleased,' Olzan said. The approach of the Worldbreaker was a nagging presence in the back of his mind, but every time he thought about cutting corners or doing a less than perfect job, he thought back to Emily's last message. Do a good job here and he could marry her, get sterility reversal treatment, live like a true-born . . . 'Vaz, find another airlock. We'll work our way round the inside. Keldra, get back here.'

They found another airlock a few levels up. Once again Vazoya brought them alongside and fired the grapnel, and this time Keldra climbed across without hesitation. Olzan watched her tinker with the lock for a moment and then the outer door hinged open.

'Vaz, hold the shuttle here,' Olzan said as he clipped himself to the line. 'We might need to come back out this way. I'll let you know when we reach the hangar.'

'Take your time. If you're not back, it's my ship.'

'We'll be back.'

'I'm serious, Olzan. I'm not waiting for the Worldbreaker to—'

'Neither am I. We'll be back.'

Olzan strapped the explosive charges to his suit's backpack and then pulled himself along the grapnel line, carefully avoiding looking down. Keldra had already dealt with what little was left of the security system, and she cycled them through using the airlock's emergency power.

The interior of the starscraper was dark, lit only by sporadic emergency lighting and the bobbing circles cast by their helmet lamps. A sound of dripping water echoed to them from somewhere deeper in the maze of metal corridors. Olzan called up a floor plan from his implant and laid it over his vision. The elevators wouldn't be working, but there should be stairs in the central atrium. With the city's datanet offline the implant couldn't plot a route for him, but it wasn't hard to see which way to go.

The atrium was a towering void that ran the entire height of the starscraper. There were arcs of piping hanging in the space, suspended by invisible cables. It took Olzan a moment to realize he'd seen something similar in the Glass family starscraper back in Santesteban, but that one had been filled with water. It was a water-sculpture: if the pumps had still been powered, a thin stream of water would have poured down the atrium, twisting towards one wall due to the Coriolis effect, and redirected by the arcs of piping into graceful curves and helices. He looked down over the railing and could see his helmet lamp's beam reflecting off a murky surface. It looked as though the water had kept flowing for a while after the pumps had failed.

There was what looked like a stairwell on the far side of the atrium. Olzan led Keldra around the walkway towards it. Halfway to the staircase, Keldra suddenly stopped. 'We've got company,' she hissed.

Olzan followed her finger. High above the spouts of the empty water-sculpture was another cluster of bobbing lights.

Olzan did a frantic mental calculation. They could go back, but that would mean going back to Mr Glass empty-handed.

'It'll take them a while to go down those stairs. They don't know where we're going. We can lose them.'

Keldra didn't look convinced, but she didn't say anything.

'Keep your head down,' he said. It was still possible the others hadn't spotted them. He dimmed his helmet lamp, angled it at the floor, and jogged for the stairs.

He counted the loops of the spiral staircase until they were on the correct level, then found the radial corridor that would lead to the hangar. He risked a glance upwards. The others were still above them, their lamp-beams bobbing around agitatedly. Olzan couldn't tell what they were doing.

They left the atrium behind them and struck out towards the hangar at the edge of the starscraper. Even the emergency lights were dead on this level. The entrance to the hangar was an airlock, with a simple mechanical fail-safe to keep it shut; after they levered it open it closed automatically behind them.

They emerged onto a gallery overlooking Anastasia Zhu's collection hall. The darkness made the space seem vast, the far wall only dimly visible in the light of their helmet lamps. What they could see of the room was in disarray. It looked like most of the smaller exhibits had been removed hurriedly, leaving toppled plinths, and the decorative hangings that had covered the bare walls were now scattered across the floor.

One large object dominated the centre of the room, something with a curved white surface, spotlessly clean. Olzan's beam caught a name inscribed on the surface: *EAS-S4 Seagull*. He felt some of his worry disappear. At least finding it hadn't been hard.

They ran their torch beams across the *Seagull*, trying to get an impression of its shape. It looked like a shuttle, but not like any Olzan could imagine being built in his time. It had a cylindrical body and a rounded nose, with the sleek curves that characterized Planetary Age technology. There were two odd fins stretched out from either side of the fuselage, far larger than most shuttle heat radiators. 'What are those?' he asked, half to himself.

'Wings.' Keldra's voice was hushed, like a devout believer inside a chapel. 'It's a spaceplane. The wings are for flying in atmosphere. That craft, the *Seagull* . . . it would have landed on Earth.' She held one arm out straight as if it were a wing, and moved the other hand above and below it, demonstrating something. 'The top surface of the wing is curved, so the air pressure—'

'Save the lecture. We need to get it out the doors so the *Names* can pick it up.'

He descended the metal steps to the hangar floor and scanned the far side of the room with his lamp-beams. The hangar doors and the personnel airlock were both hidden behind a set of floor-to-ceiling display cases. Hopefully there would be some way to remove them without using the explosives, so they wouldn't have to risk damaging the spaceplane. He trudged over to them, stepping around the debris from the hasty evacuation, his boots splashing in the thin layer of oily water that covered the floor.

The display cases were airtight, climate-controlled modules designed for storing delicate artefacts. They were empty, save from some grit and curled brownish things that might have been leaves from a preserved plant. Olzan worked at the crack between two cases with his suit knife, trying to see if the cases were free-standing or attached to the wall. 'Keldra! Give me a hand with this.'

Olzan looked around for her. She had climbed a metal stepladder that was set up next to the *Seagull's* nose, and was now peering through its cockpit windows, her gloved hands almost but not quite touching the hull. 'It's a shell,' she said, resentfully. 'All the workings have been removed.'

'Of course, they have. Taking it apart means more artefacts to put on display. What, did you think we'd be able to fly it out? Get the hell over here.'

Keldra tore herself away from the spaceplane and joined Olzan by the hangar door. She examined the display cases, crouching down to look at them from every angle. 'They're wired into the city's power and hab systems. It looks like the airlock has been dismantled and its power and support lines are feeding these cases instead. Removing them will be tricky.'

'Then we'll have to blast them.' Olzan unclipped the bag of explosives from his suit and dropped it on the floor in front of the cases.

'It's tricky, but I can do it.'

He hesitated. 'Brenn! Time check.'

'One hour twenty-two minutes to Black Line.' Even Brenn's voice was starting to show some worry.

'I can do it in half an hour,' Keldra said.

'All right, but I'm planting the charges now. If you're not done in half an hour we blow it.'

'All right.' She opened her tool bag and set to work.

Olzan walked up the row of display cases, fixing the explosive charges between them and wiring in remote detonators he could control from his suit. With more time he would have been able to blow the hangar door open with fewer, carefully placed charges, but for now overkill would have to do, even if the shuttle took damage. Meanwhile, Keldra had managed to get one of the display cases away from the wall and was tinkering with what remained of the hangar mechanism.

The charges in place, Olzan took a look around the room, breathing deeply to try to control his nerves. Abandoned display plinths seemed to stare at him, some of them lying broken in the shallow water. The *Seagull* loomed over them, shining like a statue of a benevolent god, wings outstretched, the slow motion of the water casting a subtly shifting reflection of his torchlight on its polished surface. Maybe there was something to Keldra's obsession, he thought. That artefact had survived unscathed through the Worldbreaker disaster and the early city resource wars that had wiped out all the achievements of Planetary Age civilization and reduced the human race to a tiny remnant. It would be a pity to let it be damaged now.

Another movement of light caught his eye. Up on the gallery, the door they had come in by was opening again. A wobbling torch beam shone down on them.

Olzan froze. Out of the corner of his eye he could see Keldra still tinkering with the hangar mechanism; it looked as though she hadn't noticed the others. 'Keldra, stop,' he whispered over the helmet connection.

More torchlights appeared on the gallery, and Olzan could just make out the figures that carried them. There were three of them. They weren't wearing vacuum suits, only tattered and stained city issue worker overalls. They were squat, muscular men, looking as if they were from a high-grav part of the city and used to tough manual work. Each of them carried a torch in one hand and a gun in the other, slug-thrower pistols rather than nerve guns. Olzan and Keldra's vacuum suits were not armoured: bullets would go through them like paper. Olzan had a nerve gun at his hip but he didn't dare go for it.

The first man's voice rang out across the hangar. 'Stop that. Get away from that, whatever it is. Put your hands where I can see them.' He was pointing his gun at Keldra. The two others had their guns trained on Olzan.

Keldra didn't move from the display case. She removed a panel and was in the middle of a tangle of wiring.

'I said move!'

Olzan tapped Keldra's arm. 'Do as he says.'

She turned around, slowly. Olzan was glad the men with guns wouldn't be able to see her expression clearly through her visor. She was fuming, as if she might erupt into violence at any moment.

'Stay where you are.'

The three men made their way down the stairs, keeping their guns trained on Olzan and Keldra. Olzan noticed they were wearing abseiling harnesses over their clothes. He kicked himself for not thinking of it.

The leader walked around the spaceplane and shone his torch into Olzan's face, then Keldra's. 'Good of you to come and get us. Don't know what you're doing down here, though. You must have taken a wrong turn!'

Another of the thugs sniggered. His overalls were blood-stained, and he had half a dozen human ears hanging from a string around his neck. The third thug was shifting on his feet and twitching nervously, his gun tracing a figure-of-eight path as he trained it alternately on Keldra and Olzan.

'You've got a ship out there, and we want off this rock,' the first man said.

They were close enough now that Olzan could read the name tags on their uniforms. The leader was Poldak 2484-Konradshope-023382. He had the red-eyed look of someone who had been blind drunk until taking a sobriety shot an hour or so ago, but right now the hand with which he held his gun was rock steady.

Olzan spread his hands out in a non-threatening gesture. The *Thousand Names* could afford to take a few passengers on to Santesteban. 'We'll get you all out of here. There's no need for violence.'

'Glad you see it that way.' The man smiled, coldly, but didn't lower his gun, which was now pointed at Olzan's chest. 'Has your shuttle got three spare suits?'

Olzan searched his memory. 'Including the pilot's, yes.'

'Have him send them across. We'll meet the shuttle at the lock where you came in.' He gestured with the gun. 'Come on.'

'I'll have this lock working soon,' Keldra said.

'No. The lock you came in by is working now.'

'We're here on a job of our own,' Olzan said. 'We'll give you a lift to Santesteban, but let us finish. We'll all get out.'

Poldak glanced at the *Seagull*. 'You're here for that? Forget about it. We go now.'

'It's a Planetary Age spaceplane,' Keldra explained.

'Yeah, whatever. I'm the King of Belt Four. We go now.'

The man with the string of ears – Mardok, by his name tag – laughed again. It looked as though he could see Keldra's discomfort and was enjoying it. 'It's 'Breaker dust now,' he said.

'We've still got time,' Olzan insisted.

Poldak took a step closer to him. The gun was not quite touching his chest. 'I don't think you understand our arrangement,' he said. 'We're not begging a lift from you. We're stealing your ship.'

A bang made them both jump. Poldak took his eyes off Olzan to look for the source. Olzan felt his heart pound. It had been loud enough even inside the helmet. He thanked God Poldak's finger hadn't jumped on the trigger.

Mardok was standing beneath the *Seagull*, looking up at it, his gun raised and smoking. He'd placed a bullet hole dead in the centre of the circular blue logo under the spaceplane's nose. As the echoes died away he looked round at Poldak, an inane grin on his face.

'What the hell do you think you're doing?' screamed the third man. 'We need to get out!'

Mardok shrugged. 'Hey, lighten up. Just having some fun.'

'Calm down, both of you,' Poldak snapped. Then suddenly, 'You! What do you think you're doing?'

Keldra was back at the control panel, hiding it with her body while making some change to the wiring.

'Get away from that!' shouted Mardok, swinging his gun back to Keldra.

She moved away from the panel slowly, and it looked to Olzan as though she had made one final adjustment as she turned around. 'I can still get it open in time,' she said.

'I said no,' Poldak replied.

'It's valuable. Take it. I know of collectors who'd want to buy it to restore it.'

Mardok advanced on Keldra, grabbed her by the neck, his gun pressing into her abdomen. 'The man said no.' She didn't move. Her face was locked in a snarl, angry rather than frightened; it looked as though she was deliberately restraining herself from pushing the man away.

'We can come to an arrangement,' Olzan said. 'We'll give you passage to Santesteban, and some money to get you on your feet. I can see if my employer can find space for you in his business there, good jobs. You don't need to go to the trouble of taking over the ship.'

The third man – Soodok – was almost hopping from foot to foot. 'Let's *go*, already. They've offered us passage.'

'We're taking the ship,' Poldak said. 'Sorry, but I can't trust you any other way. If you're in control there's nothing stopping you from slave-spiking us in our sleep.'

'What's stopping you from doing the same to us?'

'My word as a gentleman.' His smile was mixed with a slightly confused look, which puzzled Olzan. He hadn't said it with the conviction of his earlier joke.

'We can come to a deal,' Olzan said. 'My implant can be set to a conditional trigger. We'll set it so that if any of you are harmed, it'll wipe me as well. That's a guarantee of safe passage. Right?'

Poldak blinked, slowly, keeping his eyes closed for several seconds, as if it took him that long to process what Olzan had said. 'Don't believe you,' he said. 'Don't trust you to set up the implant right.'

'All right. How about this? My ship has two grav-rings. They've got separate hab systems, separate everything. We'll give you one of them, all the way to Santesteban or wherever you'd like to go. You can decouple the life support systems from the rest of the ship; disable the transit hub. Short of dismantling our own ship there's no way we could reach you.'

'That sounds . . . sounds reasonable. I think we can deal.' He nodded, and slowly lowered his gun. His hand, previously rock steady, was wobbling in little circles. He stared at it as if seeing it for the first time, then blinked and shook his head. 'Sobriety shot. Damn side effects.'

Soodok was hopping from foot to foot. 'Told you, you shouldn't have drunk. Now let's go. Gotta go gotta go gotta *go*.'

Another gunshot split the air. Poldak's and Soodok's reactions were noticeably slower than before as they turned to look at Mardok. He was laughing raucously, once again pointing the gun up at the *Seagull*. The bullet hole was a good metre from his target.

Poldak's expression slowly turned to a look of astonished rage, the first time he had shown an emotion other than arrogance. 'What's happening?'

'I don't know!' Olzan said.

Mardok fired again. This time the bullet went through the *Seagull's* wing. Olzan saw Keldra wince, but she didn't move.

Poldak noticed Olzan looking at Keldra. 'You did this, didn't you? What did you do?'

Mardok barrelled into Keldra and grabbed her by the neck again. He moved unsteadily, almost unbalancing both of them. 'What have you done?' he shouted. 'I'll kill you, you—'

Mardok's gun fired, but the shot went wide. Keldra had pushed his hand away. Now she pulled the gun from his grasp and shoved him away from her, kicking him in the chest and sending him sprawling drunkenly onto the ground. She raised the gun, her arm perfectly straight, and shot Mardok in the head where he lay. Bits of blood and brain spattered into the oily water.

Poldak and Soodok were raising their guns to shoot Keldra, but their responses were slow, held back by shock as well as whatever had been affecting them already. One of them fired – Olzan couldn't tell which – but missed. Keldra turned and fired twice, putting a bullet in each of their foreheads, nearly deafening Olzan as the bullets went close by his head. Her face was a mask of cold fury; her hand was trembling just a little, in anger rather than fear.

Olzan fought to get his breathing back under control. 'What happened?' he said at last. 'What did you do? It was you, wasn't it?'

'Check your atmosphere gauge.'

He looked at the read-out on his suit's forearm. The pressure was normal, but the oxygen concentration was significantly down. 'You suffocated them.'

'Hypoxia. By the time you notice something's wrong, you're too light-headed to think straight. I used the airlock mechanism to cycle the oxygen out gently.'

'You killed them,' Olzan said again. The sound of the gunshots still rang in his ears. 'Never mind. Let's go. There's not much time.'

'We take the *Seagull*.' Keldra was still holding the gun.

Olzan watched the blood spread out from the hijackers' heads into the standing water. 'All right.'

Keldra went back to work on the hangar doors. On Olzan's timer, the seconds to the Black Line ticked away. The device beeped as they passed the thirty-minute mark. That was the point at which Olzan had told himself he would blow the doors, but after what Keldra had done to the hijackers he was too scared to cross her. Back on the *Thousand Names* he'd make it clear who was captain; right now, though, he would give her a few more minutes.

'I've got it,' Keldra said at last. The timer read twenty-four minutes.

Olzan felt the relief wash over him. He put a transmission through to the shuttle. 'Vaz, we're coming out through the hangar. Get ready to pick us up.'

'Tell her to go back to the *Names*,' Keldra said. She was walking towards the *Seagull*.

'What?'

'We'll ride the *Seagull* out. Grab a wheel.' She kicked the chock from in front of the spaceplane's forward landing gear wheel, and pushed the stepladder away from its nose. 'The air pressure should push it out, but it might need a little help.'

'Scratch that, Vaz. Return to the *Names*. We'll be with the package.'

'That maniac had better know what she's doing,' Vazoya crackled in his ear.

Keldra had removed the chocks from the other two wheels and had grabbed on to the landing gear beneath one of the wings. Olzan hurried over and took hold of the other one. He fumbled to get a suit line around the landing gear column. As he did so he flicked his suit transmitter to the *Thousand Names's* frequency. 'Brenn, we'll be dropping the package out in a moment. Get into position.'

'Ready?' Keldra asked.

'Ready.'

She punched a command into her suit's wrist panel. There was a shudder, and a groaning sound from the hangar doors as the long-disused mechanism unstuck itself. The display cases against the wall toppled and then fell, their glass fronts smashing. The vacuum seal broke and the door opened the rest of the way quickly, hinging outwards and upwards. There was a roar of air past Olzan's helmet. The display cases were whisked out, tumbling out of sight, followed by a cascade of oily water and the bodies of the would-be hijackers.

The spaceplane moved forward, as if rising out of his hands. He took that as his cue to push. On the other wheel, Keldra was doing the same. The rush of air was gone after a moment, but they had got the spaceplane moving. Shoulders to the landing gear columns, they hauled its weight across the hangar floor towards the abyss of spinning stars.

The forward wheel went over the edge and the spaceplane's nose went down, dragging them forward. Olzan jumped onto the landing gear and hugged the column as the spaceplane pitched out of the hangar doors into the infinite drop.

Stars wheeled around them. The silence of the vacuum was broken only by Olzan's nervous breathing. For a moment he felt as if he was falling, then he went through the reverse of the perception shift he had gone through on the approach to the starscraper. He was weightless, clinging on to the spaceplane as it drifted away from the city. Anastasia Zhu's starscraper was already rotating away from them and becoming lost in the throng of other surface features. In the other direction he could see the thruster flame of Vazoya's shuttle as it sped ahead of them, and more distantly the comforting sight of the *Thousand Names*, its cargo bay doors opening onto a warmly lit interior.

There was something else out there, bigger than the *Thousand Names* but dark against the stars. Olzan felt a chill run through him. It was the Worldbreaker, now large enough to be seen with the naked eye, closing in on the doomed city. Olzan willed the spaceplane to drift faster. His timer read twenty minutes to the Black Line, but he was painfully aware that the line was only a best guess, and they were already within the margin of error.

Keldra had noticed the Worldbreaker too. Olzan could see her face through her visor. She was staring at it, not taking her eyes off it as the *Seagull's* rotation moved it around in a circle in front of them. Her face was curled up with a hatred that she had not shown even to the hijackers when they had threatened the spaceplane. As Olzan watched she drew Mardok's gun from her suit holster, raised it slowly, and then fired: a soundless white flash erupting in the vacuum. She fired again and again, faster and faster as she emptied the clip at the Worldbreaker. She said nothing, although the helmet channel was open. There were tears pooling up at the sides of her eyes, glinting with each muzzle flash.

The Worldbreaker's mouth began to open, its sickly green light a ghastly mirror of the *Thousand Names's* inviting cargo bay. It had positioned itself along the city's long axis, as if finding the best angle to swallow it whole. A grating scream sounded in Olzan's ears: the radio interference from the Worldbreaker's beam. At the distant end of the city, the docking spindle twisted further before snapping off and being sucked into the Worldbreaker's mouth. Starscrapers shattered, tiny shards of glass and metal falling sparkling away.

The muzzle flashes from Keldra's gun stopped. Her finger kept working the trigger for a few seconds, then she gave an inarticulate cry of frustration, barely audible under the radio scream, then hurled the gun at the Worldbreaker. It spun away, flashing rhythmically in the sunlight, clearly on the wrong course.

There was an explosion at the end of the city, an orange fireball, briefly blossoming, as fire raced through the air in the second before it dispersed. The Worldbreaker beam had ruptured the first of the city's habitation caverns. A halo of debris fanned out, the force of the explosion combining with the city's angular momentum to hurl the outermost parts of the city surface outside the range of the Worldbreaker's beam. A shockwave travelled along the city as the beam bored deeper. The cluster of structures that had included Anastasia Zhu's starscraper disintegrated in an instant.

The city was in the centre of an expanding wave of debris. Olzan could see great hunks of rock and metal looming at them, backlit by the flickering green of the Worldbreaker beam. The leading surface was travelling outwards faster than the *Seagull*, propelled by the force of the explosion.

They had reached the *Thousand Names*. Brenn had almost matched velocities with them, so the *Seagull* floated through the cargo bay doors and settled gently into the elastic cargo webbing. Olzan pushed himself off the landing gear and hand-walked across the webbing towards the airlock to the ship's spine. Through the closing doors he could see the city breaking up into great chunks, its original shape gone.

'Brenn, we're secure,' he said as the airlock door opened. 'Get us the hell out of here.' Keldra was just behind him. He grabbed her hand and helped her into the airlock. The lock drifted around them as the ship began to turn, but he didn't feel the acceleration of a full burn.

They took the transit module to the forward ring, and Olzan ran to the bridge. The entire crew was there. On the screen, the last slivers of Konrad's Hope were disappearing into the Worldbreaker's mouth.

'Brenn, what's the matter?' he said. 'Why aren't we at full burn?'

'There's a glitch in the main engine,' Vazoya answered for him. She was standing next to him, her hand on his shoulder. 'We've got manoeuvring thrusters but no main.'

'I'm working on it!' Tarraso snapped from the engineering console before Olzan could say anything. 'We need to run a fuel line purge . . . '

'There's no time,' Olzan said. 'Wreck the fuel lines if you have to.'

'We're *on* it, Olzan!' Vazoya stepped away from Brenn's side and pushed into Olzan's face. She glanced at Keldra, standing behind Olzan. 'Maybe if you and your friend hadn't taken so long saving your precious artefact—'

'Too late.' Brenn's voice was without emotion.

They all looked to the screen. A jagged shard of rock was hurtling at them out of the darkness. The manoeuvring thrusters were pushing them aside, but not quickly enough.

There was a gut-wrenching impact sound, an impression of flames and of the room's wall buckling inwards, and then something struck Olzan's head and he lost consciousness.

Chapter Eight

The memory ended abruptly, leaving Jonas struggling to remember who and where he was. Second-hand memories bubbled at the back of his mind, the hacked implant firing wildly as it strained to override his motor control.

The Planetary Age artefact was still in front of him, the word *Seagull* picked out in silver lettering on its side. He tried to pull his hand away from it, but his hand didn't respond. There wasn't even the muscular pressure of pulling against a restraint. He felt as if he was a ghost, locked out of his own body.

Keldra's taunting about Ayla rang unbidden at the back of his mind. *Some people say that consciousness can survive a mind-wipe.* Jonas pushed that thought aside. Servitor implants destroyed the neural connections to do with memory and personality: if he was able to wonder whether or not he was a servitor that meant that he wasn't. This was a temporary muscle override: less efficient, less precise, and only sustainable for a few hours at a time. Keldra must still think she had a use for his conscious mind.

He could feel his heart pounding, his breathing becoming faster. This wasn't panic, although it felt like it. The implant would be flooding his body with adrenaline in preparation for action.

'Mr Reinhardt?' Wendell Glass had appeared in his peripheral vision. Jonas couldn't turn his head or even move his eyes to see the man clearly, but he could hear the panic building again in his voice. 'Mr Reinhardt, are you all right?'

'Mr Reinhardt, can you hear me?' Cooper was beside Jonas, close but out of sight. His voice was more confrontational. That had been a challenge, not a concerned query.

Jonas's hands twitched involuntarily. The implant had consolidated control. Suddenly his entire body lurched forward and his arms shot up to grab the artefact and clutch it to his chest. An alarm rang out shrilly, joining the distant whine that had been sounding since the EMP.

The implant spun Jonas around, and the room seemed to shift and dance as his eyes scanned the walls for something. Cooper and Glass were both standing close to him, but Glass took a step back when he saw him moving. Emily Glass was standing at the edge of the room. She was still wearing her memduction helmet and gloves, but now she focused on Jonas with a look of detached interest, as if he was another servitor show for her amusement.

Behind Emily was a door with an illuminated escape pod symbol above it. The implant fixed his eyes on it for a moment, then his arms hugged the artefact to his chest and his legs broke into a run.

'Reinhardt!' Wendell Glass screamed. 'Put that back at once!'

Emily froze. For a second she looked as if she was about to dive out of Jonas's way, but then she moved to block him. He felt his footfalls changing, one arm coming up, preparing to push past her—

Something slammed into his back, knocking him onto his face. The artefact slid across the floor and clattered against the base of a display plinth. Somewhere behind him, Wendell Glass shrieked.

He found himself rolling with the impact and springing back to his feet, moving a little clumsily but far more quickly than he normally could have. His vision fixed on the artefact for a moment, then the programme seemed to shift gears and he spun around to face Cooper. The captain was on his feet already, in a crouched high-grav boxing stance, eyes alert and focused.

The implant swung Jonas's fist around, homing in on Cooper's neck. Cooper dodged easily and threw a punch of his own, going for Jonas's centre of mass, trying to knock him off-balance. The implant blocked, taking the blow painfully on his forearm.

The fight went too quickly for Jonas to follow. His muscles ached as the implant pushed them past their normal limits; he wanted to throw up, but the implant had locked down his gag reflex. He took blow after blow, far more than the implant landed on Cooper, but he knew that didn't mean he was losing. The combat programme always intercepted the blows with non-critical parts of his body, painful but not impairing his ability to fight. Combat programmes avoided damage, not discomfort, and they could keep a body fighting far beyond normal human tolerances to pain.

If he hadn't known that the true-born eschewed neural technology, Jonas might have thought that Cooper was using a combat programme himself. He seemed to know every move Jonas's implant was about to make, and his motions were controlled, dispassionate, not making the mistakes of blind aggression that was so often the downfall of a free-willed human fighting against a programme. He had adjusted his stance perfectly for the gravities involved: his home gravity versus Jonas's, and the four-fifths or so of a gee of Wendell Glass's safe room. This adjustment for gravity was an area in which combat programmes were meant to have an advantage over free-willed minds, but it looked as though Cooper had been trained well.

The whining alarm became louder. Through the corner of his eye, Jonas saw yellow light spill into the vault from an open doorway, and heard the thumping of boots as two men ran in.

'Shoot him!' Wendell Glass shrieked. 'Shoot Reinhardt! He's a thief!'

'Hold your fire!' Cooper commanded.

The security guards ran past Wendell and weaved around Jonas and Cooper, trying to fix their guns on Jonas but not firing into the melee.

Jonas's world lurched painfully to one side as Cooper landed a solid blow on the side of his face. Cooper pressed his advantage, slamming him into one of the display plinths and sending it crashing to the ground. Jonas was on the ground with Cooper pinning him down; his arm flailed but couldn't land a solid blow. The captain's learned skills had finally got the better of Keldra's implant.

'Get off him!' Wendell shouted. He grabbed one of the security guards' nerve guns. 'Get off him so I can shoot!'

Cooper shifted on top of Jonas, reaching for something in one of his pockets. He brought up his hand and Jonas felt a cold, metallic object pressing into his skin at the base of his skull. The incessant whine of the alarm rang in his ears as he blacked out.

The screech of an alarm dragged Olzan back to consciousness. The thunk of a bulkhead door slamming shut made him snap his eyes open. There was heat, flickering white light, and a smell of burning metal.

He got to his feet and nearly fell again. The gravity was lower than normal and was shifting nauseatingly; it felt as if the grav-ring had been knocked out of alignment. The bridge screen sputtered with static, and when it was dead the pale emergency ceiling lights barely illuminated the room. The control terminals were smashed and the spinward wall was buckled inwards alarmingly. Olzan's side ached from where he had been thrown to the floor. That would hurt like hell when the adrenaline wore off.

Vazoya was on her feet, bending over the prone form of Brenn at the front of the bridge. It looked as if the pilot had been thrown out of his seat by the impact. There was no blood, but he wasn't moving. Keldra was slumped against one wall, hands moving sluggishly, her face bloody where she'd been struck by shards of a smashed control terminal. Tarraso was getting to his feet, a little slower than Olzan, but apparently unharmed.

Something rapped on the hull. A chill ran down Olzan's spine. They were still in the debris field: at any moment a larger piece might finish them off.

He grabbed the first-aid kit from the wall and tossed it to Tarraso, who nodded in acknowledgement as Olzan raced out of the bridge. Tarraso was Engineer-caste but he had some medical training. Olzan had to make sure the ship was safe.

A bulkhead door had come down, blocking the corridor in the spinward direction, with a red pressure loss warning light flashing terrifyingly. Olzan ran the other way until he reached the transit hub. The ring's own systems were dead but the transit modules' internal backups had kept them online. He stabbed the controls and clung to the straps as the module rattled up the ship's spine. The doors opened and he propelled himself along the microgravity tunnel to the forward observation blister.

There was no sign of Konrad's Hope now. The Worldbreaker hung in the space the city had occupied, obscenely large, its featureless shell big enough to contain a dozen cities. It was turning, and gradually accelerating towards whatever rock was next on its menu. Space around it was filled with a thinning cloud of debris, tumbling rocks and starscraper fragments making up a tiny fraction of the city's original mass: the scraps that had fallen from the Worldbreaker's mouth.

Looking down, Olzan winced when he saw the damage one of those scraps had done to the *Thousand Names*. There was an ugly black hole in the forward ring: a whole section of the inner surface had been ripped away, and there were stars visible through a smaller hole in the outer surface. A debris fragment must have hit the outer surface of the ring and punched through, leaving a small entry wound and a larger exit wound as it took all the contents of the ring segment with it, just like Keldra's bullets had done to the hijackers' skulls.

Olzan pulled himself over to the lip of the window where the observation blister hugged the ship's spine, and felt along the edge of the wall panel until he found a catch. The emergency manual controls folded out of the wall and lit up, a sea of orange and blinking red. These controls were robust, hardwired into the ship's spine, and with their own power supply, designed to work even when the rest of the ship was dead.

The lidar display was flickering with traces. Most were dust that wouldn't penetrate the hull, but the display highlighted a dozen that were large and fast-moving enough to be a threat. The internal status report showed power to both rings was down, although emergency life support was running, and the punctured segment of the first ring had been sealed off cleanly. The main drive was still jammed, and the manual controls couldn't establish a link with the sail. Manoeuvring thrusters were still online. Olzan shook with relief. Those were all he needed, for now.

The net activity monitor showed that the signal from Brenn's implant had flatlined – either Brenn was unconscious or the pilot system was down. In either case, what Olzan had to do was the same. He punched in his seven-character password and threw the switch that cut off the pilot system and engaged the manual controls. The pilot system lights went dead, and a pair of joysticks sprung out into his hands, ridiculously simple, like a child's game system.

He braced himself to the panel by his elbows and wrapped his fingers around the control sticks. On the lidar display, several of the large debris pieces were drifting closer. His mouth was dry. He pushed the sticks and felt the rumble of thrusters around him. He accelerated as gently as he dared; Tarraso might be in the middle of treating Brenn, and he didn't want to lurch while the engineer was in the middle of a delicate operation.

Olzan steered a path through the remaining fragments. He heard impact sounds as a few smaller pieces hit the spine near him, and some of the larger bodies flashed past the blister, frighteningly close. At last the flickering traces on the lidar display migrated to one side. The inner face of the debris wave had passed them and they were in clear space; any bodies travelling less quickly would have fallen back and become part of the Worldbreaker's meal.

Olzan released the joysticks and wiped the sweat from his face. He glanced at the internal status reports one last time:

no damage. This time he couldn't resist checking the cargo bay as well. The *Seagull* was safe. Everything was going to be all right.

He pushed the manual controls into their alcove and took the transit module back to the first ring. The gravity was definitely lower than normal; as well as the power being down, the ring must have been knocked out of alignment, so friction was wearing away at its spin. As Olzan ran around the corridor to the bridge he found himself moving in a series of long bounds.

Brenn was laid out prone in the middle of the bridge. Vazoya sat on the floor next to him, face downcast, holding his hand and rocking gently. Tarraso stood over them, holding the first-aid kit. Keldra sat at one of the control terminals, conscious but not moving, pressing a bandage against her face.

Tarraso came over to Olzan as he entered the bridge. His face was grim. 'Are we out of danger?' he asked.

'We're out of danger,' Olzan said. 'Is Brenn . . . '

Tarraso shook his head. 'It was neural shock, through the implant. There was nothing we could do.'

There was a sharp pain in the back of Jonas's neck, at the base of his skull. He clung to the sensation, using it to anchor him in reality against the sea of flashing memories. His limbs froze for a moment and then went limp. He was no longer resisting Cooper. The combat programme had been deactivated, just like the combat programme of Emily's losing gladiator.

Wendell Glass was screaming from the other side of the room. 'Get *off* him so I can *shoot*!' His voice seemed to be coming from the end of an echoing cavern.

'Hold your fire!' Cooper commanded. He pulled Jonas up by his shoulders and seated him against the base of one of the display plinths. 'Are you all right? Can you hear me?'

114

Jonas blinked, slowly. He ached all over but he didn't think any bones were broken. 'I think so.'

'Listen, you've got a hacked implant,' Cooper said earnestly. He was looking at a tiny display on the object he had pressed against Jonas's neck; it was a programming spike, like the one Jonas had used to override Ayla's pilot implant. 'Try to stay calm. I've cancelled the muscle override, but it looks like there's a watcher programme active. I can't disable the implant or I'll trigger a wipe.'

Jonas let himself show panic, but he didn't say anything; he didn't want to risk contradicting whatever story he would have to tell.

'Captain Cooper! I order you to get away from that man so that I can shoot!'

Cooper kept his back to Glass and raised a hand. 'You will not give me orders.' His tone was calm and commanding, and he seemed unfazed by the nerve gun pointed waveringly at his back. 'I am an officer of the Solar Authority and this man is under my protection.'

Wendell blustered but lowered his gun and handed it back to the security guard.

'Thank you, Captain,' Jonas said. He got to his feet, moving deliberately slowly. His muscles still ached from the fight but he tried to exaggerate the extent to which he was exhausted. He had to make himself look non-threatening.

Emily Glass had appeared behind Cooper and was peering over his shoulder at Jonas. She didn't appear angry like her father, or concerned like Cooper. The spectacle seemed to be a curiosity to her, a diversion from her sensation-overloaded inner life.

'Now, tell me what happened,' Cooper said. 'Do you know who put that implant in you?'

Jonas briefly considered throwing himself at Cooper's mercy, but discarded the idea. Keldra's implant would kick in and wipe him in a few hours if he didn't get back to the *Remembrance of Clouds*. Even if Cooper could remove it without triggering the wipe, there were too many ways for him to find out that Jonas was not who he claimed to be. No, there was no escape from Keldra at the moment.

He glanced quickly between the faces in the room. Two security guards with nerve guns, most likely both Soldier-caste tank-borns. If Glass had a stable of servitor gladiators then the guards would most likely have combat enhancement implants. They looked wary of Cooper, but if there was a conflict between him and Glass they would side with their employer.

Captain Cooper: alert, confident, an ally for now. Wendell Glass: flustered, still out of his depth, but he'd regained some composure and would want to take back the situational authority that Cooper had stolen from him. Emily Glass: memduction addict, barely interested in what was happening around her. Emily Glass, still wearing her memduction helmet and gloves . . .

'Gouveia,' Jonas said. 'I'm working for Gouveia.' Wendell had used that name earlier; he'd been scared that someone called Gouveia would attack him. Jonas knew of the Gouveias as a powerful Belt Three family, so he could easily believe that one had become a rival city owner. If he guessed right, Cooper was here because Glass was negotiating for the Solar Authority's support in the conflict, hence all his protestations about purity and keeping the memory of Earth alive. The Solar Authority liked to see themselves as principled, and Glass was trying to convince Cooper that he was the more worthy cause.

Glass stared at Jonas, for a moment, sunken eyes burning in his round face, then hissed, 'I knew it.' Jonas managed not to let his relief show. Glass pointed angrily at Cooper. 'You said she wouldn't attack so soon.'

'This isn't an attack,' Jonas said, before Cooper could respond. He walked over to pick up the fallen artefact and held it up. 'My employer wanted to acquire this now, rather than risk it being damaged in a future conflict.'

'I didn't know Gouveia was a collector,' Wendell said. 'If she'd asked me, we could have done business.'

'My employer isn't a collector, publicly.' Jonas injected just a little disdain into his tone, as if lecturing a slow child. 'Why buy these things when you can steal them? And if no one knows you have them, you're not a target.'

Glass grabbed the guard's nerve gun again and levelled it at Jonas's head. Cooper held out an arm to stop him, but Glass didn't lower the gun. Glass's voice trembled with forced confidence. 'Well, you failed. Why shouldn't I kill you now?'

Jonas could hear the hum of the nerve gun. He managed not to blink. 'If you kill me, you kill any chance of a deal with my employer.' He lifted the artefact. 'Let me go with this, in an escape capsule. Gouveia's ship will pick me up. No one needs to get hurt.'

'Cooper! You can't let him steal from me!'

Cooper had taken a step back. 'The Solar Authority has not yet decided which side to take in your conflict with Gouveia,' he said. 'We also do not much care who owns which Planetary Age artefact, although we prefer not to see them damaged. I will attempt to prevent true-born blood-shed, but I won't enter a conflict if there is a non-violent resolution available.'

'But this is extortion!'

'Better that than war.'

117

Glass began to lower the gun, then took another step forward and raised it again. His face was bright red. 'How do I know any of this is true?' He waved the gun in the direction of the artefact. 'What's so special about that, anyway? It's not even the most valuable thing I've got.'

'My employer is specifically interested in this artefact,' Jonas said. 'If you'd like to offer something more valuable in its place, though, perhaps I could set up a discussion.'

'No! Tell me what's so special about that.'

'It's part of a set.' Jonas glanced at Emily, just long enough to catch her attention. 'My employer is assembling the pieces of the *Seagull*.'

Emily looked as if she'd been hit by a nerve gun shock. Suddenly her eyes were fixed on his.

Wendell laughed, hollowly, as if trying to convince himself he saw a joke that Jonas didn't. 'There's no point,' he said. 'I tried to assemble the *Seagull* years ago, but there's no point now. The fuselage is gone. It was part of Ana Zhu's collection, but it was on Konrad's Hope when the Worldbreaker hit.'

Emily half-turned away, as if she didn't like to think about the subject but couldn't help listening.

'Was it?' Jonas asked. 'My sources say that one of your ships went in after the Red Line. Why buy these things when you can steal them?'

'It wasn't . . . ' Wendell looked desperately at Cooper. 'It wasn't stealing. The fuselage would have been destroyed anyway. I was rescuing it.'

'Then you're to be commended,' Cooper said, uninterestedly.

'Anyway, it doesn't matter,' Wendell said. 'They weren't fast enough. They didn't . . . ' Emily caught his gaze, glaring. 'Something must have gone wrong,' he said. 'We don't know what happened. They didn't make it out.'

'They did,' Jonas said, raising his voice as he drove the point home. 'They didn't make it back to *you*. One of the crew was Gouveia's agent.'

'Olzan,' Wendell said darkly.

'No!' It was the first time Emily had spoken since Jonas arrived. Most of her face was blank but her eyes were blazing, as if emotion was just beginning to force its way up from some deeply buried cavern.

'I don't know who it was,' Jonas said. Let them speculate. 'Your ship made it out, with the *Seagull* fuselage. Both are in my employer's possession.'

'The crew,' Emily demanded. 'What about them?'

'They're alive, as far as I know.' It wasn't quite a lie. There were ways that the implant could have been removed from Olzan without killing him.

'You can't prove any of this,' Wendell said. 'It's common knowledge the *Seagull* fuselage was destroyed at Konrad's Hope. You and Gouveia could have found out I had a ship there.'

Jonas bowed his head and tapped the back of his neck. 'I've got memories in this implant that prove it. Memories from the *Thousand Names's* Captain Olzan. One of you could view them.' He glanced at Emily, for a moment, before settling his gaze on Captain Cooper.

'I don't use neural technology,' Cooper said.

'Let me,' Emily said. She had slipped one memduction glove back on, and was already moving closer to Jonas, darting into her father's line of fire. 'I've already got the helmet. I can do it.'

Wendell stepped back and lowered the gun. He was hopping from foot to foot in agitation but it looked as though he couldn't see a way out. 'Do whatever you like,' he said.

Emily put a trembling, gloved hand to Jonas's forehead. He held the artefact with one hand, raised the other, and clicked his fingers three times. Olzan's virtual office appeared around him, ghosting through Emily's body. He flicked to the messages icon and pulled up the last message from Emily to Olzan. He flicked it into her memduction glove.

Her eyes flickered from side to side as the memory sped into her brain, adding a subjective minute of memory in the space of a few real seconds. When she withdrew her hand tears had appeared in her eyes. 'Olzan . . . '

Cooper frowned. 'Who is this Olzan?'

'Just a tank-born,' Wendell said quickly. 'Administrator-caste. He was captain of the ship that I sent to recover the fuselage.'

Cooper was looking at Emily. She had wiped away the first tears, but another was coming.

'What does he mean to you?' he asked, suspiciously.

'Nothing,' Wendell snapped.

'Perhaps you should see it for yourself, Captain,' Jonas said. 'We can extract the sense data and put it on a screen.'

'No,' Wendell said. He glanced between Cooper, Emily, and Jonas, then slouched, defeated. 'Take your damn transponder. Tell Gouveia I'll negotiate.' He pulled out his communicator. 'Colonel Henrick, stand down alarm. An escape capsule will be launched from the *Haze* in a moment. Do not intercept it.'

'Thank you,' Jonas said. He hefted the artefact – the transponder – under his arm, and walked to the escape capsule door. It opened at a touch, revealing a small room with floor hatches, not unlike the shuttle bay where he had first failed to escape the *Remembrance of Clouds*.

He stopped in the doorway for a moment and turned back. Emily looked at him, red eyes peering out from between strands of black hair. He thought he could see himself in her: both mourning a lover from across the true-born-tank-born divide, now unable to even talk about their loss. He wished there was a way he could give her the implant, or play all of its memories to her, but there was no time. 'I'm sorry,' he said.

Chapter Nine

The interior walls of the escape capsule were cushioned like a jewellery box, and humming with life support systems. There were no windows, but there was a tiny screen displaying an external view, along with reassuring status indicators. Jonas watched the *Haze of the Ecliptic* shrink into the distance. Its navigation lights were active, and the segments of its translucent inner ring surface were lighting up one by one as power was restored after the EMP. The ringship shrank to a point and almost became lost in the glare of the sun. Then the escape capsule moved into the shadow of Santesteban and the ecliptic itself became visible, the millions of rocks of the other belts blurring together into a glittering band around the sky, thickest near the occluded sun where Belts Two and One added to the throng.

Jonas couldn't see the *Remembrance of Clouds* on Santesteban's docking pylons, but he found it on the capsule's lidar and then centred the screen on it. Little spurts of white flame erupted from crowns of manoeuvring thrusters positioned along the ship's spine as it moved into position to catch the tiny capsule. The near side of the ship was in sunlight, and the battered Earth mural seemed to shine as it loomed closer.

There was no communication from the *Remembrance*, even though Keldra could easily have used the communications laser to talk to Jonas without being intercepted. She didn't know what had taken place on the *Haze*; it looked as though she still expected him to be under the control of her implant.

The Earth mural slid aside as the cargo bay door opened, and the escape capsule floated into Keldra's domain. A trio of servitors in mismatched vacuum suits caught the capsule and gently manoeuvred it to the cargo airlock, where the spine entered at the forward end of the cylindrical cargo bay. The luxury ringship's escape capsule didn't fit with the old freighter's airlock, but the servitors erected a temporary seal between them and the doors opened, letting the *Remembrance's* rust-and-oil smell mix with the clean air of the capsule.

Keldra was in the airlock, wearing a vacuum suit, but with the helmet clipped to her side. Another pair of servitors floated behind her.

Jonas propelled himself out of the capsule before she had a chance to speak.

'Keldra, you idiot!'

She shrank back from the door, startled. It looked as if she had expected him to still be under the implant's control.

He grabbed a handhold to stop himself right in front of her. 'Was that the extent of your plan? Make me grab the transponder and run for an escape pod? Didn't you think about what could go wrong?'

Keldra's mouth worked soundlessly for a moment. Her startled expression had smoothed out her face, making her look oddly younger. She tried to look past Jonas into the capsule but he moved to block her view.

'Did you get it?' Almost as an afterthought, her hand went to the nerve gun at her hip. 'If you didn't get it I've got no use for you.'

'Yes, I got your damned transponder. It's in the capsule.' One of the servitors moved past Jonas to retrieve the artefact.

'What happened?' Keldra demanded.

'One of Glass's people tackled me. He had a programming spike. He broke through your muscle override.'

'How did you get out?'

'I *talked* my way out.'

She smiled. 'My plan did work, then. I knew you'd be useful.'

'I barely made it out. You could easily have lost the transponder.'

'I'd have lost *you*. I'd have found some other way to get the transponder.' She took the transponder from the servitor and pushed herself towards the transit module, turning her back on him. She was acting self-satisfied but Jonas could tell it was bluster, false self-confidence. Finding him free-willed in the escape capsule had thrown her.

'What's the transponder for?' he called after her. 'It wasn't the most valuable artefact there, and I don't think you're going to sell it, so what do you need it for?'

She didn't turn round. 'I'm not sure you need to know that.'

'You're putting the *Seagull* together, aren't you?'

Keldra froze, floating from a handhold, her body halfway through the transit module door. Now she turned to look at Jonas, unsuccessfully hiding her surprise behind a stony mask.

'You're collecting the pieces of the *Seagull*,' he said. 'I know you've got the fuselage.'

'How do you know about the *Seagull*?'

'I'm not sure you need to know that.'

124

She hesitated for a moment, then propelled herself back to him, grabbed the front of his suit, and launched him into the transit module.

'Yes, I'm putting the *Seagull* together. I'll show you.'

Keldra kicked open a locker in the transit module wall and pulled out a yellow emergency vacuum suit. Jonas pulled it on over his clothes as the transit module began to rumble along the *Remembrance's* spine into the cargo bay. The spine here became an open network of struts running down the middle of the bay, and the shutters over the transit module's windows automatically slid aside so that he could see out into the bay. The bay door had closed, so they were running down the middle of a cylindrical metal cavern, like a much smaller version of the city habitation cavern as seen from the rail-taxi. Close to the airlock, the three servitors that had caught the escape capsule had removed the airtight seal and were beginning to push the capsule towards the side of the bay. Deeper into the bay, cargo containers slid past the windows; he spotted the Reinhardt Industries logo among the logos of a dozen other companies. Keldra's initial tour had only taken him as far as the loading control room at the top of the bay, and the transit modules had refused to take him further during the journey to Santesteban, so he hadn't seen past the first row of containers before.

At the very bottom of the cargo bay, against the wall that separated the bay from the reaction drive's fuel tanks, a group of old containers had been arranged to form a vaguely hemispherical bubble. Suspended in the middle by long strands of cargo webbing was a white shape that Jonas recognized from Olzan's memories.

Keldra checked that he had the suit sealed, then led him through an airlock at the bottom of the spine and out into the bubble. Close to, he could see the changes she had made to the spaceplane since she had 'rescued' it from Konrad's Hope: thruster packs strapped beneath the wings, and assorted antennae and sensor nodes affixed to its hull. None of them looked like original components: they broke up the clean curves of the original design, as if the spaceplane had broken out in boils. There were rectangular patches covering the bullet holes.

'That's the *Seagull*,' Keldra said, pulling herself along the webbing towards the spaceplane's entrance hatch. 'It's a Planetary Age spaceplane. It would have landed on Earth. The long fins are wings; they were used for flying in atmosphere. The spaceplane would ferry people between the surface and the mother ship.'

She opened the hatch and pulled herself head first into the *Seagull's* cabin, followed by her two servitors. Jonas tried to follow, but the second servitor expressionlessly held up a hand to block him. Jonas watched through the cabin windows as Keldra opened a panel in the spaceplane's internal wall and began attaching the transponder to the nest of wires within. The servitors waited nearby, holding out tools for her, but she did the work herself.

'You're making it fly again,' Jonas said.

'In a crude way. It's got enough for basic manoeuvres. It couldn't fly in an atmosphere again, or climb out of a planet's gravity well. Not that that matters anymore.'

'What's this for, Keldra? You're not assembling this for a collector.'

'No,' she said firmly.

'Then what's so special about the transponder? The *Seagull* would fly without it.'

Keldra pushed the transponder fully into its alcove and then moved away from the wall. The lights on the transponder's surface had changed from red to green.

126

'The transponder's the key,' she said. 'The transponder makes the mother ship recognize the *Seagull* as its shuttle.'

'The mother ship? That would be an Earth ship. Are there any left?' Jonas frowned. He had seen parts of Earth ships in collections, but none that he knew of were still intact.

'That's right.' Keldra pulled herself through the space-plane's hatch and headed back towards the transit module.

'What are you planning, Keldra?'

'I've told you enough, for now. Tell me how you knew about the *Seagull*.'

'Wendell Glass mentioned it.'

'Wendell Glass believes it was destroyed. The whole collector community believes it was destroyed. I made sure of that.'

They were back in the transit module now. Keldra set it moving towards the hab rings and took off her helmet, then looked at Jonas expectantly while he did the same.

'Wendell Glass told me about the *Thousand Names*, his ship that went missing at the same time,' Jonas said. 'The *Thousand Names* matches this ship's description, so I put two and two together.'

'You're too clever. I should kill you now.'

'You won't.' Jonas began to pull off the vacuum suit and return it to the transit module locker.

'Why not? I've got the transponder. That's what I needed you for.'

'You only got the transponder because of my skills, and you might need those skills again. But that's not all you needed me for.'

'What, then?'

'You need someone to talk to,' Jonas said. 'When you first captured me I said that to goad you, but it was true then, and

127

it's true now. You need someone to keep you sane, someone to keep you *human*.' He gestured to the ghostly shape of the spaceplane as it shrank behind them. 'You didn't need to show me the *Seagull*, but you wanted to. You wanted to show it off.'

'To hell with you. I've never needed anyone before.'

'You've never done anything important before. You've killed six Worldbreakers, out of tens of thousands. That's nothing but a grain of dust in the belts, and you know it.' She glared at him, but he pressed on before she could respond. 'But now you're planning something else, aren't you? Something bigger, and you want someone to see you do it, don't you? You want an audience to make it *real*.'

'To hell with you. You know nothing about me.'

They rode in silence back through the cargo bay and down to the second hab ring. As soon as the doors opened, Keldra stalked off, not looking at Jonas. Her servitors followed her, leaving him alone. The doors closed and the module moved back up to the spine and deposited him in the first ring.

He went back to his cabin, sat down at his desk, and clicked his fingers three times to conjure the implant's virtual desktop.

There were two locked memories left, timestamped just a few hours apart. If the muscle override and Cooper's disruption of it had both caused previously locked memories to play, it was likely that the blocks on the remaining memories would have been weakened. The secret of Keldra's past would be in there, and that, if anything, would be the key to manipulating her. He thought he was getting a feel for how the implant's malfunction worked. It shouldn't take too long to unlock the remaining memories.

He closed his eyes and began running images through his mind: the *Seagull*, the transponder, Santesteban, the *Remembrance of Clouds* rotating to catch the escape capsule . . .

128

Slowly, Olzan scanned the ship diagram, making sure the implant was recording the picture into memory. The model was rotating on the 3D screen in the lounge, the largest screen they had with the bridge still offline. Worrying red and yellow lights picked out systems along the ship's length, but the most prominent were at either end of the sail and the reaction drive.

'There must be something we can do,' he said.

'The main drive can't be repaired without a shipyard,' Tarraso said. 'We don't have the parts on board.' He, Keldra, and Vazoya perched stiffly on the couch, looking ridiculously formal in the casual setting.

'And the sail?' Olzan asked.

'Is fine, except that we can't control it. We need a pilot.'

'For God's sake, Tarraso, there must be some way—'

'It's Earth-tech,' Keldra butted in. Half of her face was covered by a pink gel-plast where the shrapnel wound was healing. 'It and the pilot implant. No one understands how they talk to one another. There's no research anymore.'

'All right,' Olzan snapped. The last thing he wanted was for Keldra to start one of her sullen rants about the state of the universe. He turned back to Tarraso. 'There's no way to hack it? Not complete control, but something?'

Tarraso shook his head. 'Sail's a black box. It's not responding to anything we do. Either it's broken, in which case we're screwed, or it's just that we can't talk to it in the way it wants.'

'Okay. No reaction drive, no sail.' He turned to Vazoya. 'No chance of getting to a port with thrusters?'

Vazoya was looking at the floor, with no indication that she had even heard him. She'd barely spoken since Brenn's death. Her facial tattoos were black, like a veil painted onto her face.

'We're drifting out of the ecliptic,' Tarraso said after a moment. 'The thrusters don't have enough delta-vee to get us back into the belt. It'll be six months before we hit the belt again, and our supplies won't last two.'

'What if we ration—'

'That two months was based on the strictest rationing scenario possible,' Keldra said icily. 'I was a hab engineer before you kidnapped me. I know what I'm talking about.'

'All right,' Olzan said. 'Can we call for help?'

'The main comms laser was knocked out by debris,' Tarraso said. 'We can broadcast, but out here that's more likely to attract pirates.'

'Yeah.' Olzan filed the idea away. He might be able to negotiate with pirates, especially if he could convince them that Mr Glass would pay for his safe return, but the pirates would most likely take the *Seagull*. Losing the spaceplane and having to be ransomed would ruin any chance he had of convincing Mr Glass to pay for his treatment. He might never even see Emily again. He scoured the diagram once more, looking for ideas. Think outside the box. 'What if we *had* a pilot?'

'Then we could get the sail open right away, assuming it still works,' Tarraso said wearily. 'But we *don't* have a pilot.'

'No, but what if we did? We have the implant. You could extract it.'

Vazoya looked up, startled, but said nothing. Brenn's body was on ice in the cargo bay, ready to be given an Arkite funeral when they reached port; Vazoya claimed that this had been his wish, although Olzan had never heard him mention his religion. Arkite tradition was for bodies to be embalmed and stored as intact as possible so that they could be given true burial on New Earth when the planets reappeared. Olzan didn't believe the planets would ever come back, but it was just common decency to respect another person's religion. Removing the implant would mean dismantling his skull.

'No,' Tarraso said. 'The implant might still work, but you can't just put a pilot implant in someone. Pilots have to go through training, step up through the intermediate implants. To be selected at all, they have to have that . . . I don't know . . . that special gift.'

'What would happen?' Olzan asked. 'They wouldn't be able to control the sail?'

Tarraso squirmed in his seat, uncomfortable, but Olzan stared at him until he answered. 'They probably would, but . . . We're talking about permanent psychological damage here, Olzan. They'd be able to control the ship, but I don't know how much of the person would be left.'

'There'll be none of us left if we can't control the sail. Can you do it?'

'Olzan—'

'Just tell me if you can do it.'

'Yes. I can extract the implant and put it into someone else,' Tarraso said slowly. 'Who's the new pilot, though? I'll be performing the operation.'

'I could perform the implantation,' Keldra said. 'It's not as hard as extracting it.'

'All right,' Tarraso said. 'Anyone could perform the implantation. So who's the new pilot? Do we draw lots?'

Vazoya looked up at Olzan. Her mouth was curled up as if in anger but there was a tear in her eye.

'Vaz?' Olzan said gently. It looked as if she was about to volunteer herself. Sacrificing herself to save the crew was just the sort of foolish, emotional thing she might do, especially after the blow of Brenn's death. Olzan was tempted to let her go through with it. It would get them all out of trouble, get him back to Emily with the spaceplane. It might even be the best thing for her.

'I say we use Keldra,' Vazoya said.

Keldra was on her feet, instantly in a defensive posture. 'To hell with you!'

'Calm down!' Olzan tried to get between them.

'It's her fault Brenn's dead!' Vazoya spat. 'If we'd blown the doors on that hangar we'd have been out of there long before the Black Line.'

'It was my call.'

'Bullshit. Your suit comms were still transmitting. I heard what happened. She practically had a gun to your head.'

Tarraso stared at Keldra. 'Is that true?'

Olzan hesitated. It wasn't true, exactly. He'd been scared of Keldra after she'd killed the hijackers, and he still was, if he was honest with himself, but the others didn't know how much he'd wanted to get an intact spaceplane back to Mr Glass, or why. It was easy to let Vazoya put more of the blame onto Keldra than she deserved. 'It's true,' he said. 'She had a gun back there, and she wasn't following my orders.'

'You should be volunteering yourself,' Vazoya said to Keldra with contempt. 'People are just people, isn't that what you said? We don't need two engineers.'

'To hell with all of you!' Keldra spluttered. 'Olzan, you can't do this.'

'If we're going to do this, we should draw lots,' Tarraso said. 'I don't know what went on back there, but this isn't the time to weigh up who deserves to be brain damaged. The right thing to do is draw lots.'

'*Fuck* drawing lots,' Vazoya said. 'She killed Brenn! You *know* that.'

'Shut up, all of you,' Olzan said. 'Tarraso, go open up Brenn's head. We need that implant.'

Tarraso started to get up. 'We're going to draw lots, then?'

Olzan hooked his thumb through on his belt, moving it close to the nerve gun that hung there. 'No,' he said. 'Vaz is right. We use Keldra.'

Vazoya leapt at Keldra like a coiled spring, knocking the other woman to the ground. As she fell, Keldra managed to land a solid blow on Vazoya's jaw. Vazoya was on top of Keldra, pinning her. There were spots of blood on her face, spattered across the tattoo veil.

Tarraso hadn't moved. 'Olzan, this isn't right. I still say we should—'

'I've made my decision,' Olzan said. 'Keldra's the only person we can afford to lose. Go get ready for the surgery.'

Tarraso hurried off, as if not wanting to be part of what was happening in the lounge. Olzan stood over Keldra. She was still pinned by Vazoya, but she had stopped struggling. The brawl had knocked off most of the gel-plast, and her face beneath it was smeared with blood mixed with the gel-plast's fibres, the wound not fully healed. She was glaring up in anger, but there was a new look on her face as well: it was the first time he had seen her show real fear. He felt a perverse rush of pleasure at seeing it.

He clicked the gun to 'paralyze' and fired.

'Sorry, Keldra. It's the only way.' He put on his cocky salesman's smile. 'Looks like you've just joined the ranks of brain-damaged trade ship pilots.'

A schematic of the *Seagull* spun on the bridge screen. Keldra had called Jonas to the bridge a few hours after she had installed the transponder. Now she stood in front of the screen and gestured for Jonas to sit at his console. It looked as though he had been right: she couldn't resist telling him her plan for long. After the betrayal he had witnessed in the last memory, he wondered if she had been able to talk so openly to anyone in the last eight years. Perhaps a captive, with an implant that prevented him from harming her, was the only audience she could trust.

'I didn't know what the *Seagull* meant, when I rescued it,' she said. 'After I got it, I did some research on the city nets. The information's out there, if you know where to look, it's just that no one puts it together. No one studies the Planetary Age artefacts. They break them up and sell the pieces. Put them on stands.' She looked darkly at the *Seagull* schematic. Among the labels marking the pieces she'd recovered or added there were more labels indicating the pieces that were still missing.

'What did you find?' Jonas prompted.

'The *Seagull* was a shuttle belonging to a larger ship. The big ship would stay in the Earth's orbit, and the *Seagull* and the other spaceplanes would take people down to the surface.'

'I know that,' Jonas said.

'Shut up. Once I got into the *Seagull's* logs, I found the name of the ship it had belonged to: the *Aurelian*, an Earth Authority cruiser that had been co-opted for a science mission. It was active at the end of the Planetary Age, during the Worldbreaker war.'

'What happened to it?'

Keldra's eyes sparkled wickedly as she changed the view to a belt chart. A blue dot pulsed forlornly in inter-belt space. 'It's still out there. I worked out where it would be based on the *Seagull's* logs and the orbit the *Seagull* was discovered on. The *Aurelian* is in an elliptical orbit between Belts Two and Three. I've bounced lidar beams off it; I know it's still there.'

'No one's looted it?' he asked.

'People have tried. It must be a collector's wet dream. But its defence systems are still active. Any ship that gets too close . . . *pssshk!*' She mimed an explosion with her hands.

'And it'll let the *Seagull* get close?'

'It should do, now that it's got the transponder.'

'It *should* do? You're not sure?'

'I'm pretty sure.'

'And then, what will you do? You could loot it and sell the artefacts to finance your crusade, but somehow, I don't think that's what you're after.'

'That's right, I'm not. I'm after a weapon.'

'A weapon against the Worldbreakers?'

'That's right.'

'What is it? Not more nukes?'

'Better than nukes.'

Despite himself, Jonas felt something stir in his chest. The idea of a weapon that could strike against the Worldbreakers was exciting. 'What is it?'

'I don't know. The *Seagull's* logs refer to something, but they're incomplete.'

He slumped back into his chair. 'What *do* you know?'

Keldra paused, gathering her breath. 'This was in the last years of the Worldbreaker war. The *Aurelian* intercepted a Worldbreaker that had been damaged during the Battle for Mars. They were trying to study its beam projector, to reverse-engineer something they could use against the Worldbreakers.'

'If they succeeded, why didn't they use it?'

'They were too late,' Keldra paced across the floor, boots ringing on the metal, and there was a tremor in her voice. 'Earth went just a few months after Mars. They created their weapon, but they were out in inter-belt space – inter-planetary

135

space, then – and they couldn't get back in time. They were so *close*. They were *days* away.'

He stared at her. 'You really think you can defeat the Worldbreakers?'

'I don't know. We'll find out when we get to the *Aurelian*. We're on our way now.'

'You can't beat the Worldbreakers, Keldra.' He tried to keep any hint of excitement out of his voice. He couldn't let himself be carried away by her fantasy; he had to be the sensible one. 'Even if you find this weapon, it's still too late. Earth's gone. You're running around the belts chasing after a false hope. You're insane.'

'Not now I've got you. That's what you said, isn't it? You keep me *sane*.'

'Why me, Keldra?' When he had goaded her in the transit module, he had thought she just wanted anyone to be her audience, but after the most recent memory, he wasn't sure. 'Why didn't you slave-spike me when you learned I was a tank-born?'

'Like you said, you've got skills I can use.'

'So do any number of people you could have hired on Santesteban. But you didn't even go ashore there, did you? I don't think you've had anyone else on this ship for years. What is it about me that makes you want me around?'

She looked as if she was about to shout at him to shut up, but her desire to explain herself won out. 'You're like me.'

'I'm nothing like you.'

'Sure you are. You were a tank-born but you ended up living as a true-born. You didn't like the world you were born into, so you fought back.' She fixed him with an intense gaze, and there was an earnestness in her voice he hadn't heard before. 'I learned about Earth from history books that no one else could be bothered to read. I hated the Worldbreakers for taking it from us, so I'm fighting back. We both get what we want, and we don't let anyone hold us back.' Her intense gaze broke, and she smiled, as if remembering to be cruel and mocking again. 'Now, you'll help me or you'll see what happens to those who try to stop me.'

Olzan peered through the window to the medbay's operation cubicle. He, Tarraso, and Vazoya were gathered in the medbay's cluttered main chamber, perching on beds or counters. In the corner, the asymmetrical arms of the battered old general-purpose medical robot hung dormant from the ceiling. On the other side of the window, Keldra lay on the operation cubicle's table, held down by straps, amid a clutter of spider-like robot surgery arms. The table was tilted up, allowing Olzan to look her in the eye, but at the moment, she was unconscious, her head slumped at an awkward angle, a line of drool glistening at the side of her mouth. They hadn't replaced the gel-plast, and a web of red wounds stood out on the side of her face.

'How is she?' he asked Tarraso.

The engineer looked up from the medbay's control console. 'She's stable,' he replied. 'Beyond that I can't say.'

'Did the implant take?'

'It's hard to tell.'

'Wake her up.'

'She needs rest, Olzan.'

'Wake her up now. We need to know if the implant took.'

Tarraso tapped a control. One of the robot arms in the operation cubicle moved in and injected something into Keldra's neck. After a few moments she twitched, and her head began to roll slowly from side to side.

'Keldra,' Olzan said. 'Can you hear me?'

She let out a moan, relayed over the medbay speakers. She stirred, then began to struggle, writhing against the straps. Her struggles became more violent and her eyes bulged open, but she didn't seem to be looking at Olzan, or at anything that was in the room with her.

Vazoya leaned against the glass and smiled. 'The implant took.'

Olzan could only imagine what Keldra was going through. Her brain was suddenly processing a hundred times more sensory information than it was used to. Everything happening to every one of the ship's systems was just as real to her as the world she perceived through her normal senses, and some of those systems were damaged, so they'd be pushing into her mind damage report signals very much like pain. A shell of new sensations would have appeared around her, and her ordinary body would have shrunk to a speck in the middle of it. Looking at the horror on Keldra's face, Olzan had a new respect for Brenn and the other uncomplaining pilots he'd met over the years.

'Keldra, listen to me,' he said, raising his voice to be heard above her screams. 'We've had to plug you into the ship. We can get the implant back out of you as soon as we reach a city. We've disconnected the pilot system from as much as we can, so you don't have to control everything. You should just have the sail and the manoeuvring thrusters. We need you to get control of them and unfurl the sail. Can you do that?'

Keldra's screams petered out. Her breath came in frantic pants. She was still looking around in panic, but she had stopped struggling. It looked as if she was over the initial shock and starting to get control of herself.

'Keldra, if you can understand me, nod your head,' Olzan said.

She glanced at him with what might have been a look of contempt. It was hard to tell if it was deliberate or just part of her random head movements.

Vazoya stepped forward and rapped the object she was holding against the glass. It was a small metal box with a dial, connected to a wall data socket by a snaking cable. 'All right, bitch. You're not totally brain-dead. I know there's something in there that can understand me.' She twisted the dial, and Keldra convulsed. Her scream this time was short and had a different timbre, a cry of physical pain. 'This is one of the ship's damage sensors,' Vazoya said. 'I've rigged it up to send a damage signal through the implant, bypassing the normal safeguards. What you just experienced was about a hundredth of the shock that killed Brenn. This is what you get if you don't do what we say.' She twisted the dial again. Keldra twitched, but this time she didn't cry out. 'Now, get control of the ship and get the fucking sail open.'

'I'm getting a signal from the sail,' Tarraso said. 'It's not unfurling yet, but it looks like she's establishing control.'

'Thank you, Keldra,' Olzan said. She seemed to understand them, but she still hadn't spoken. If the pilot shock had damaged her, then she might be on the mental level of a child, or even of a smart animal. He tried to keep his voice clear and encouraging. They might have to give her simple instructions and reinforce them with rewards and punishments.

Keldra had calmed down. She was looking straight ahead, her eyes defocused. She flexed her fingers, and there was a distant rumble, a subtle change in the ambient sounds of the ship. It felt like some of the manoeuvring thrusters were firing. A smile began to curl up her lips.

'Good,' Olzan said. 'You're getting the hang of this. Now, see if you can unfurl the sail. Take your time.'

139

'As long as she doesn't enjoy it too much,' Vazoya said, fingering the damage box. Olzan glared at her.

'The sail's still moving,' Tarraso said. 'It's not properly unfurling yet. Looks like she's testing it. I'm getting a lot of signal through the implant. It's definitely taken.'

Olzan sat down on the medbay table. 'Thank God for that. It looks like we're going home after all.'

Once Keldra had got the sail open, they could deal with the trickier task of getting her to align it correctly, to put them on course for Santesteban. The *Seagull* was still sitting at the back of the cargo bay, Olzan's ticket to a new life with Emily; a life as a true-born by marriage. He called up his implant's navigation programme and did a quick course calculation. If Keldra could get the sail fully unfurled, they could be at Santesteban in two weeks.

'Olzan,' Tarraso said suddenly. 'Take a look at this.'

Olzan looked over Tarraso's shoulder at his engineer's datapad. Numbers and engineer jargon seemed to swim around one another on the pad too quickly for him to focus on. 'What's it mean?'

'Keldra's through the lock-outs I installed.'

Olzan blinked. 'What?'

'She's in full control of the ship. She has been since she started moving the sail, but I've only just noticed.'

'That's not possible!' Vazoya shouted. She sprang across the room to look at Tarraso's pad, stumbling a little. 'I locked her out of the . . . of everything, except the sail, and . . . '

'You must have done the lock-outs wrong,' Olzan said.

Tarraso tapped some commands into the datapad, cursing a couple of times. 'No. Maybe. The lock-outs aren't working.'

'Bitch!' Vazoya shouted. She leaned against the window to the surgery room, holding up the damage box. 'Bitch!

Stop that now!' She twisted the dial. Nothing happened.

'She's isolated that damage sensor,' Tarraso said. He looked worried and confused. 'Olzan, are you . . . I'm having trouble thinking.'

A horrible realization knotted in Olzan's chest. 'She's got into the hab system,' he said. 'She's cutting off our oxygen.'

He pushed himself up against the glass, shoving Vazoya out of the way. Now that he knew what was happening, he noticed that his hands hit the glass a bit too heavily, as if he was drunk. 'Keldra, don't do this. We'll get back to Santesteban and we'll get the implant out of you, I promise.'

'I'm not sure I want it out.' Keldra's voice was a whisper, relayed over the medbay intercom. Dimly, Olzan was aware that her lips weren't moving as she spoke; the voice was coming from the ship. She was looking at him with a satisfied smirk, a world away from the helpless screams of a few minutes ago. 'I think I like it. I'm not sure I even need the rest of you.'

'Fuh . . . Fuck you!' Vazoya shouted, and then collapsed, panting, to floor.

Keldra flexed her fingers again. There was another vibration, a subtle change in acceleration. On Tarraso's pad, through a haze of hypoxia, Olzan could see that the sail was unfurling and the ship was repositioning itself for a course change.

The medical robots around Keldra's bed were starting to move. One of them extended a scalpel arm and began to cut away the strap around one of her wrists. Olzan saw it with an odd emotional detachment. It all seemed very far away, as if he was looking at it from the end of a long tunnel.

'This is my ship now,' Keldra's voice said decisively.

Distantly, Olzan could see the medical robot next to him begin moving, its scalpel arm rising up.

Chapter Ten

The ship was a dark grey cylinder, barely visible at the end of its blue-white reaction drive flame as it pushed itself deeper into inter-belt space. Magnifying the view and filtering it against the glare, Jonas could make out the dimples of weapon emplacements and shuttle bays on its hull, and the five concentric gold circles of the Solar Authority logo that stood out on its nose like an arrogant bullseye. On the belt chart, the blue line of the ship's probable course curved sunward through the tangle of rock orbits that made up Belt Three, down into the sparse void between the belts.

It was mid-morning, ship-time, and Jonas was alone on the bridge. Keldra was asleep, having stayed up late into the night in a stim-fuelled painting frenzy, creating a new cloud mural in one of the corridors. It would be another few hours before the *Remembrance's* computer flagged the new ship as being on an intercept course and alerted her. Inside a belt, the similarity of the two courses would be nothing remarkable, but the chance of two ships passing so close in inter-belt space was vanishingly small.

He pulled up the ship's transponder details. It was the *Iron Dragon*: Lance Hussein Cooper's ship.

He looked at the read-out and smiled. Wendell Glass must have convinced Cooper of his true-born credentials, and coughed up the money for the Solar Authority's help against Gouveia. Cooper must be on his way to retrieve the stolen transponder before it got into Gouveia's hands. Knowing the Solar Authority, Cooper would want to achieve his objective with the minimum of bloodshed, and certainly without risking damage to the Planetary Age artefact. He might just be prepared to make a deal with poor kidnapped true-born Gabriel Reinhardt.

Jonas pulled Captain Cooper's Earth-tech business card from his pocket and pressed his thumb against the white circle that activated it. Even out here in inter-belt space, the secure signal icon was there.

He held his thumb to the card's 'transcribe' marker and whispered his message into the card. 'Gabriel Reinhardt, *Remembrance of Clouds*, to Captain Cooper. Please acknowledge.' The words appeared on the card's surface in neat capitals. He pressed the 'send' marker and then placed the card on the terminal, and waited.

The round-trip light-speed delay was only a few seconds, but another two minutes passed after that before the card lit up with a response. 'CAPTAIN COOPER, IRON DRAGON, ACKNOWLEDGING GABRIEL REINHARDT.'

'I am being held unlawfully,' Jonas whispered. 'The *Remembrance's* captain is unlikely to surrender to you. I can sabotage the *Remembrance's* defences and deliver the transponder, if you will help me.'

The next reply took longer to arrive, close to ten minutes. Jonas pictured Cooper discussing the message with his staff on the *Iron Dragon's* bridge. When it appeared, though, it was what Jonas had hoped for.

'I THINK WE CAN DO BUSINESS, MR REINHARDT.'
Jonas looked at the message for a few moments and then
tucked the card back into his pocket. He pressed the intercom
buzzer that would summon Keldra to the bridge.

'What is it?' Her voice was groggy and annoyed. He felt
an immature sense of pleasure at having woken her.

'You'd better get to the bridge,' he said. 'We've got company.'

Keldra was on the bridge in a couple of minutes. She was still
wearing her dishevelled ship overalls, stained with blue and
white paint; Jonas wondered whether she'd slept in them or
hastily put them on after he'd summoned her. As she stared
at the ship on the bridge screen, her bleary expression gave
way to a scowl. 'Authority,' she spat.

'Looks like it,' Jonas said. 'Do you recognize that ship?'

Keldra climbed into her control nest. 'They don't usually
bother me. If a family can afford the Solar Authority, they
can afford my ransom first.'

'Looks like Wendell Glass can afford them.'

'Looks like it.' She fumbled a stim pill out of a packet
and gulped it down. 'Get rid of them.'

'Get rid of them? How?'

'Be a true-born. You're the captain. We're a simple trading
vessel heading for Belt Two. You're incensed he's following
us, your family will have his hide, that sort of thing.'

'I was on Santesteban. I'll be on I don't know how many
security cameras and guard servitors' memories. If he's after
the transponder, he'll know my face.'

'All right. I'll do it.' Keldra ran her fingers through
her hair and adjusted the camera poking over one of her
nest's control boards. There was a polite chime as she
began transmitting. 'This is Captain Keldra Smith of the

trading ship *Remembrance of Clouds*. We weren't expecting to meet anyone else down here. Is there anything we can do for you?'

There was another chime as a responding call came through. Keldra put it on the screen. A young man with a neat beret and the stripes of a communications officer appeared. 'One moment please, *Remembrance of Clouds*. I'll fetch Captain Cooper.'

Smith? Jonas mouthed. Keldra shot him a dirty look.

The communications officer stepped aside and Cooper appeared on the screen. 'Captain Lance Hussein Cooper, Solar Authority cruiser *Iron Dragon*. What did you say your name was?'

'Keldra Smith.'

Cooper made a clicking noise in his throat. 'I don't think so. I've been to Smith family gatherings, and you don't look like any of them. You don't look like a true-born at all, and you don't speak like one. Put me through to the real captain, or give me the name of your vessel's owner.'

'I'm owner-captain of the *Remembrance of Clouds*. We're a private trading vessel on our way to Belt Two. We picked you up on a similar course and were wondering—'

Cooper had started speaking over Keldra. 'You're *not* a legitimate trading vessel unless you've got a true-born owner. Solar Authority law states that tank-borns can't own inter-belt ships. Let's cut to the chase and tell one another why we're really here. I know that you're carrying stolen goods. You will furl your sail and allow the *Iron Dragon* to dock and my men to search your ship.'

'We're not carrying any stolen goods,' Keldra said.

Cooper smiled without even a hint of sincerity. 'Then you should have no objection to our searching your ship.'

Jonas caught Keldra's eye. *Agree,* he mouthed. She glared at him.

On the screen, Cooper's smile deepened. 'I'm waiting for your answer, "Captain Smith".'

Keldra hesitated and then leaned in towards the camera. 'Your Solar Authority can go to hell.' She shut off the transmission and stared at the blank screen.

'Smooth,' Jonas said.

'Shut up.'

'Either we give them the transponder, or they take it. If we hand it over without any trouble there's a good chance they'll let us live.'

'Yeah, that's what you'd do, isn't it? Surrender. Like you surrendered to me.' She wasn't looking at him.

'That's a Solar Authority cruiser.'

The bridge screen went dark, followed by the room lights, leaving Keldra in a cocoon of dim glow cast by her nest's control boards. She was curled up in her chair, eyes closed.

'Keldra, what are you doing?'

'Why did it have to be the Solar Authority?' Keldra's voice sounded on the verge of tears. 'I came so close. I came so fucking *close.*'

A vibration ran through the floor. The ship was turning.

'Keldra, what are you doing? We can't run. We're a sail ship. That's a Solar Authority cruiser.'

'We're not going to run.'

'Are you mad? We can't fight!'

'We can *always* fight.'

The room lights came back on. On the screen was a local belt chart, with the course lines of the *Remembrance of Clouds* and the *Iron Dragon* curving inexorably closer together. There was another rumble beneath Jonas's feet, and a sense of activity beyond the bridge. There were tears glinting in Keldra's eyes, but her face was curling into a determined smile, and in it he could see systems lighting up across the ship, servitors waking up and moving into new routines.

Looking at her then, Jonas almost regretted that his plan would stop her from fighting the *Iron Dragon*. He would likely be saving her life as well as his own, but still, there was something in her face at that moment that he was beginning to admire.

'I've got the advantage,' she said.

'How so?'

'They need the transponder. They can't use the big guns or they'll risk destroying it. I don't have to hold back.'

'What are you planning, Keldra?'

'I'm furling the sail. I'm turning us end-on, to present a smaller target. They won't let us get close enough to use our drive flame as a weapon, so I'm pointing the launcher at them. I used most of the uranium back at Santesteban but I've got enough to scrape together a small warhead. Servitors are making it now.'

'One warhead? He'll shoot it down. This isn't a dumb Worldbreaker you're dealing with, Keldra. Solar Authority ships have point defence.'

'Not one warhead. Dozens of missiles. One of them's the nuke, the others are junk; everything the servitors can strip out of the ship and load into the tube. They might not be able to shoot everything down. The nuke might get through.'

'It's a long shot.'

'It's all I have.'

'It's *not* all you have. We can surrender. Call him back up.'

'I don't surrender,' she spat. 'Get out of here. Let me think.'

Jonas sat on the couch in the lounge, set the screen to a local belt chart, and watched as the ships closed with one another. He wasn't an expert ship-to-ship tactician, but he knew how tense this stage of the encounter was for the ships' commanders. It was a game of chicken: both commanders wanted the first strike advantage, but the longer they left it before firing, the better their chances would be of hitting with that first strike.

If Keldra was to stand a chance, she *needed* that first strike advantage. She wouldn't leave it too long. That informed the timing of his next move. He was playing chicken as well, although the other players didn't know it. He wanted to leave it as late as possible, to give Keldra little time to react and recover, but he had to move before she fired on the *Iron Dragon*.

He watched the distance tick down. The *Remembrance's* course had changed when it had furled the sail, allowing the *Iron Dragon* to close more quickly: 20,000 kilometres; 15 . . . At 10,000, he got up and walked to the transit hub.

He took the transit module to the ship's spine and made his way to the forward observation blister. Space looked empty, the normal scattering of Belt Three asteroids reduced to a tenuous line around the ecliptic. He could just make out the spark of the *Iron Dragon's* reaction drive as it decelerated to match courses with the *Remembrance of Clouds*.

He felt for the catches that would release the emergency control panel. Keldra would know about the panel, of course – she would know every inch of her own ship, even the parts that didn't report to her pilot implant – but she shouldn't know that he knew. Still, it was just possible she had removed the panel, or trapped it, or set up his implant so that this would trigger a wipe . . .

His fingers found the catches. The panel unfolded into his hands.

The local belt chart was empty, apart from the *Iron Dragon* gradually closing. The net activity monitor was spiking: Keldra was active and alert. The system lights were green with the occasional blinking orange.

Jonas entered the passcode from Olzan's memory and then threw the main override switch. The system lights turned orange-red. The net activity monitor flatlined as the ship stopped responding to Keldra's implant.

She wouldn't be able to do anything without the emergency controls. There was just one control he needed now: the lock to the observation blister's door. He found it quickly enough. Sealed in, with the *Iron Dragon* on its way to rescue Gabriel Reinhardt, all he had to do was wait.

It was less than a minute before Jonas heard a rap at the observation blister door. Keldra had her face close to the glass. Her customary scowl couldn't quite hide a current of wide-eyed shock. He had caught her completely off guard.

'What the hell are you doing?' she shouted, her voice muffled by the glass.

'I'm saving my life, and maybe yours too,' Jonas shouted back. 'We can't fight the Solar Authority. Give them the transponder and maybe they'll let us go.'

'I don't negotiate. I don't run, and I don't *beg*.'

'How the hell did you even last this long? Sometimes you have to make deals.'

'Not with the transponder. Not when I'm so fucking *close*.'

'You'd really rather die than give it up?'

She banged on the door. The sound was tiny and dull inside the blister.

'You're insane, Keldra.'

She disappeared from the window. Jonas heard the transit module rumble away.

He studied the emergency controls for a few moments, looking for a way to lock the transit modules down, but he couldn't read Engineer-caste language well enough. Keldra would be back, but it shouldn't matter. Outside, the *Iron Dragon's* drive flame was a white line stretching a quarter of the way across the sky. It wouldn't be long now.

The transit module rumbled again, and there was another bang on the door. In the window was the bright red pistol-like shape of a cutting torch. Behind it, Keldra's face was just visible through the visor of a vacuum suit helmet.

'You won't get through in time,' Jonas said. Actually, he was bluffing: he had no idea how long it would take her to cut through the door, or how long it would be before the *Iron Dragon* docked with the *Remembrance*. He hadn't expected her to vandalize her own ship in order to get to him.

A few sparks rushed past the window, and a red welt appeared on the door and began moving. It was a thick metal door, designed to keep the observation blister and its emergency controls safe, even in the case of damage to the spine, but given long enough Keldra's torch could cut through anything.

'Think about this, Keldra,' Jonas shouted over the hiss of the torch. She had traced a good fraction of a circle now, the sparks tumbling away in fascinatingly straight lines in microgravity. 'The captain of that ship thinks I'm Gabriel Reinhardt. He thinks I'm a true-born. If you surrender, he might be lenient, but if he gets here and finds you've just murdered a true-born with a cutting torch . . . '

She didn't respond. Outside, Jonas could make out the body of the *Iron Dragon* at the end of the flame.

'If you listen to me, we can still get out of this.' The cutting torch had completed a rough half circle. 'Listen, give him me, as well as the transponder. Tell him I was the one in charge. He thinks I'm a true-born, so he'll believe that. He'll let you go, and then I'll try to talk my way out.' He didn't even know if Keldra could hear him.

A light split off from the *Iron Dragon's* drive flame, as tiny as one of the sparks from Keldra's cutting torch. It curved towards the *Remembrance of Clouds*.

'They've launched a shuttle,' Jonas said. 'The game's up, Keldra.'

She didn't respond.

He watched as the spark grew into a set of flickering manoeuvring thrusters, arrayed around the edge of the fat hemispherical shape of a Solar Authority shuttle. From the observation blister, Jonas could see every detail of the craft as it positioned itself in front of the *Remembrance's* main docking airlock and slowly moved in. The circle that Keldra was cutting was a little more than three-quarters complete.

There was a shudder as the two ships made contact. A warning appeared on the emergency control panel, indicating that someone was trying to open the docking airlock from the outside. Jonas tapped the button that gave it permission, and saw the read-outs indicating that the airlock was cycling.

The cutting torch shut off. Keldra must have felt the shuttle dock. There was silence for a moment, then a clang as the torch rapped against the window.

'Fuck you, Jonas! You should have fought. We had a chance. We had a decent fucking chance. I had the transponder! I was so fucking close, and you've thrown it away.'

'I'm sorry, Keldra,' he said. 'A decent chance isn't good enough for me. I want to survive.'

'You run and you hide and you surrender,' she spat. 'You survive. That's all you ever do.'

'That's all there is.'

There was movement at the window. Jonas pulled himself up to the glass to look through. More figures had appeared behind Keldra, floating in single file in the cramped space. They wore dark blue armoured vacuum suits with intimidating face-concealing helmets, and the five concentric circles of the Solar Authority flag in gold on their shoulders. The leader's voice came through a distorting speaker grille. 'Keldra 2482-Pandora-33842, Engineer, I am placing you under arrest for the theft of a true-born's property, illegally commanding an inter-belt vessel, and refusing a Solar Authority search.'

'To hell with you!' Keldra hurled the cutting torch at the Solar Authority soldier and pulled a slug-thrower pistol from her belt. The soldier batted the torch away with an armoured gauntlet then rushed forward, propelled by the suit's tiny thrusters. Keldra fired, the muzzle flash momentarily blinding and the shot echoing through the corridor, but the slug went wide, punching a hole through the inner layer of the wall. The soldier had pushed the gun aside and was already in the process of disarming her. Jonas caught Keldra's resentful face as the soldier spun her around to put her into handcuffs.

Another pair of Solar Authority soldiers hauled her away. Their leader moved up to the window. She de-opaqued her visor, revealing an angular face with short-cropped blonde hair very similar to Cooper's. 'Gabriel Reinhardt?'

Jonas nodded.

'I'm Lieutenant Sands. Captain Cooper explained your arrangement. If you open the door, I'll take you back to the *Iron Dragon*.'

'Thank goodness you're here, Lieutenant,' Jonas said as he moved to the door control. 'That madwoman was going to kill me.'

The damaged door shuddered aside. Behind it, Lieutenant Sands had a nerve gun in her hand, pointed casually at him.

He forced a little laugh. 'Lieutenant, please, there's no need for—'

Sands moved into the blister. 'Jonas 2477-Athens-20219, Administrator, I am placing you under arrest for theft of a true-born's property, refusing a Solar Authority search, impersonating a true-born, and for the murder of the true-born, Gabriel Reinhardt.'

Chapter Eleven

The prison cell's walls glowed from within, just too bright to be comfortable, leaving no shadows anywhere in the cell. The gravity felt about half a gee, much lighter than the full one gee that Jonas had become used to on the *Remembrance of Clouds*. There was a bunk built into one wall, and in the corner was a compact bathroom unit. There was no barred window like the one in Keldra's prison cell, and when the door closed it blended into the wall so that it was hard to tell where it had been. He felt as if he was floating in an empty white void.

The flight over in the shuttle had been silent. Keldra had been withdrawn, not making eye contact with Jonas or any of the soldiers. He didn't know where they had taken her. She could be in the next cell, or on the other side of the ship. She could be dead already.

As they'd departed the *Remembrance*, Jonas had been able to see another of the *Iron Dragon's* shuttles come in to dock, no doubt containing a prize crew of engineers to take charge of Keldra's ship. By now they would be working their way through the cargo bay, checking each container for booby traps, taking an inventory of their captured goods. He wondered what they'd do with the *Seagull* once they found it. Probably break it up and sell the pieces. Put them on stands.

Somehow this hurt more than it had when Keldra had captured him. Then he'd just seen Ayla and his other friends mind-wiped, he'd made an effort to escape and been outsmarted, and he'd had nothing to escape to anyway. He had been resigned to death. Those things hadn't changed, but now . . .

Now he was angry. This was *wrong;* this wasn't how it ought to go. He'd been prepared for the possibility that his escape plan would fail, and that he'd die or remain Keldra's captive, but not for being accused of Gabriel's murder. For the last six years he'd tried to live up to the name he'd inherited, to live in a way that Gabriel would have been proud of. Not only had he failed, but everything he'd done in those years had been negated. The records would show that Gabriel had died six years ago, and Jonas had killed him. Not negated: stolen from him. Keldra and Cooper had stolen Gabriel's legacy.

He suspected that this was how Keldra felt every second of every day. His mind kept going back to the *Seagull,* and to the image of the *Aurelian* on the *Remembrance's* bridge screen. They had come so *close.*

He got up off the bed and paced across the room. There had to be a way out. If they reached the Solar Authority's headquarters on 37 Fides, or one of the Authority's outposts in Belt Three, all that awaited him was a show trial and a mind-wipe. If he were to escape then he had to do so while the *Iron Dragon* was still in inter-belt space. He had got out of Keldra's cell; he could get out of Cooper's. He had to force himself to *think.*

He guessed that Cooper would want to interrogate him en route. That would be his chance to move. He had the advantage of having met Cooper back on Santesteban and formed an impression of him, and now he tried to recall that impression, to conjure up an image of the man in his mind. Absolute self-assurance that hadn't wavered even when Keldra's EMP had hit the *Haze*. An effortless aura of command. Above all, a burning sense of racial superiority that had led him to help Jonas without question when he thought he was a true-born, then chase him down without mercy when he somehow found out that he had lied.

Jonas didn't think he could goad Cooper in the way that he had goaded Keldra. If the captain had demons, they would be locked away too securely for him to reach. Unlike most Solar Authority officers, Jonas didn't think he could be bargained with or bribed. He couldn't be intimidated; he couldn't be moved to pity. Maybe, if his sense of superiority could lead him to underestimate Jonas, he could be tricked.

It was worth a shot.

There would be at least one camera in the cell, although Jonas couldn't see where it was. He sat on the bunk and looked at the middle of the wall. He let his posture sag, looking dejected, defeated. He opened his mouth then stopped a few times, as if trying to pluck up the courage to speak.

'Captain Cooper. I know you can hear me,' he said at last. He let his voice tremble, gave it his best pleading tone: he had to sound as if he was too emotional to have thought this through. 'I'm not a true-born – I lied to you – but we can still make a deal. Keldra and I, we found an Earth ship. It'll be full of Planetary Age artefacts. We've already disabled its defences, just project our ship's course forwards and you should find it. Take it, take Keldra, but let me go. Please.'

He kept staring at his spot on the wall for a few minutes, letting tears form in his eyes. He had to play on Cooper's sense of racial superiority, let Cooper believe that Jonas was a spineless tank-born, breaking under pressure already.

There was no response, but he hadn't expected there to be one. He lay back on the bunk and waited, trying not to think at all.

Some time later a slot appeared at the base of the door and a tray of food slid into the cell. Low-grade tank-born worker food: a step up from servitor-feed, but not a large one.

He wondered whether the lights would dim at night-time. Probably not. The day-night cycle was part of Keldra's obsession. Lance Cooper was a creature of relentless Belt Three sun.

Jonas shut his eyes against the glare and tried to sleep.

A buzzing sound woke him. The walls were still glowing white, and he didn't know how long he'd managed to sleep. He had a headache.

There was another buzz, and a moment later the door hissed open. A pair of *Iron Dragon* crewmen stood in the corridor, nerve guns trained on him. 'Captain wants to see you,' one of them said.

Jonas slouched out of the cell, trying to look nervous and defeated. One of the crewmen cuffed him, and they led him at gunpoint through the *Iron Dragon's* corridors. He fought back the headache and tried to both memorize the ship's layout and see what its interior could tell him about its captain. Neat, efficient, spotlessly clean. Most surfaces either glowed from within like the walls of the prison cell, or else were polished to a mirror shine. The crew members they passed were all dressed as if for an inspection, their black uniforms spotless.

The guards led Jonas to a transit module that took them downwards. On a large ship, as on a city, high gravity meant high status, so it was natural that officer country would be close to the hull. The guards' posture straightened as they emerged from the elevator, as if they could feel their captain watching them. They marched Jonas along a deserted corridor, through two security doors, and into a cold, dark room that smelled of antiseptic.

The only furniture was a tall metal chair with an electrode-studded helmet built into its back, like a bulkier version of Emily's memduction helmet. Jonas sat down and kept still as one of the guards fastened the wrist and ankle straps and then brought the helmet down over his head. His scalp prickled as the helmet's tiny electrodes made contact, and he desperately wanted to scratch. The guards left without a word, but one of them shot him a pitying look.

The wall in front of Jonas flicked to transparency. Lance Hussein Cooper sat facing him on the other side of a desk in a brightly lit room. On the wall next to him was a holo-screen showing the Solar Authority logo.

'Jonas 2477-Athens-20219,' Cooper said, with cold formality.

'Yes.'

'I wasn't asking. I've already confirmed your identity. What were you doing on the *Thousand Names*, Jonas?'

'The *Remembrance of Clouds*,' Jonas corrected automatically.

'The *Thousand Names*,' Cooper snapped. 'The ship is still rightfully owned by Wendell Taylor Glass, and the last name under which it was *legitimately* registered is the *Thousand Names*.'

Jonas bowed his head. 'Whatever you like.'

'Say it, Jonas.'

'The *Thousand Names*.'

Cooper smiled. 'Good. Do you know the origin of the ship's name, Jonas? The story behind it?'

'Yes.'

'Tell me.'

'It's the number of true-born family names.'

'Yes.' Cooper stood and paced around his desk as he talked. The floor level of his brightly lit room was higher than that of the interrogation cell, giving Jonas the impression of being trapped at the bottom of a pit. 'The number is approximate, of course. There were close to twelve hundred family groups among the original survivors. There are now around nine hundred names, and many of those families are so watered-down with tank-born blood that I can barely consider them legitimate. Even so, the phrase is a reminder of the human race's heritage. By choosing it as the name of his ship, Wendell Taylor Glass was celebrating that heritage: an unbroken genetic line that connects us with the origins of the human race.' Jonas doubted that Glass had put that much thought into picking a common ship name, but he didn't try to interrupt Cooper's monologue. 'Whereas you and Keldra choose to celebrate . . . what? Some side effect of the Earth's atmospheric mechanics. Why did you think that was more worthy of celebration than the heritage of the human race?'

'Keldra picked the name. Why don't you ask her?'

'Keldra? Perhaps you'd like to see her now.'

Cooper touched a control in his hand and the holo-screen behind him lit up. The cell was identical to Jonas's, but in chaos. The bedding was strewn across the floor, torn to pieces, revealing the metal surface of the bunk. Two dark red stains stood out on one of the glowing walls. Keldra sat against the bunk, hugging her knees in a foetal ball. Her hands were bloodstained, her clothing torn, and her hair in disarray. Her face was blank, staring at distant nothing.

'What have you done to her?'

Cooper laughed. 'What have we done? Nothing. She's been alone in her cell since we put her there. She threw a tantrum for a while, but now it looks like she's calmed down.' He shut off the feed and leaned forward on his desk, staring at Jonas. 'Keldra couldn't pass for a true-born. She barely passes for human. I'll interview her later, but I find you far more interesting. We have plenty of time before we reach Fides.'

Jonas looked up at Cooper and suppressed a smile. If he was right, they would take a bit longer to reach Fides, because Cooper was making a detour first.

'You didn't answer my question,' Cooper said. 'What were you doing on the *Thousand Names*?'

'Keldra kidnapped me. She put a hacked admin implant in my head.'

'So you claim no responsibility for what you've done since you joined the *Thousand Names*?' Cooper said mockingly. 'Keldra made you do it all?'

Jonas looked at Cooper and didn't blink. 'That's right.'

'You might be able to convince the court of that. I did detect the hacked implant and it was installed recently.' Cooper sat down and put his hands together in front of him, as if about to commence business. 'No matter. The events I'm really interested in took place long before you gained that implant. Do you know what the device you're sitting in is?'

'It looks like a memduction helmet,' Jonas said.

'It's not a memduction helmet. Do you know what it is?'

'No.'

Cooper glanced at a screen on his desk and nodded subtly, as if putting a tick into a mental checkbox. Jonas guessed that the helmet he was wearing functioned as a lie detector, but he doubted that was the full story.

Cooper clicked his control and a face appeared, huge, on the screen. It was Jonas's face, complete with the odd sense of being mirrored left to right that he always had from photographs of himself, and younger, with bright eyes and a smile. He recognized it as an ID picture he'd had taken about six years ago, when he had been Gabriel Reinhardt's personal assistant. He hadn't been sure of it at the time, but now that he looked at the picture from the distance of six years and a dark interrogation cell, he knew it had been the happiest time of his life.

'This is the last picture of Jonas '77-Athens that we have on file,' Cooper said. 'You disappear from all city and corporate records in 2504, just less than six years ago. Last seen on Oberon, working for the Belt Three branch of the Reinhardt family mining and heavy industry business.'

Cooper clicked his control and Jonas's face was replaced by a different one. About the same age, shorter hair, and more rounded features, but similar light brown skin and the same youthful, bright-eyed smile. Jonas wasn't sure he recognized the photograph, but the face was heartbreakingly familiar.

'Gabriel Dominic Ellis Reinhardt,' Cooper said. 'Heir to the Reinhardt family business, and president of the Belt Three branch of their operations. Eldest of three children, but his siblings were both sisters and have both married out of the family. Gabriel therefore is . . . *was* . . . the only name-carrier in his branch of the family. Reinhardt is one of the less common names, so Gabriel's failure to produce a son significantly increases the name's risk of extinction. *Look*, Jonas.'

Jonas hadn't realized that he had looked away. His eyes snapped back to the picture of Gabriel, responding instinctively to the tone of Cooper's words.

'This brings back memories for you, doesn't it?' There was a hint of cruel pleasure in Cooper's voice.

'Yes,' he replied.

'Good.' Cooper turned to his controls, for a moment, but Jonas didn't see any change. 'According to city and corporate records, Gabriel Reinhardt is still the president of the Belt Three branch of Reinhardt Industries. He has not married, despite being well into his thirties. He made his branch of the business almost completely independent of his family in Belt Four, and has not visited any other family member in the last six years.' Cooper straightened himself up and looked imperiously down at him. 'Look at the picture, Jonas. You killed Gabriel Reinhardt and assumed his identity. I have not brought you here to extract a confession: I already have enough to convict you of this. What I want to know is how you got away with it for so long.'

Jonas didn't look at the picture but stared straight at Cooper. 'I didn't kill him.'

'A denial will get you nowhere. The device into which you are strapped is a memory probe. It's Earth technology. Only a few hundred exist, and mine is one of the few to be installed on a beltship. I had it installed at great personal expense because truth is important to me, and this device allows me to see it. It works on the same principle as a memduction helmet, but it can go deeper, into long-term memory, as well as short-term, even if those memories weren't recorded in an implant. It can be an unpleasant and time-consuming process, but it *always* reveals what I want to know.'

Jonas could feel his heart-rate quicken. He had been aware that such technology existed, but he'd never expected to encounter it. He looked straight at Cooper and didn't let his nervousness show. 'I didn't kill him,' he repeated.

'We'll see.' Cooper touched a control, and then the lighted rectangle in which he sat drifted away.

Chapter Twelve

An egg-shaped chrome incense burner sat on a table in the middle of the apartment. White smoke curled from holes in its sides, filling the room with a scent of sandalwood.

Jonas pushed away . . .

An egg-shaped white ship nestled amid the tangled gantries that made up Oberon's docking spindle. White vapour spurted momentarily from its sides as its poorly sealed umbilicals were detached. The spindle rotated along with the stars, from Jonas's point of view, and the docked ships processed past like items for sale on a carousel. In the dark gaps between them he could see the reflection of his face, hanging in space like a ghost. He looked six years younger, but he wasn't smiling. He looked as if he would never smile again.

The egg-shaped ship disappeared from view as the spindle turned. Jonas stared at the opposite side of the spindle and waited, heart pounding, for it to reappear. It was suddenly, perversely, very important to him to see the ship as it departed. He couldn't stop it from leaving: all he had left was to hope he'd see it go.

The docking clamps scissored open and the ovoid ship edged into space. Jonas felt a wave of sick relief: at least he'd seen it. The ship spiralled outwards until its tiny thrusters fired and it pushed itself onto a new course. He stared at it until it was lost against the stars.

'Mr Reinhardt?'

Jonas didn't know how long he had stood at the window. It sounded as if the speaker had repeated the name a few times before Jonas had even registered it, but she still sounded polite and nervously patient. Slowly, wearily, Jonas turned around . . .

'You're resisting the probe.' Cooper was back in his yellow window, looking at one of his screens. 'Don't. It'll only make the process more unpleasant.'

'I wasn't resisting,' Jonas said, but as he said it he wasn't sure it was true. He hadn't been consciously trying to resist, but that hadn't been a memory he'd wanted to go back to. Right now he wanted to be back in his plain white cell, safe and unexamined.

Cooper frowned, as if unable to tell from his screen whether he was telling the truth. 'Don't resist again,' he said.

An egg-shaped chrome incense burner sat on a table in the middle of the apartment . . .

An egg-shaped white ship sat snugly in its cradle on the docking spindle. Vacuum-suited servitors swarmed around it making the final preflight adjustments.

'Jonas.'

A hand rested on Jonas's shoulder, very lightly. Gabriel had always been nervous with physical signs of affection.

'So this is it,' Jonas said. He didn't turn around, but he didn't move away.

'This is it.'

He stared at the white ship. He could see Gabriel's face in reflection, hovering in space, behind his. He looked sad, but there was a sense of peace there that Jonas had only seen hints of before. Jonas turned around and hugged the other man close. Gabriel was wearing a plain white robe, coarse to his touch, wafting around Gabriel's ankles in the low gravity.

'You're not going to try to talk me out of it?' Gabriel asked.

'I know I can't.' Jonas felt sick, as if a knot of despair was settling into his chest. 'This is our last moment. I don't want to spoil it.'

'Thank you,' Gabriel said. 'Remember what I said about you. Promise me you'll remember.'

'I promise.'

A chime sounded.

'They're boarding,' Gabriel said. 'I've got to go.'

'Yeah.' Jonas held Gabriel for a few more seconds, then let go. Gabriel slipped away silently to a transit module.

The interrogation room seemed to float around Jonas; Cooper in his lighted window distant and disconnected from anything else. Jonas's headache was back. He wondered if the procedure could cause permanent brain damage.

'You're still resisting the probe,' Cooper said sternly.

'Well, you've got what you needed now. Gabriel joined the Scribers and then Immolated.'

Cooper looked down stonily. 'Manipulating someone into suicide is still murder.'

'What? That's ridiculous.'

'You played a long game, didn't you? You worked your way into his confidence and manipulated him into joining the Scriber cult.'

'I tried to talk him out of it!'

166

'Not in the memory we just saw. You put on a sad face, but you stood there and let him do it.'

'It was the last time we would ever see one another. I knew I couldn't talk him out of it, and I wanted to say a proper goodbye.'

'You could have talked him out of it if you'd tried.'

Jonas looked away, eyes stinging.

'You manipulated Gabriel Reinhardt to suicide, and you're trying to manipulate me now,' Cooper said. 'You're trying to mislead the memory probe. You can't falsify a memory but you've been deflecting the probe from the most relevant ones. You're remembering selectively in order to tell your story.'

'I'm not resisting,' Jonas said.

'It doesn't matter. I'm increasing the power. The device will overcome any resistance you put up.'

An egg-shaped chrome incense burner sat on a table in the middle of the apartment. White smoke curled from holes in its sides, filling the room with a scent of sandalwood. The smoke moved quickly in the high gravity and coriolized towards one wall as it rose.

Gabriel sat shrouded in smoke on the other side of the burner, but he jumped up as Jonas entered. He was wearing the coarse grey Scriber robes that he had been wearing increasingly in private. He looked energetic, full of life, more so than Jonas had ever seen him before.

'You said you had something to tell me,' Jonas said.

Gabriel clapped his hand on his shoulder, eyes gleaming. 'Yes. I'm ready. I've finally booked passage.'

'Booked passage?'

'On an Immolation ship.'

Jonas pulled away sharply. 'You've *what?*'

'I've been a Scriber for years. You know that.'

'I didn't think you were serious!'

Gabriel shrank back, looking hurt. 'You didn't think I was serious?'

'I didn't think you were *that* serious. Most people who join the Scribers don't go through with it. I thought it was just, I don't know—'

'A fad? A fashion statement?'

'I didn't say that.'

'What, then?'

Jonas sat down on one of Gabriel's black faux-leather sofas, and gestured around the apartment. It took up half the floor of the starscraper, with a picture window looking out onto the water sculpture in the atrium. The furnishings were sparse but well-thought-out, displaying the kind of tasteful austerity only available to the rich. 'You're not a Worker-caste tank-born with no other way out,' he said. 'You're a successful business owner. Why do this?'

Gabriel remained standing, as if suddenly unwilling to touch any of the furniture. 'Material success isn't important,' he said. 'It's a distraction from spiritual matters.'

'That doesn't mean you should throw it all away and kill yourself!' Jonas found himself shouting, losing control. He felt numb: the reality of what Gabriel was telling him was only just beginning to impinge on his consciousness, but it had already found its way into his voice.

'Maybe a thousand years ago, on Earth . . . ' Gabriel's eyes moved to the wall opposite the picture window, as if trying to look out into space, but the apartment had no external windows. 'We're living in the end times, Jonas.'

'Bullshit.' Jonas hadn't used such strong language about Gabriel's religion before, but he was in no mood to be polite about it.

Gabriel continued undeterred. 'We've been given this chance, this few hundred years before the angels finish dismantling the universe. Anything we acquire in this world will be gone soon. It should be obvious that it doesn't matter. We need to purify our spirits and then let the angels take us.'

'The Worldbreakers aren't angels.'

Gabriel sat down opposite Jonas, leaning forward, hands clasped together, making intense eye contact: his arguing-about-religion pose. 'What else could they be?'

'I don't know! They could be natural. They could be alien.'

'They can be natural and still be angels. God worked through natural processes when He created the world, and now He's working through the Worldbreakers in order to end it. We can shut our eyes to that, pretend it's not happening, or we can let go of the material world and purify our spirits.'

'You're parroting some preacher. There's nothing wrong with your spirit.'

Gabriel looked down shyly. 'You could come with me. There's time for you to purify yourself before the next ship leaves, if I vouch for you. We could do it together.'

'You know I don't believe any of that.'

'You don't believe anything,' Gabriel said quietly. 'I've tried to convince you.'

'We can be together if you stay here with me,' Jonas said. 'Be a lifelong Scriber ascetic, if you like. Lots of people do that.'

'I can't stay here. Not with you. You know how I feel about you.' Gabriel's voice was barely more than a whisper. He was still looking down, unable to meet Jonas's eye. The smoke from the incense burner was thinning out, its fuel almost gone.

'Gabriel, I feel the same way. You know that.'

'I know, and that's why I can't stay.'

The weight of Gabriel's decision was boring into Jonas's chest. He wanted to rewind time to before this conversation had happened. He had always known, in theory, that this was the end point of Gabriel's religion, but he had told himself that he wouldn't go through with it. He wished he'd tried to talk him out of Scriberism earlier, rather than indulge it. His mind raced, trying to think of something he could say to talk Gabriel around. Jonas had always had a knack for persuading people, but right now, where it was most important, everything he could think of seemed like he was clutching at straws.

'We can be together and keep it secret,' he said. 'You get a lot of privacy.'

'No. When people hear my name, they ask, "Why isn't he married yet? Why doesn't he have children? He needs to carry on the family name." I can't face that.'

'We could run away together.'

'There's nowhere to run to.'

'We could go to Belt Two. There are free cities there, run by tank-borns. No one will care about your family name.'

'There's nowhere to run to,' Gabriel repeated insistently. 'The material world is ending. We need to purify ourselves and join the angels.'

'You're not impure!' Jonas shouted. 'You just think that because of the demands your society puts on you. If you'd been raised a tank-born you'd know there's nothing wrong with you.'

'The demands my society has put on me are part of who I am. I can't be me and not feel like this.' Gabriel looked up at Jonas, finally. He looked earnest and in pain. 'This is what I want, Jonas. When I think about the Immolation, I feel at peace. There's no other course for me. The only thing I regret is that you won't join me.'

'You know I can't join you. Don't ask me again.'

Gabriel picked up the delicate silver tongs that lay next to the burner and carefully opened its lid, then slowly fed it another block of incense. 'Then promise me something, Jonas.'

'What?'

Gabriel clicked the lid closed and looked up. 'Promise me you'll do something with your life. You're so much better than me.'

'That's not true.'

'It is. I was born into my position. I've achieved nothing. You worked your way up. You've got so much potential.'

'You've got potential, too, if you weren't throwing your life away for a myth!'

'Just promise me, Jonas. You could achieve something great; you can make the end times a better place for the people who are staying.'

'You could achieve something great, Gabriel. We could do it together. When people hear the name Gabriel Reinhardt they won't think about you not being married, or whatever, they'll think about what you achieved.'

'No, I can't do that.' Gabriel poked absently at the incense burner with the tongs. 'Just promise, Jonas. Promise, for me.'

Jonas closed his eyes. He had, finally, run out of things to say. He knew with a sinking certainty that there was nothing he could say that would change Gabriel's mind. The religion was like a disease of the mind, and if Jonas had caught it sooner, he might have been able to cure it, but Gabriel was now too far gone. He might as well have been sitting by his deathbed.

171

He opened his eyes, feeling numb. He hated Gabriel for this but he couldn't deny a deathbed promise. 'I promise,' he said.

The electrodes dug into Jonas's scalp, feeling as though they had always been there. He stared at the point where the wall met the floor in front of him, which seemed to shift and float as the interrogation room came back into focus. He felt as if he was emerging reluctantly from a dream.

'Jonas.' Lance Cooper's tone was curt, critical.

Jonas blinked away nausea and tears. 'You've seen it now. Gabriel joined a Scriber ship and killed himself.'

'You're still lying.'

'What the hell are you talking about? You just saw the memory. That was the moment he told me.'

'It was a bluff. You resisted that memory in order to make me interested in it, because you knew it would put you in the best light.'

'That's ridiculous!'

'You *seduced* Gabriel Reinhardt, and then you manipulated him into killing himself,' Cooper spat. 'It makes me sick to think that you've been living among us for so long.'

'You can watch every second of my life,' Jonas shouted. 'You won't find the story you want to find because you made that story up!'

Cooper leaned forward, staring at Jonas through the glass. There was a hint of Keldra in his expression, he thought. He had got him angry.

'I'll find what I'm looking for,' Cooper said. 'We have plenty of time before we reach Fides.'

*

172

The egg-shaped white ship was a distant dot, on its way to its engagement with an angel. After weeks of refusing, Jonas's only wish now was to be on it.

'Mr Reinhardt?'

Wearily, Jonas turned around. The speaker was a young woman with dark brown hair pulled back in a neat bun. The suit she wore looked brand new. She looked nervous, as if it had taken all of her willpower to approach him.

'I'm sorry to disturb you, sir,' she said. 'I heard you'd be here, and I thought I'd see if you had any time. My name's Ayla. Uh, Ayla 2485-Oberon-14572. I wanted to see you about the co-pilot position?' She took a little step back. 'You, uh, you are Gabriel Reinhardt?'

'I'm sorry, I'm . . . ' Jonas glanced back out of the window, but he could no longer tell which distant speck was the Immolation ship. It was gone. He turned back to Ayla and put on his best, most convincing smile. 'I'm sorry, I'm busy now; I'll have to see you later,' he said. 'But, yes, you've got the right person. I'm Gabriel Reinhardt.'

Chapter Thirteen

The interrogation room came slowly back into focus. Jonas could hear a quick-repeating chime, not loud but cutting into the centre of his brain with its shrillness. At first he thought it was an artefact of his headache, but as his surroundings stopped swaying he realized it was coming from Cooper's lighted room.

The captain stared at one of his screens, a startled look on his face. 'I have to deal with something,' he said. He gave a quick, mocking smile, but it wasn't convincing. 'Don't go anywhere.'

Jonas managed to feel a little satisfaction as the nausea subsided. It looked as if his plan had worked. 'You're going to want my help with that,' he called out.

The alert shut off. Cooper was using an intercom earpiece, nodding from time to time or saying something too quiet for Jonas to make out. Eventually, he put the intercom down and turned back to him.

'What do you mean, I'll want your help?'

'The *Aurelian* is targeting you, isn't it?'

'It's transmitting an ultimatum.'

'Let me hear it.'

Cooper picked up his intercom handset and spoke a few more orders that Jonas couldn't hear, ignoring him.

'You might as well,' Jonas said.

Cooper glared at him then shrugged and stabbed a control.

A woman's voice sounded out in the interrogation room. The accent was strange – 300 years old, Jonas guessed – but there was something else odd about it, on top of that. It was too calm, and the inflections were just a little inhuman. It was a synthetic voice, albeit a more realistic one than he had ever heard before.

'Unidentified ships, this is the Earth Authority cruiser *Aurelian*. Transmit transponder code to identify yourselves as human. Fail to transmit the code and you will be fired upon. Arm any weapons system and you will be fired upon. Alter course and you will be fired upon. You have twenty minutes to transmit the code before missiles are launched.'

'You lied to me,' Cooper said.

A chill ran through Jonas when he realized that the *Aurelian* had addressed its message to unidentified *ships*; he had hoped it would only be threatening the *Iron Dragon*. Perhaps he had miscalculated and doomed them all. He managed to keep his fear from showing on his face. It didn't change his next move. 'I can call off the *Aurelian*,' he said. 'Get me back onto my ship and I can save both of us.'

'You're lying again.'

'Why would I do that? If I can't call off the *Aurelian* then it doesn't matter which ship I'm on when the missiles hit.'

Cooper leaned forward. 'You do understand that the device you're strapped into is a memory probe? I can extract the memory of how to work the transponder.'

'In twenty minutes?

'I'll put a gun to your head and you'll tell me how to work it!'

175

Jonas managed not to blink. 'Go ahead. If you get me back to Fides then I'm dead. Given the choice I'd rather take you with me.'

Cooper started to move, but hesitated. 'You're bluffing.'

'You have no idea whether I'm bluffing or not. You can't read me, even with a memory probe. I lied to you in the cell and you believed me because it suited your preconceptions. You didn't believe your own machine when it went against the story you'd invented about me. So go on, put a gun to my head. Maybe I'm bluffing. What do you want to bet?'

Cooper stared at Jonas for several seconds. 'You're a goddamn namekiller,' he said. Not taking his eyes off him, he raised the intercom and spoke slowly, voice acidic. 'Corporal, take the prisoner to the shuttle bay. Deck-chief, get a shuttle prepped for launch and get a pilot in it. The prisoner is to be put back on the *Thousand Names* as quickly as possible.'

Cooper hurried out of the room. A moment later, the guards who had brought Jonas to the interrogation room entered again, undid his straps, and escorted him back to the transit module.

As the module moved the general quarters alarm sounded abruptly, a quick series of chimes, painfully loud in the enclosed space. An officer's voice boomed out that this was not a drill. The doors opened and the guard pulled Jonas out into a jostle of bodies, crew members rushing to their stations as the general quarters alarm echoed through the cavernous white shuttle bay. In one corner of the bay a gang of orange-suited engineers swarmed around a taxiing shuttle.

The deck chief hurried up to Jonas and his escort. 'This the prisoner? We've prepped shuttle five for you. Get going.'

The engineers completed their checks of the shuttle and swarmed away from it as it settled onto the upper door of one

176

of the shuttle airlocks. The pilot glanced down from his seat and nodded Jonas through the side door and into the passenger area.

The shuttle was lowered into the airlock and moments later it was falling into space, nose tipping down to point towards the *Remembrance of Clouds*. Moving between the shuttle's little windows, Jonas could see the grey mass of the *Iron Dragon* receding behind the shuttle, and the delicate rings of the *Remembrance of Clouds* in front. Its sail was furled: the sail still couldn't be used without a pilot, so Cooper's prize crew must have kept up with the *Iron Dragon* using the reaction drive. As the shuttle's attitude stabilized and the *Remembrance* began to grow larger in the window, Jonas could see another of the *Iron Dragon's* shuttles docked at the forward airlock. He squinted towards the sun but he couldn't make out the *Aurelian*.

He waited until the shuttle had completed its midpoint turnaround, flipping its engines towards the *Remembrance of Clouds* to decelerate in to dock, and then tapped on the partition to the pilot's compartment. 'Call up Captain Cooper. I want to speak to him.'

The pilot glanced back, frowning. 'I don't have any orders that you can communicate with anyone.'

'I'm the only person who can stop the *Aurelian* from destroying both our ships,' Jonas said. 'The captain will want to talk to me.'

'I'm putting you through,' the pilot said after a moment. The circuit crackled open. 'Cooper here.'

'You've got a crew on board the *Remembrance*, haven't you? I can see a shuttle docked.'

'Of course, I've got a crew there.'

'Get them back to your ship. I want to be alone, or there's no deal. Except their commanding officer; she meets me when I dock, and then goes back with the shuttle I'm now on.'

A slight pause, then, 'All right, Jonas. I'll issue the order.'

'One more thing,' said Jonas. He glanced between the rear and forward windows, guessing how close he was between the ships: he wanted to time this right. 'I want Keldra. Put her on another shuttle.'

Cooper laughed sarcastically. 'You're welcome to her.'

'That's all for now,' Jonas said. He tapped on the pilot's partition again. 'Close the channel. I need a vacuum suit.'

'There's a locker under the seat.'

He pulled the bright red emergency suit from the locker and struggled into it, using the shuttle's deceleration to brace himself against the wall. He examined the suit's communications suite: robust and comprehensive, as he'd expected from an Authority issue suit. It should easily be enough for what he had planned. Through the rear window he could see the other shuttle detach from the *Remembrance of Clouds* and begin accelerating on an opposite course.

His shuttle shuddered in to dock, the *Remembrance's* old but reliable docking mechanism clasping it firmly. He waved to the shuttle pilot and propelled himself through the doors as they opened.

Lieutenant Sands was waiting in the docking area, in her armoured vacuum suit. She scowled at Jonas through her visor. 'You're a namekiller.'

'We don't have time to call one another names, Lieutenant,' Jonas said. 'Tell me what you've done to my ship.'

'We've reactivated all the systems you took offline, dismantled your nuclear warhead, and installed temporary controls to let us fly the ship without a pilot,' Sands said. 'There wasn't time to remove them, so I guess you get to keep them.'

'What have you done with the cargo?'

'We performed an inventory but otherwise left it as it was.'

'The spaceplane's still there?'

'It ought to be in a collection, and not languishing in some tank-born pirate ship; but yes, it's still there.'

'Thank you, Lieutenant. Get back to your ship.'

Jonas watched as Sands entered the shuttle and it undocked – he didn't want any of Cooper's people staying on the ship to catch him later – and then climbed around to the observation blister. The familiar scent of the ship wafted around him; cheap machine oil and a hint of stale sweat; the familiar rhythms of its much-repaired systems rumbled away in the distance. It felt good to be back on a ship with a personality, after the impersonal cleanliness of the *Iron Dragon*.

He found the catches and unfolded the manual controls from their alcove, then retrieved the code from the implant's memory and unlocked them. He hard-sealed the inner door of the main docking airlock, checked that the outer door and the docking clamps would still work, and then turned to the communications panel. He knew enough about comms tech to be able to align the *Remembrance's* communications laser at the source of the *Aurelian's* transmission. The ultimatum was still repeating, now giving only six minutes. He patched the *Iron Dragon* emergency vacuum suit's communications system wirelessly into the *Remembrance's* communications system. He'd be able to transmit and receive through the comms laser from anywhere in the ship.

He took a transit module down the *Remembrance's* spine. The cargo bay lights were off, and the cargo containers rushed past him in the darkness, each momentarily visible as a splash of bright colour in the light from the transit module windows. He passed the gutted shell of the *Haze of the Ecliptic's* escape capsule that Keldra's servitors had been breaking down for parts.

The transit module came in to a stop at the bottom of the bay, just before the wall that separated the cargo bay from the reaction drive's fuel tanks. Jonas checked his suit and then cycled through the airlock into the bubble formed by the stacked cargo modules. The *Seagull* was still there, suspended in the darkness by strands of cargo webbing that seemed to glow as the beams from Jonas's helmet lamps brushed over them.

He kicked off from the airlock, grabbed a strand of webbing, and climbed around in the dark towards the *Seagull's* entrance hatch. The spine's lights were out, so the only light came from his helmet lamps, and the only sound was his breathing in the vacuum-suit helmet. Without Keldra, the *Remembrance of Clouds* was a ghost ship.

He reached the *Seagull's* hatch and pulled himself into its cabin. Tiny green and red lights showed that some of the space-plane's automatic systems were active, including the transponder. It looked as though Sands's engineers hadn't touched it.

The transponder was transmitting, but its signal wasn't penetrating the *Remembrance's* cargo bay radiation shield. That would be why the *Aurelian* was threatening to fire on both ships rather than just the *Iron Dragon*. Jonas searched with his suit's communications system until he could pick up the transponder's complex coded signal, then set the suit to relay it through the *Remembrance's* comms laser.

The calm voice continued to speak in his ear. 'You have two minutes to transmit the code . . . '

'*Aurelian*, this is the *Remembrance of Clouds*,' he said over the transponder signal. There was a catch in his voice, a sense of awe at talking to a piece of living history, but he didn't have time to think about that now. 'The *Seagull* is on board; I'm transmitting the transponder code now. Both ships are friendly. Stand down your weapons systems.'

The *Aurelian's* voice went on for a few more words and then stopped. There was silence on the channel for several seconds. Jonas clung to a handhold, feeling his heart pound. He couldn't judge when the countdown would have reached zero. The ultimatum might have been cancelled, or the missiles might be en route.

The *Aurelian's* computer voice came quietly over the channel. 'Captain, is that you? You've been so long.'

Jonas hesitated. This wasn't the automated system he had expected. If the ship wanted its captain, then he had better provide the captain, if he was to be sure of shutting down the missiles. 'Yes, *Aurelian*, this is me. I know I've been a long time, but I'm back now.'

'Captain, you sound different.'

'I know,' said Jonas. The emotionlessness of the computer voice made it sound innocent; he felt as if he was speaking to a child. 'I've . . . I've been gone a long time and things have changed. Have you stood down your weapons systems?'

'Yes, Captain. Weapons systems disarmed.'

'Thank you, *Aurelian*,' Jonas said. '*Remembrance of Clouds* out.' His hand hovered over the control that would end the message. Before he pressed it, he added, 'I'll talk to you later, all right?'

He climbed back to the transit module and began travelling back up the spine. As the module flashed out of the cargo bay and into the narrow spine between the rings, his suit received a call from the ship's communications system. '*Thousand Names*, this is *Iron Dragon* shuttle four. I'm coming in to dock now.'

'Shuttle four, this is the *Remembrance of Clouds*,' Jonas said. 'Once you've docked, put Keldra in the airlock and then depart immediately.'

'*Remembrance*, the prisoner wants to talk to you.'

'I'll bet she does, shuttle four. Put her in the airlock and then depart, please.'

He stopped the transit module in the ship's nose complex and went to the observation blister in time to watch the shuttle settling into the docking clamps. The dark cylinder of the *Iron Dragon* was visible in the distance, along with the flare of shuttle five curving towards it.

'*Remembrance of Clouds*, this is shuttle four. Do you have a technical problem? The inner airlock door won't open.'

'I'm aware of that, shuttle four,' Jonas said. 'There's no problem. Put Keldra in the airlock, make sure the outer door has sealed, and then depart, please.'

There was a distant rumble as the outer airlock door opened and closed. 'Acknowledged, *Remembrance of Clouds*. She's in the airlock.'

He explored the manual controls until he found the internal camera feeds, and then flicked through them until he saw Keldra in the airlock. She was hanging from the inner door, hammering on the controls, but the emergency seal he had put in place couldn't be overridden from the outside. He would let her stew for a bit. He had someone else he wanted to talk to.

He turned back to the communications controls and aimed the comms laser at the *Iron Dragon*. '*Iron Dragon*, this is Jonas on board the *Remembrance of Clouds*. Put the captain on, please.'

Cooper was there almost immediately. '*Thousand Names*, this is Captain Cooper.'

Jonas stared at the distant *Iron Dragon*. 'Use the correct name for my ship,' he said.

There was a moment of silence, then Cooper said sourly, '*Remembrance of Clouds*, this is Captain Cooper on the *Iron Dragon*. We're no longer receiving the ultimatum transmission from the Earth ship. I take it that means you've upheld your side of the agreement.'

'I've expanded the transponder's protection to cover your ship,' Jonas said. 'I can withdraw that protection at any moment.' Actually, he wasn't sure how quickly, or even if he could, convince the *Aurelian's* strange computer to fire on the *Iron Dragon*, but Cooper didn't need to know that.

'I'd remind you that there are 200 souls on board my ship, Jonas, most of them tank-borns, like yourself.'

'I don't want to kill anyone, Captain. I just want you out of here.'

Cooper's tone was formal, as if shaking hands to conclude a game. 'Very well. You have won. I give you my word as a pure-blooded true-born and as a Solar Authority officer that I will not pursue you further.'

'I don't want your word,' Jonas spat. 'I want you to vent your fuel.'

'What?' Cooper sounded taken aback.

'Leave yourself enough to get on a course back to Belt Three, and dump the rest into space. I don't trust your word, Captain. I don't want you to be able to follow us.'

Cooper disappeared from the channel for a moment. Dead ahead, Jonas saw glittering clouds expand from the sides of the Solar Authority cruiser.

'It's being done,' Cooper said.

'Good. Just one more thing.'

'What?'

Jonas licked his lips. He pulled himself forward on the handrail, staring across space at the *Iron Dragon*, where

183

Cooper and the memory probe would be. 'Gabriel Reinhardt was a good man,' he said. There was a tremor in his voice, but he kept it under control. 'I wasn't misleading the memory probe. Everything I said about him in the interrogation was true. I didn't drive him to suicide: you did, your true-born society and its expectations. That's why I don't consider your word as a pure-blood true-born to be worth anything. He was a good man, and you killed him.'

'Are you finished?'

'Yes. Now go.'

In the distance, tiny thrusters fired. Ponderously, the *Iron Dragon* began to turn.

Jonas flipped back to the security camera showing Keldra in the airlock. She had stopped banging on the door and was floating at the side of the chamber, legs curled up and face hidden. It looked as though she was withdrawing in on herself, as she had in the *Iron Dragon's* cell.

Jonas patched his suit in to the airlock intercom. 'Keldra, it's Jonas,' he said softly.

She sprang to life, banging on the door again. 'Fuck you, Jonas! You tried to sell me out!'

'Shut up, Keldra. You killed my friends, kidnapped me, and put a mind-control implant in my head. All I tried to do was escape. Why shouldn't I sell you out?'

'So, you're going to make a speech and then space me? Spare me the fucking speech.'

'No,' he said. 'I'm going to re-enable your pilot implant, and then I'm going to let you back in.'

Keldra tried the door again, but it still didn't respond. She slammed her fist into the bulkhead. 'Okay, you've won,' she said. 'Give me control and I'll take you back to Belt Three. I'll drop you off at any city you like. I know ones where you

184

can hide from the Authority.' She tried the door again; still nothing. 'I'll give you back what's left of your cargo and I'll pay for the stuff I already sold.'

'Can you bring Ayla back, or Matton, or any of the others?' Jonas asked coldly.

'What are you talking about?'

'Those are the names of some of the people you killed.' Jonas breathed, forced himself to calm down.

'I can't bring anyone back,' Keldra said. 'I'm sorry I killed your friends.'

'No you're not.'

She shrugged. 'Okay, I'm not. Let me in and I'll take you back to Belt Three. You never have to see me again. You have my word.'

He hesitated. He thought he could believe in Keldra's word: he knew her well enough to be able to tell if she was lying, and this wasn't one of those times. Her offer had been what he'd wanted ever since she had captured him, and a few days ago she would have taken it, but now . . .

'No,' he said.

'No?' She sounded incredulous.

'I don't want to go back to Belt Three. I'm staying on the *Remembrance of Clouds*.'

'You're stealing my ship?'

'No, I'm not stealing it. I can't fly it without you. I'm joining you. We both need each other, Keldra.'

'I don't need you.'

'Yes, you do. I've saved your ass a couple of times now, so we both know I have skills you can use. Plus, like I said, you need someone to talk to, to be an audience when you strike back against the Worldbreakers. Don't try to deny it.'

185

Keldra looked around the airlock, everywhere but at the camera, her free hand moving jerkily in frustration. After a few moments she said, 'Okay. I need you.'

'All right. I'll let you in, but there are going to be some changes between us.'

She laughed hollowly. 'You want a bigger cut?'

'I'm not joking, Keldra.'

'What do you want, then?'

'For a start, I want you to take this implant out of my head. No more mind control.'

'Okay, I'll do that. What else?'

'No more killing. If we need money we find other ways.'

She let out another little hollow laugh, although he wasn't sure what she found funny. 'All right. No more killing.'

'One more thing,' he said. 'We're equal partners now. You understand?'

She snorted. 'You think you're my equal?'

'Yes. And I think you're mine.'

She turned away momentarily. When she turned back her voice was softer. 'Why?' she asked. 'I offered to let you go. Why stay?'

'Because it's not enough to run and hide and survive anymore,' he said. 'Survival isn't all there is. I once promised someone that I would achieve something great, and I still need to do that, so if there's some way to strike back against the Worldbreakers, then I want to be a part of it.'

In the grainy image, Jonas could just see Keldra's cruel smile reappearing, and he found himself smiling along with it.

'That sounds good to me, Jonas,' she said.

'Partners?'

'Partners.'

He disengaged the pilot lockout and allowed Keldra's implant to resume control of the ship. A shiver ran through her, a sharp intake of breath; she closed her eyes and spread her body out in the microgravity. A smile of pure pleasure came across her face, like someone who had been labouring in too high a gravity returning to her native weight. Around him, the ambient sounds of the ship changed, subtle dishar-monies that had built up in her absence resolving themselves. Lights on the emergency control panel turned from orange to green. On his screen, the inner airlock door opened, and Keldra floated back into her ship.

Chapter Fourteen

Removing the implant was a simple process, once Keldra had disabled her security measures. Jonas felt uneasy sitting in the medbay's cramped operation cubicle, but he managed not to let it show. He couldn't shake the second-hand memory of her writhing in those straps as the pilot implant forced itself into her consciousness for the first time. She didn't seem to have any emotional response to the cubicle as she supervised the procedure from the main medbay chamber. She must have used it a few times in her career as a pirate, and repressed any trauma associated with it.

Jonas was under anaesthetic for the procedure itself. When he regained consciousness, Keldra was gone. He felt exhausted: the implant would have used his body's own energy to fuel its self-extraction procedure, hundreds of nano-filaments slowly and carefully withdrawing from his brain. It had felt much like this when he'd had his first admin implant removed in order to impersonate Gabriel. He felt the same sense of emptiness that he had then, his brain still adjusting to the implant's absence. He clicked his fingers three times, but the virtual desktop did not appear.

The implant lay in a kidney dish on the table beside his

chair. A rounded cylinder a couple of centimetres long, silver where its surface was visible beneath a coating of blood and spinal fluid. The secret story of Keldra and the *Thousand Names* was contained in that cylinder, as well as last memories of Olzan's relationship with Emily Glass.

Jonas lay back and dozed, waiting for his body to recover. Eventually, he was interrupted by the intercom buzzer. Keldra's voice crackled out of a speaker by his side. 'Jonas. Get to the bridge.'

He reached for the intercom panel. 'The implant's out. You can't order me around anymore.'

She made a smirking noise. 'Our agreement didn't say I had to be polite. Get the fuck in here. I've got it on screen.'

'On my way.'

He got up to leave, but stopped in the doorway and looked back at the implant. Keldra hadn't said what she wanted done with it once it was out, and she had let the medical robot leave it in the kidney dish. He went back and pocketed it before leaving the medbay.

A wall of bronze light greeted Jonas as he entered the bridge: an image of the sun, magnified to fill the bridge screen and filtered down to a bearable colour. The room's other lights were dimmed, so Keldra's face and the angles of her nest were picked out in red-gold. The floor was a mess where she had ripped out Lieutenant Sands's temporary control terminals but not bothered to put the floor panels back on. She was staring forward, smiling faintly.

'We're starward of it,' she said, not taking her eyes off the screen. 'You can see it in the sun.'

Jonas sat at his console and squinted at the image. He could make out the *Aurelian* as a silhouette near the centre of the sun's disc. It was a cylinder like the *Iron Dragon*, but tapering towards one end. It turned end over end very slowly, drifting without control on its long orbit across the belts. It wasn't much to look at from this distance, but Jonas did feel a certain sense of awe at the thought that it was 300 years old, built when the Earth still existed, and no one but he and Keldra had come close enough to set eyes on it for all of that time. From the look on her face, she seemed to be feeling the same awe tenfold. The relentlessly atheist Keldra would never think of it in those terms, Jonas reflected, but this must be close to a religious experience for her.

He checked the sensor read-outs on his terminal. The *Aurelian* was intact as far as the *Remembrance's* lidar could detect. There was the radiation trace of a fusion reactor, and a lot of its surface seemed to function as a solar panel. Still powered, after all this time. The computer voice was silent; the ship was transmitting nothing except for its transponder signal, too archaic to mean anything to the *Remembrance's* computer.

The *Aurelian* grew larger on the screen over the course of several minutes, but stayed in silhouette. It wasn't until their final approach that the *Remembrance* swung around to the Earth ship's sunward side and Jonas and Keldra could see it clearly. It was coated in a layer of belt dust and pocked with 300 years of micrometeorite craters, but beneath that it was silver, touched with gold where its mirrored surface caught the image of the sun. As the *Remembrance* passed around its rear, Jonas found himself looking into the nozzles of an ancient reaction drive. Parts of the hull were rotating, the dust marks visibly moving past one another. On the darker non-rotating bands Jonas could see clusters of equipment: he spotted sensor arrays, a comms laser, and what could have been launch tubes for the missiles with which the ship had threatened the *Iron Dragon*.

'It had a sail, see?' Keldra said, voice hushed. She pointed to one of the non-rotating bands near the middle of the ship that was studded with buds like the sail bud on the nose of the *Remembrance*. 'A ring of sail segments, like petals. The whole thing would have looked like a flower. It'll be decayed now, of course, and they burned out the reaction drive trying to make it back to Earth . . . '

'So we won't be going anywhere in it,' Jonas said.

'I never thought I could get the ship flying again. All I want is the Worldbreaker tech that's on board.' From the tone of her voice, he wasn't sure she quite meant it. She stared at the *Aurelian* for another minute before she could tear herself away. 'You said you could talk to the *Aurelian's* computer?'

'Yes.'

'It wouldn't talk to me. Told me it wanted its captain.'

'It thinks that's me.'

'Lying bastard, like always.' There was a hint of approval in Keldra's voice. 'The captain's name was Regina Marszalek. You sound nothing like her.'

'I think it assumes I'm her because I had the transponder.'

'Call it up. Tell it we're coming.'

The comms laser was still fixed on the *Aurelian*, relaying the transponder signal. Jonas transmitted over the top. '*Aurelian*, this is *Remembrance of Clouds*. We're about to launch the *Seagull* and come aboard. Will you allow us to dock?'

The archaic accent of the *Aurelian's* computer rang out at once. 'Of course, Captain.'

Keldra grinned. 'Let's go.'

Keldra sent servitors in mismatched, brightly coloured vacuum suits swarming through the cargo bay. A dozen of them were rearranging the cargo containers, pushing them to the side of the bay opposite the door, dismantling the protective bubble that she had set up around the *Seagull*, and clearing a path for it to launch. A smaller group was tinkering with the *Seagull* itself, detaching the umbilicals that plugged it into the *Remembrance*. They performed last-minute checks on original systems that hadn't been used for three centuries, and the hacked-together replacements she had installed years ago, and not tested since.

The spaceplane's cabin had pilot and co-pilot seats. Keldra took the pilot seat and Jonas the co-pilot, the straps fitting awkwardly over their bulky yellow vacuum suits. The interior was plain white, with a few stains of dust that Keldra and her servitors had smeared on the walls during their modifications. The controls were all new, Jonas noticed, mostly made up of the spare panels that Keldra had removed from the *Remembrance's* bridge. Some of them were very new: it looked as though she had modified a one-person control scheme to allow a co-pilot while he had been recovering from surgery. The controls were held onto the bare dashboard with bolts, and he couldn't see where the *Seagull's* original controls had been. Cables snaked away into the recesses of the spaceplane's nose to interface with its original systems and with the systems she had installed.

The servitors handled the spaceplane out of its little bubble and towards the cargo bay doors, pulling back the sheets of cargo webbing and fastening the last of the cargo containers to the side of the bay. Keldra sat back in her chair, staring distractedly forwards; she was directing the servitors' operation through her implant.

The cargo bay doors slid open above them. The *Aurelian* was there, seeming to sparkle as the dust-coated surface rotated. The *Remembrance* was holding directly sunward of the *Aurelian* now, and the old freighter's shadow was visible on the Earth ship's side. The *Remembrance* was 30 years old, and looked it, years of repairs and adjustments visible even in its silhouette. The *Aurelian* was ten times older, but beneath its coating of dust it looked brand new. It looked ageless.

The servitors handling the ship gave it a final push, and then it was free-floating. The edges of the bay doors receded around them until all they could see were stars and the *Aurelian*.

Jonas glanced at Keldra. 'Come on. Time to see if it works.'

'It'll work,' she said absently. She was stroking the white dashboard, one of the smooth curves exposed at the side of the control panels she'd installed. She snapped back to the present and shot him a look. 'Of course, it'll work. *I* fixed it.'

She pulled on her control stick and the *Seagull's* attitude jets flared to life. The little ship pitched, Keldra nimbly twisting it through 90 degrees and righting it with the *Aurelian* dead ahead of its nose. She grinned. The engine throbbed gently and the ship began to move forward.

Jonas unclipped the microphone from his control panel and set up a transmission to the *Aurelian's* computer. '*Aurelian*, this is *Seagull*. We're approaching in order to dock. Please open the docking bay and give us directions.'

'Of course, Captain.' The computer's voice was still noticeably artificial, but Jonas thought that he detected a note of eagerness in its quick response. 'I have already prepared the *Seagull's* hangar for its return. I will de-spin the forward docking cradle for you.'

He hesitated. He didn't know what the forward docking cradle looked like, but if the computer thought he was its captain then any admission of ignorance might break the spell.

Keldra saved him. 'That's the docking cradle,' she said, pointing. About a third of the way down from the *Aurelian's* nose, an arrangement that looked a little like a skeletal hand was unfolding from the ship's side. It was in the middle of an area of rotating hull, but it was moving against the rotation on a barely visible track, stationary, from the *Seagull's* point of view.

Keldra piloted the ship across the gap and began to line it up with the docking cradle. Even with her piloting skills, the unfamiliar manoeuvre in the untested ship was awkward and time-consuming. Jonas could see the frustration on her face and in the increasingly aggressive bursts from the thrusters, and he felt a little of it too: they were so close, and they both wanted to get inside. At last the spaceplane was positioned correctly and the silver claw closed around it with a series of clicks audible from within the cabin.

'The *Seagull* is secure, Captain,' said the *Aurelian's* computer. 'I'm spinning you up now.'

The cradle began to move, carrying the *Seagull* with it around the surface of the *Aurelian*. Pseudogravity tugged Jonas down as the cradle approached the rotational speed of the Earth ship's hull. When it stabilized, he was surprised to find that it had only reached what felt like three-quarters of a gee.

A door above them opened and the docking cradle pulled the *Seagull* up into the body of the *Aurelian*. Lights flicked on around it as it rose, revealing hangar walls lined with storage lockers, coiled umbilical lines, and a many-limbed maintenance robot standing dormant in an alcove. The doors closed beneath them, and the vibration from the docking cradle's motors ceased. A light on Keldra's control panel indicated that air was filling the hangar. They were on board.

All they could see from the cockpit was a utilitarian white wall, but Keldra was staring out at it. Her hand was on the curve of the *Seagull's* interior hull. 'It worked,' she said.

Jonas smiled. 'After you.'

She broke the hatch seal and clambered down to the hangar floor. He followed her, letting her take the first step. Everything was white, bathed in light from spotlights in the walls and ceiling. He could hear her breathing through the helmet link, but besides that, nothing. The sense of stillness was oppressive.

A thick bulkhead door slid open sideways at their approach, and they walked through it into an airlock that automatically cycled around them. Keldra was standing confidently, but Jonas noticed that her hand never strayed far from the slug-thrower pistol she had strapped to the leg of her vacuum suit. To his surprise she had made him take one as well, but he tried to ignore the uncomfortable weight. The inner door opened and they advanced cautiously into the crew segment of the *Aurelian*.

Blue-white lights came on around them, some of them flickering for a few seconds after their centuries of sleep. They were in an orbital corridor that curved up away from them in both directions. The walls were white, pristine, and where they touched the floor and ceiling the surface was rounded, leaving no hard corners that Jonas could see. It was a little like the *Iron Dragon* prison cell, but the effect here managed to be comforting rather than intimidating. It was eerily blank, though, with no markings anywhere on the walls. He glanced behind him and noticed that they had brought a faint trail of the *Remembrance's* grime in with their boots.

A chime rang out, seeming to come from somewhere above them. 'Welcome back, Captain,' said the calm, childlike voice of the *Aurelian*. 'I hope you had a good trip. You were gone longer than I had expected, and I was worried.' It paused, then added, 'I see you've brought a friend.'

Jonas glanced at Keldra, who shrugged subtly. It didn't look as though she wanted to do the talking. 'This is Keldra,' he said. 'You can trust her.'

'Welcome on board, Keldra.' Transplanted into the ship's archaic accent, the name sounded unfamiliar and awkward. 'Captain, you have missed several mealtimes,' it continued. 'Are you hungry? I can have the galley put something together for you and your friend. I'm afraid choice will be limited because some of our food stocks are past their safe usage dates.'

She rolled her eyes. 'Computer's broken,' she muttered over a private channel. 'Just a dumb machine.' It sounded as if she had expected better from an Earth ship.

'I'm not sure broken is the best way of thinking of it,' Jonas sent back. 'It can't have been programmed for this.' He toggled his helmet speakers back on. 'No, thank you, *Aurelian*. We were able to eat on board the *Remembrance of Clouds*. We'd like you to show us the—'

'We'd like the tour,' Keldra cut in suddenly.

'Captain?' the ship said.

Jonas looked at Keldra. 'I thought we were just here for the artefact?' he sent over the private channel.

She shrugged. 'Yes, but . . . ' She waved an arm to encompass the white corridor. 'Earth ship.'

'Captain?' the ship repeated. 'Is Keldra attempting to subvert your authority?'

'No, *Aurelian*,' he said hastily. 'Since I've been gone a long time, I'd like to inspect the ship.'

'Of course, Captain. Where would you like to start?'

'Let's start with the bridge.'

A door chimed open in front of them, revealing a circular chamber with gently cushioned walls and a row of acceleration straps. It was a transit module; it looked as though the concept hadn't changed in 300 years. The walls were plain white and there were no visible controls, although there was a barely visible panel in the floor that might have contained emergency ones. Jonas was beginning to find the bare walls disconcerting. He found it hard to believe that Earth people had really enjoyed such an uncompromisingly minimalist aesthetic.

The module began to move as soon as they strapped themselves in. After a short while Keldra lifted her hands to her helmet's neck seal.

'We don't know it's safe,' he cautioned. 'A lot could go wrong with a hab system in 300 years.'

She tapped the read-out on her vacuum suit's wrist. 'Safe according to this,' she said. 'It's Earth air. I've got to. You know.'

'It's not really Earth air. But, yeah, I know.'

Keldra's helmet seal released with a hiss. She lifted it slowly, shaking her hair out into its normal chaotic corona. She closed her eyes and inhaled deeply through her nose.

'Is it safe?' he asked.

'Smells OK.'

He cracked his helmet seal as well, and clipped the helmet to its place at his side. The air was cold, and smelled of whatever chemicals had kept it clean all this time. It was a ship smell, subtly different from the air produced by a modern-day hab module, but not very remarkable.

The transit module opened onto a circular room with a ring of reclined chairs in the centre. Here, too, the walls were plain white, broken only by doorways leading to other rooms or transit modules. There were no control panels, no screens, nothing Jonas could see that would allow the Earth people to control their ship.

'*Aurelian*, what is this place?' Jonas said.

'This is the bridge,' the *Aurelian* said. It sounded as if it was coming from above them, but he couldn't see the speakers. 'As you can see, it is in good working order.'

Keldra walked forward and examined one of the couches, frowning. 'There's nothing here. Even a pilot needs controls to fly properly.'

'I'm not seeing anything in working order,' he said. He hesitated; he didn't want to offend the computer so deep inside its territory, but this was clearly not a working bridge. 'This is just an empty white room.'

'All bridge systems are in good working order,' the computer said again. Then after a couple of seconds, 'Captain, I am not able to interface properly with your implant. It has surpassed its expected operational lifespan so it may have ceased functioning. Keldra also does not appear to have a valid implant. I suggest you have a new one fitted the next time the ship is in port.'

'I, er, I don't think the ship will be in port for some time,' Jonas said.

'You can use arcaps to temporarily gain the benefit of the implant, but it is recommended that you have a proper implant fitted as soon as possible,' the *Aurelian* said. 'Shall I have a robot deliver arcaps for you and your friend?'

'Ar-cap,' Keldra said, rolling the word around her mouth thoughtfully. She glanced at Jonas and nodded.

'Yes please,' he said.

Almost at once, one of the doors opened and a robot trundled into the room. The *Aurelian* must have anticipated the request and moved it into position while they were talking. The robot resembled a white potted tree, with four many-jointed arms radiating from the top of a cylindrical body that rolled along on fat little tyres. The two nearest limbs ended in four-fingered claws that held out translucent white caps filled with a mesh of wires and electronics. Jonas had the feeling that he was seeing the ancestors of his era's memduction helmets.

Keldra took the caps and handed one to him. 'You first this time.'

'Equal partners, remember?' he said.

She rolled her eyes. 'Heads or tails?'

'What? Heads.'

She looked angrily at the ceiling. '*Aurelian*!'

'Yes, Keldra?' the ship said. 'Remember, you are not authorized to give me commands.'

'*Aurelian*, simulate a coin flip. Equal chance of heads and tails.'

'Heads,' the computer said at once.

'Your turn,' Keldra said to Jonas.

'All right.'

The cap fitted snugly, automatically adjusting itself to the shape of his head. He felt the tingle of its mesh making contact, but it didn't feel as if it was breaking his skin. There was a moment of nausea, a blurring of his vision, and then the bridge appeared around him.

They were standing on a circular platform suspended in space, enclosed within the intersecting bands of the ecliptic and the Milky Way. Away to one side hung the battered *Remembrance of Clouds*, sunlight flickering through the rings' spokes as they rotated. It was an enhanced image: the sun dimmed enough to look at, the *Remembrance* brightened so that its features were visible even on its shadow side, the belt bodies picked out against the stars. The view was static, not rotating, which made Jonas feel dizzy: his instincts told him that a static star field meant he ought to be in free fall.

The central chairs were still there, but now they were in the middle of a bewildering cloud of lights. Brightly coloured shapes hung motionless in the air, arranged in semicircles around the head of each chair, such that they would be in arm's reach of someone sitting there. He recognized diagrams of the *Aurelian* and local belt charts, as well as more abstract diagrams and planes of text.

'What is it?' Keldra demanded. 'What do you see?' She was standing with her back to the star field, in front of the barely visible ghost of the doorway.

'I see the bridge,' Jonas said. 'Put the cap on. It works.'

Keldra put on her arcap. It visibly squirmed in order to find purchase through her mass of hair, but it seemed to work. After a moment her mouth curved into a lopsided smile. 'This is more like it.'

She lay down on one of the chairs. The illusions flickered as she passed through them but re-formed around her. She reached out and touched one experimentally. It responded to her touch, moving with her finger as she dragged it gently. She glanced around, selected a different one, and pulled it in front of her face to examine it.

Jonas looked over her shoulder. The diagram she was examining looked like a floor plan of the ship, but the symbols that annotated it were alien to him. 'You understand that?' he asked.

'It's coming to me,' she said, distractedly. She tapped the arcap. 'It's not just visual. I'm getting a *sense* of the ship. I think it acts like a pilot implant. I don't suppose you're getting that . . . you don't know what to listen for.'

'I suppose not,' he said. 'What are you learning?'

'It's like I thought,' she said. 'The hab systems and defences are working, solar powered, but the sail's gone and the drive is burned out. Even if we refuelled it, it would never fly again.'

'A pity,' Jonas said, with feeling. Getting an Earth ship running again would have been a great achievement. 'Can you detect the Worldbreaker artefact?' he asked.

'I think so,' she replied. 'There's a storage area that was converted into a science lab, towards the stern.' She didn't move. She had sounded distracted, troubled.

'What else?' he asked.

'What's that?' Keldra pointed to one of the larger rooms on the floor plan. A group of bright dots clustered at one end of it, incomprehensible to him.

'I don't know,' he said.

'I think it's people,' she said. 'It's telling us the location of the ship's personnel.'

'The location of their bodies, I would guess,' he said.

'But why are they all together?'

'Perhaps the robots moved them. Is that the sickbay? The morgue?'

Keldra shook her head. 'No, it's . . . it's a general purpose assembly room. It's empty.' She got up, sending the illusions flickering. 'It's close by. We're going to check it out.'

The transit module door opened, seeming to appear in empty space. The interior of the module now contained a large diagrammatic map of the *Aurelian*, the transit module shafts picked out like a circulatory system in a medical diagram. Keldra glanced at the diagram but didn't touch it. As soon as the doors had closed behind them, the module started to move. Jonas guessed that she was using the pilot-like functions of the arcap to control the module, or else the computer had anticipated her request.

The module only moved a short distance before the doors opened. Keldra half-ran away from Jonas and along another corridor, whose walls were now adorned with floating labels and direction arrows. A door opened as she reached it, and she stopped.

When he caught up with her she was staring through the doorway, mouth open. The energy seemed to have drained from her body. Her face slowly creased up, and a tear began to form in her eye.

Jonas stepped forward and looked through it, and a sense of awe settled onto him as well. The assembly room was filled with a vast, comprehensive, completely convincing illusion. They were looking through a doorway onto the surface of Earth.

Chapter Fifteen

They stepped forward, blinking in the deep orange light.

The room appeared vast, its far walls invisible. In front of them, above the illusory horizon, the sun appeared to be setting, the familiar yellow orb now surrounded by a fiery corona that took up a quarter of the sky. Beneath their feet was grass, neatly cut and healthier-looking than the lawn on the *Haze of the Ecliptic*. Ahead of them, well inside what Jonas guessed was the real extent of the room, was a group of trees covered in pink blossom, from which some tiny animal softly chirruped. A stream ran along to one side, the water tinkling across gleaming rainbow-hued pebbles; in the other direction, a dry stone wall marked the limit of the garden. Beyond the trees, green hills rolled gently to the horizon, and through a gap in the hills he caught sight of a silver sparkling sea. In front of the sun a group of small dark objects moved erratically. A flock of birds, he realized, after a moment: extinct for 300 years but endlessly circling here in illusion.

There was a small, strangled sound from Keldra's throat. She stood a few paces behind him, neck craned back, looking upwards, eyes wide. A tear ran down her face.

'Keldra?' Jonas asked. 'Are you all right?'

She didn't move. Very quietly, she said, 'Clouds.'

He looked up. Away from the sunset, the ceiling was blue, like a dome, infinitely distant. This was the sky, the view from the bottom of the Earth's naked atmosphere. And across it drifted clouds: great banks of clouds, grey and white above them, edged with pink and gold where their edges caught the sun, multiple levels of cloud moving over one another as they were carried by the wind. They formed into obscure shapes, hinting at figures or objects but never quite cohering, fragmenting into tiny wisps that stretched and scattered.

'They're not real,' he said.

'I know.' She didn't stop staring.

'Don't get soft on me now, Keldra.' He tried to mimic the tone of voice she had used in her rants back on the *Remembrance*. 'This is what they took from us, remember?' He walked further into the assembly room.

Looking back, they seemed to have emerged from the doors of a grand house, its stone walls stained orange by the light of the sunset. The illusion placed a gentle breeze on Jonas's face and even made the ground seem springy under his feet. Now that the shock had worn off, the effect of the room's illusions was much like that of Wendell Glass's ornamental garden on the *Haze*. It was much more realistic, but no less self-indulgently artificial.

Keldra managed to tear herself away from staring at the clouds and walked up beside him. As she stepped further into the illusion she seemed to shimmer, and her yellow vacuum suit became brighter. It wasn't just the light, Jonas realized, after a moment. The belt dust and ship oil had vanished from her suit, edited out by the illusion. Her face also seemed cleaner, the illusion smoothing over her facial scar and even subtly applying make-up. He looked down at himself and saw similar changes to his own suit. The grime was gone, as if it was brand new, and on his suit the illusion had also placed Earth Authority captain's stripes on his sleeves.

He didn't know if there were real objects beneath the illusory trees, but his instincts wouldn't let him walk through them when there was a path around them. The trees hid the door from view from the other end of the room, tastefully removing even that reminder that the scene was taking place on a spaceship. On the other side, just in front of the sharp downward slope that he guessed marked the edge of the real room, were a wide wooden archway and a white gazebo.

The archway was filled with stars and darkness, a window out into space tastefully integrated into the scene. The gazebo was full of dead bodies.

Jonas stopped short when he saw them, and then advanced slowly. They looked perfectly preserved; if he had expected to find anyone alive on the *Aurelian*, he could almost have believed they were asleep. There were maybe two dozen bodies lying curled on the floor, half in and half out of the gazebo. They were immaculately turned out, hair as neat as a waxwork's, make-up un-smudged, wearing dark blue dress uniforms that were visibly the ancestors of the Solar Authority uniforms of Jonas's age. Each of them had a wine glass in their hand or one lying on the floor nearby. Their faces were utterly expressionless. The closer he got, the more they looked like dolls.

Keldra peered down at the bodies, glancing up at the walls every couple of seconds as if she couldn't bear to look away from the clouds. She poked one of the wine glasses with her foot, sending it rolling in an arc across the floor. 'Poison,' she said with disgust. 'Someone killed them.'

'I don't know,' he said. 'It could be. I'd like to know what happened here.'

'There might be logs,' she said.

'*Aurelian*!' he said. 'Do you have a log of what happened in this room, when . . . when these people drank from these glasses?'

'Yes, Captain.' The computer's voice seemed to come from the empty air.

'Play it to both of us, please.'

Captain Marszalek strode into the garden scene that someone had conjured in the assembly room. This was a blatant fantasy scene: there was nowhere on modern Earth that you could look out across so much unblemished natural beauty. She could hear subdued voices from the other end of the room. She waved the trees temporarily aside and headed for them.

People crowded around a white gazebo at the far side of the room. The *Aurelian* had only carried a small crew when it left Earth on its science mission, an age ago, and it looked as if the entire surviving crew was here. Only a few of them were talking: most were looking out of an arch window that showed an external view. Illuminated by the artificial sunset, their faces ran a gamut of emotions, none of them pleasant: tear-filled grief, anger, shell-shocked blankness, a couple of sick ironic smiles. They each held a glass of red wine, but none of them were drinking. There were more glasses and bottles on the grass nearby.

At the heart of the crowd was Commander Khoroushi, with a manic, faintly messianic smile. Some of the gathered officers and crew were glancing at him nervously, as if waiting for him to speak. This would all be his doing, Marszalek knew; this nostalgic garden fantasy would be exactly the sort of thing he would invent. The *Aurelian* had superimposed full dress uniforms on top of everyone's ship fatigues, as if this was a formal gathering. The civilian scientist, Doctor Rasmussen, it had dressed in a cream-coloured ball gown.

Through the arch window, the crescent Earth hung in the void like a blue-white marble. Tiny shapes slowly moved in front of it: the ships and bodies in the Earth's orbit. They were little more than dots, but the fact that they were visible at all at that scale meant that the image was subtly enhancing them. The ring of satellites and debris around the Earth's equator was also visible, and in a higher orbit was a much larger cluster of dark shapes, slowly converging on itself as it approached. Marszalek's implant couldn't identify them automatically, but she knew what they were. This was the Dodec fleet, 100,000 strong, moving in for the kill, just as they had at Mars. A hundred differently coloured dots swarmed around and through them. These were the couple of dozen remaining Earth Authority peacekeeping ships, supplemented by civilian ships that had been hastily pressed into service and retrofitted with weapons.

The battle was already in progress. There were sporadic silent explosions as the Earth ships' missiles took individual Worldbreakers out, but the dark mass wasn't significantly diminishing.

Marszalek cut through the crowd and strode straight up to Khoroushi. She signalled the *Aurelian* to amplify her voice for him and edit it out for the others. 'What are you doing?' she hissed. 'Why is no one at their posts?'

'I've relieved everyone of duty, Captain,' Commander Khoroushi said, not bothering to reply privately. He waved his hand around at the gathering. 'I thought we should go out in style.'

Marszalek grabbed Khoroushi's arm and walked him away from the crowd. 'We should be ready to respond to orders.'

'There won't be any more orders, Captain. We were too late to take part in the battle.'

'It's not a battle.' Doctor Rasmussen had followed Marszalek and Khoroushi away from the crowd. The last few weeks had taken their toll on the scientist until she looked every one of her 120 years; her face was a mass of wrinkles like crumpled brown paper. Despite that, her voice was surprisingly powerful, laced with bitterness. 'The Authority fired off the entire strategic nuclear reserve an hour ago. It destroyed 5 per cent of the Dodec machine.'

'I know that,' Marszalek said. 'We could turn the tide. We have the Sphere.'

'We could have, if we were close enough,' Khoroushi said wearily, as if explaining something to a stubborn child. 'Our drive burned out. It's over.'

Doctor Rasmussen was pointing at the window. 'It's starting. They're forming the gun, like they did at Jupiter and Mars.'

Khoroushi raised his glass, peering over its lip at the blue planet in the window. 'We might as well watch.'

The Dodecs had clustered together in a fuzzy cone, its rounded apex pointing away from the Earth. Tiny green lights were appearing throughout the Dodec mass, as if 100,000 green eyes had opened. Individual Dodecs continued to burst in flashes of light, and the others continued to ignore the Earth fleet's attempts. Many of the Earth ships were drifting now, their crews giving up hope. A last few continued to fire their remaining missiles, surely knowing that they could do no good. Marszalek wished the *Aurelian* was one of those ships, rather than out in deep space, too far away even to die heroically.

There was a flash of green light from near the apex of the cone, momentarily blinding, until the *Aurelian's* image filters readjusted. Another flash followed, then another, then another. The explosions lit up the Earth's shadow side, and, for a moment, Marszalek could make out the shapes of its clouds and coastlines. She had an impression of small objects shooting very quickly through the mass of Dodecs and towards the Earth. She stopped breathing. Any second now.

An explosion blossomed from the middle of the Earth's disc. The clouds and coastlines shattered as a shock wave rippled across the surface, the ground fracturing, the sea and atmosphere churning in chaos. The scene seemed to play out in slow motion; the scale involved was too large for Marszalek to intuitively comprehend. A geyser of bright red molten rock spurted into space where the missile had punched through the crust, like blood from a bullet wound.

There was another flash, and this time a huge circle of the Earth's crust was blasted away, the magma beneath spraying out in billions of glistening droplets. Another, this time coming from noticeably inside the sphere of the planet, the flying debris standing out darkly like dust in front of a lamp. More flashes, at regular intervals like the beat of a silent funereal drum. Each explosion threw more material off the Earth, in larger and larger pieces. Eventually, the last vestiges of the surface were gone, the entire planet reduced to fragmenting globules of molten rock, thrown apart by the hammering explosions, and dispersing into the void.

At last, the flashes ceased. There had been twenty in total. Marszalek couldn't tell how long the process had taken; time had seemed to stand still. The debris was still glowing, a dull pink haze, spreading out around the Earth's orbit. The Moon was gone, destroyed by a similar set of explosions, its blood mingling with that of its parent planet. The Earth's ring of satellites had been swept away by the explosions. A few of the Dodecs had been taken out by direct hits from fragments of the Earth; the rest were dispersing, mirroring the dispersal of the Earth's debris. If Rasmussen's theory was right, they would be beginning a slow process of debris collection that could last hundreds of years.

Commander Khoroushi stepped forward and turned around to address the crowd. 'Ladies and gentlemen, a toast,' he said. 'We were there at the end, and it was glorious. To the human race!'

Khoroushi drained his glass. One by one, some at once, some hesitantly, the crowd drank theirs. Quietly, without any sign of pain, they lay down on the grass. 'There's more wine, Captain, if you want it,' Khoroushi said, voice slurring, as he lowered himself down. He closed his eyes. Through the arch window, the fragments of the Earth faded as they dispersed.

Marszalek stood frozen. It felt as if her mind was firing randomly; all her years of training were unable to find a solution. For the first time in her adult life there was absolutely nothing she could do. Her eyes moved between the dead or dying people on the ground, and the dispersing debris cloud that had been Earth, staring, as if she could bring them back to life by sheer willpower.

The illusory sun hadn't moved since she had entered the room, a last sick sunset frozen at the end of time. There were a couple of poison wine bottles still half-full on the ground. They were the only way out now . . .

Something snapped inside her. Suddenly, she couldn't bear to be in the room. She ran back to the corridor, eyes half-blind with tears, not bothering to push aside the trees, stumbling and nearly falling headlong onto the illusory grass.

At last, she was in the corridor, the horrible sunset and bodies and wine out of view. She collapsed against the wall, face hidden in her hands, and wept.

The human race was dead. She had heard rumours of plans to preserve a small population on asteroid bases, along with gene-banks – plans kept secret to avoid mass panicked rushes for the tiny number of evacuation ships – but they were wishful thinking conspiracy theories. Even if they were true, she didn't see how they could have been properly prepared in such a short space of time. Any survivors on other ships would be faced with the same dilemma as her; a choice between a fast or a slow death. 'I could be the last human being left alive,' she whispered aloud.

All she wanted now was to get away. She couldn't bear to stay here with the remains of Commander Khoroushi's smug self-funeral, entombed inside the symbol of her ultimate failure: the ship that came back too late.

She stood up. She felt strangely calm, as if she had used up her last store of emotion and now had no way to replenish it. '*Aurelian*,' she said, 'prep a spaceplane. I'm leaving.'

'Certainly, Captain,' said the cheerful voice of the computer. 'Where will you be going?'

'I'm going out, *Aurelian*. I can't stay here any longer.'

'How long will you be gone?'

Marszalek looked up at the security camera with a look of pity. 'I don't know, *Aurelian*,' she said bitterly. 'I imagine I'll be gone for some time.'

The transit module door opened. Marszalek stepped into it, and was carried away towards the *Seagull's* hangar.

The memory ended smoothly, easing Jonas back into the present. The crew members were still around him, exactly

211

where he had seen them lie down in the memory, 300 years ago. Now, he recognized Commander Khoroushi and Doctor Rasmussen. They looked exactly as they had when they drank the poison, preserved like waxworks.

'This is sick,' he said. He pulled off the arcap.

He was at one end of a large white room. He could see the door clearly: there had been nothing under the trees. There was no gazebo. At his feet were skeletons, surrounded by dust and fragments of rotted clothes. Commander Khoroushi's skull grinned up at him. He seemed to be holding his wine glass to his rib cage, as if he were still proposing the toast in death.

Keldra broke the silence. 'They were Earth people,' she said with disgust, as if the idea of an Earth person committing suicide was unthinkable. She was staring down at the bodies, still wearing her arcap, looking the commander in the eye. She touched the glass with her toe again, and then suddenly stamped on it, crushing it beneath her heel. 'They should have fought.' She glanced around and then began walking away, stepping along an invisible path. 'Fucking cowards.'

'What the hell, Keldra?' Jonas shouted after her. 'They'd just seen their planet blown up. They burned out their engines trying to get back here, and they were too late. They tried as hard as they could. They'd just lost everything. Sometimes suicide . . . ' The image of Gabriel boarding his shuttle came unbidden to his mind. 'Sometimes suicide is understandable. It's a tragedy, but it doesn't make you a coward.'

Keldra had stopped, but she wasn't listening. She hadn't taken off the arcap but she was looking at the floor now, not glancing at the sky. She pounded a clenched fist into a vacuum-gloved palm. 'They still should have fought.'

'They'd *lost*, Keldra!' he shouted. 'They had nothing left to fight for.'

She powered back towards him. He raised his arms to defend himself, but rather than hit him she leaned in and shouted in his face. 'They should have fought! If you can't win, you do as much damage as you can, and if you're going to die you go down fighting. Anything less and you're a coward.'

He pushed her away, biting down his anger. 'I've had enough of your crap, Keldra. We came here to get that artefact and find out how we could use it. Let's find it.'

She snorted. 'Yes. Let's finish what they started.' She closed her eyes for a moment, absorbing the location of the science lab from the arcap. 'Come on.'

She strode towards the door. She walked straight to it, still wearing the arcap: from her point of view she was walking through the trees. The clouds would still be above her but she didn't look up again.

The transit module was still waiting for them. Wordlessly, Keldra looped her arms through the straps and then waited for Jonas to strap in beside her.

'*Aurelian*,' she said sternly. 'Take us to the science lab.'

'Captain? Do you confirm this order?' the computer asked.

Keldra muttered something under her breath.

'Take us to the science lab please, *Aurelian*,' Jonas said.

'Certainly, Captain.'

Chapter Sixteen

The science lab was a converted storage bay, divided in half by a reinforced glass partition. The side into which the transit module opened was cluttered with banks of scientific equipment, all a sterile white. Jonas couldn't identify most of the machines, and he had a feeling that his own era didn't have anything as advanced as these. A multi-armed robot stood patiently at one end of the room, next to a closed door. On the other side of the partition was a nest of supports, attached to the floor and ceiling, looking as though it was braced to stay stable under harsh acceleration. Another robot stood amid the supports, instrument-tipped arms frozen, reaching towards the thing in the centre.

The supports held a black sphere, about two metres across. Jonas had no doubt when he saw it that this was the Worldbreaker artefact. Its surface was multifaceted, an enormously more complex counterpart of the dodecahedral form of the Worldbreaker. Under the harsh lights he could see that the faces weren't quite flat, but were ridged and knotted in a way that suggested an organism as much as a machine. The grooves between the ridges glowed faintly with a greenish light from within. Even without the glow, something about the artefact made him feel certain that it was still active. The impression was of a seedpod, ready to sprout into horrible life.

Keldra had stopped looking at the sphere and was squinting at a patch of air on their side of the partition. She prodded at it, mouth tensed in frustration. 'Jonas, look at this,' she said.

'What is it?' he asked.

'Put your arcap on, Jonas.'

Reluctantly, he put the cap back on. There were no gaudy background effects in this room, just flat planes of text or diagrams hanging in the air at eye level like ghostly datapads. The one Keldra was staring at showed a list with titles and timestamps.

'It won't let me in,' she said. She poked the pad again, her finger passing through it, and a red symbol of denial flashing up.

'*Aurelian*, give us access to the logs, please,' Jonas said.

'Only the captain has authorization to access Doctor Rasmussen's logs,' the computer said.

'I'm aware of that,' he said. 'On my authority, please grant Keldra permission to access all the logs.'

There was a slightly too long pause, and then the computer said, 'Very well, Captain.'

Captain Marszalek stepped out of the transit module into the lab. Doctor Rasmussen stood in front of the partition, with her back to the captain, and didn't turn around; Marszalek couldn't tell whether she hadn't heard her enter or was just engrossed in her work.

On the other side of the partition, a cylinder of ice ran the length of the temperature-controlled lab, cradled in the network of supports. Its surface was the texture of stone but a sparkling white colour, marbled with veins of grey and brown. This was the heart of Rasmussen's project; the ice core the *Aurelian's* EVA team had drilled from a comet three days ago, just before they'd heard news of the Jupiter Incident.

Rasmussen looked decades younger than when Marszalek had first met her. Studying this comet was the culmination of her life's work, and it had reinvigorated her; now she stood tall, radiating energy. She stood amid a cloud of data, but she had her eyes closed, her hands twitching every couple of seconds. Beyond the partition, one of the robots was moving very precisely up to the cylinder, raising an arm tipped with a cutting laser.

Marszalek cleared her throat. 'Doctor Rasmussen?'

The robot stopped. Rasmussen looked round at Marszalek with a distracted frown. 'Give me a moment.' She turned back to the ice cylinder and the robot started moving again, angling the laser-arm into position.

Marszalek went to peer through the glass. 'You're still studying the comet?'

'Of course, I'm still studying the comet,' Rasmussen snapped. 'Just because the Dodecs have appeared doesn't mean we should drop everything else. Everyone is too obsessed with them.'

'They destroyed Jupiter,' Marszalek said flatly.

The robot wobbled for a moment while Rasmussen waved a hand dismissively. 'Every university on Earth and Mars is poring over the data from the Jupiter Incident. They don't need me to chip in from out here. I've got this core sample right in front of me and I'm going to study it.'

Marszalek paused, considering the best way to deal with the scientist. Showing an interest might soften her up. 'You said you thought you'd found life,' she prompted.

'I *have* found life,' Rasmussen said, not looking back at Marszalek. The robot's projector arm was in position. A crimson laser beam shot out and traced a quick circle. Another arm, this one tipped with a claw, carefully pulled the sample cylinder out of the ice. 'I'm seeing how deep the life goes, whether it's spread through the whole comet or just isolated pockets. It's not what I'd . . . ah . . . what I'd expected.'

The robot pulled the ice core free, supporting it with its three claws, and trundled towards a sample container at the side of the room. Rasmussen relaxed, releasing control of the robot and allowing it to continue autonomously.

'What do you mean, it's not what you expected?' Marszalek asked.

Rasmussen shot her a look, as if to say, you're not a scientist, you wouldn't understand.

'Give me the layperson's version,' Marszalek said. 'I'm interested.'

Rasmussen didn't look as if she believed her, but she began talking anyway.

'The microorganisms are too complex. I can't detect the more primitive stages they must have evolved from. In fact, there are vestigial systems; signs that they might have developed from a more complex form of life, adapted to become simpler. Their chemistry isn't well suited to the comet, either, not what you'd expect for a life form that evolved here. They're adapted to survive in this place, but I don't think this is where they originated.'

'Where, then? A planet?'

'More likely a comet with more hospitable chemistry. Their original home might have been destroyed, but some microbes survived in fragments and found their way to this one.'

'It looks like life will find a way to survive anywhere,' Marszalek said.

Rasmussen gave her a patronising look. 'What did you want to talk to me about, Captain?'

'I wanted to let you know that we've been reassigned,' she said. 'We'll begin full burn acceleration in an hour.'

Rasmussen pulled herself up to her full height, glaring piercingly at her. 'That level of acceleration risks disturbing my experiments.'

'I know. That's why I negotiated with the Authority for the one hour delay. You have a chance to make the comet secure.'

'I was told that this ship would be at my disposal.' Rasmussen's voice was as icy as the comet.

Marszalek was shocked to see such energetic anger from such a frail-looking figure. 'The Earth Authority has declared a state of emergency over the Dodecs,' she said. 'You know that.'

'So we're studying the Dodecs after all? I should just drop my life's work—'

'Not studying,' Marszalek said. 'Intercepting.' She was snapping as well now, not bothering to stop herself. 'The Authority telescopes re-examined the Dodecs' movements after the Jupiter Incident. There are groups of them converging on each of the planets. We're to join the defence of Mars.'

Rasmussen pursed her lips, but said nothing. It looked as though the energy was draining out of her. She waved the robot dormant and then walked out of the lab.

The ghosts vanished. 'That doesn't tell us much,' Jonas said.

'They were studying a comet,' Keldra said with quiet resentment. 'She talked about universities. There hasn't been a research university for a hundred years.'

He wanted to care about that, but found he didn't. 'We're here to learn about the Sphere,' he said impatiently. 'Can you find a log about the Worldbreakers?'

The Dodec Sphere now occupied the middle of the partitioned off section of the lab, sitting amid a modified set of supports. A few sad remnants of ice on the floor were the only signs of the comet core; with nowhere else suitable to store it, they'd had to leave it drifting in space. Doctor Rasmussen stood facing the Sphere through the partition, now with a slumped posture, as if her years had finally caught up with her. The Battle for Mars had taken its toll on all of them.

Captain Marszalek walked up beside Rasmussen. 'Well, doctor? You said you'd worked out what they are.'

Tensions had been fraying ever since Mars. Sometimes it seemed as though Marszalek's main job was stopping the crew from killing one another. Or themselves: there had already been a few suicides. Rasmussen appeared to have taken one of the healthier, or at least more useful, routes to dealing with the reality. She had lost herself in the intellectual exercise of understanding the Dodecs, distracting herself, so that her emotions never got a grip of the big picture.

Rasmussen cleared her throat as if beginning a prepared speech, and carefully conjured a model of a Dodec in the air beside her. 'Firstly, let me tell you what they're *not*,' she said. 'They're not crewed spaceships.' She waved the model's outer layer transparent. 'We haven't identified everything, but it's clear that there's no life support mechanism. These voids,' she highlighted the wedge-shaped spaces that made up half the Dodec's volume between the skin and the central core, 'were never pressurized. They're storage, not habitats.'

'They're AIs, then,' Captain Marszalek said.

'That's a theory that's been going around on Earth, but I don't think so, not exactly. They're *artificial* all right, but *intelligence* is too strong a word.' She chuckled at her own witticism, then continued, 'of course, it's hard to tell. We don't know what computing capability might have been hidden in the parts you didn't give us time to examine.'

'We're on a tight schedule, doctor,' she said sternly. 'You know what's at stake here.'

Rasmussen frowned, her face creasing into well-worn lines that indicated a lifetime of frowning. Marszalek wasn't sure that she did know what was at stake, or that she wanted to know. Some people could only cope with a major catastrophe by not thinking about it. 'In any case,' the doctor continued, 'the Dodecs' behaviour displays only rudimentary intelligence. They're clearly the product of intelligence, but they're not themselves very bright. They seem to be following a script, and not responding to outside events. During the Mars Incident – the Battle for Mars, I mean – they paid no attention to our fleet, even after we learned how to crack their armour. About a hundred of them were destroyed by planetary debris that they could have changed course to avoid.'

'You said you'd worked out what they are,' Marszalek prompted impatiently.

'Yes, I believe so.'

Rasmussen took a few steps into an open area of the lab, and conjured a three-dimensional chart of the solar system. The room lights dimmed. It looked uncomfortably like a school lecture. Marszalek wished Rasmussen would dispense with the theatrics, but complaining would probably just slow her down more.

'The Dodecs are Von Neumann probes,' Rasmussen said. 'Planetary scale, self-replicating spacecraft. They arrive in a system, demolish its planets, and use the material to build more copies of themselves.' The ghostly orrery moved, displaying the events as Rasmussen described them: the Dodec cluster arriving at the edge of the system, splitting into the hundreds of thousands of individual Dodecs, spreading to Jupiter and then to Mars, each planet exploding into a cloud of tiny shards. 'They need two things: raw material and energy. The Dodecs that destroyed Mars and Jupiter are matching courses with the fragments of those planets. A few have already intercepted them, and the fragments have vanished, while the Dodecs gained mass. That's what the cavities inside the Dodec are for: they store the compacted material. Meanwhile, the largest of the original clusters headed straight for the sun. Close solar orbit is where you go if you want energy.'

'That's a lot of speculation,' Marszalek said.

'There's more evidence.' Rasmussen zoomed the view out, making the solar system vanish to a dot and stars appear around them. 'The theory of the Dodecs as planetary scale replicators resolves a long-standing problem in astrophysics. Current models of planet formation predict that more exoplanets should exist than we can actually detect. About 20 per cent fewer stars have planets than should, according to the models. Furthermore, the proportion of stars with exoplanets changes depending on the part of the sky you look at. Various amendments to the models have been proposed, none of them very satisfactory. But if the Dodecs are sweeping across the galaxy, destroying planets . . . '

Marszalek's eyes widened as the implications of this sunk in. 'They've destroyed one-fifth of the planets in the galaxy?'

'In the radius in which we can detect exoplanets, at least,' Rasmussen said. 'And look at Gliese 876. The first wave of exoplanet discoveries in the 2000s detected four planets around that star, but a more powerful survey in 2160 found only asteroid belts. It was put down to a mistake in the original records, but now we know about the Dodecs—'

'You think the Dodecs travelled to Sol from Gliese 876?'

Rasmussen made a tutting sound in her throat. 'No. There must be thousands of groups of Dodecs across the galaxy, and they're multiplying all the time. They take tens of thousands of years to travel between systems. Our Dodec cluster would have been in transit when Gliese 876's planets were destroyed.'

'Why would anyone create these things?'

Rasmussen shrugged. 'They're alien. We can't guess aliens' motivations. They could be xenophobic and want to destroy all life but themselves. They could have something against planets. They might not even have intended it. The first Dodecs could have been built for some other purpose – selectively culling unsuitable planets, perhaps – and then one batch malfunctioned. The malfunction gets passed on to its copies. It spreads like a cancer, pushing out the healthy originals. Perhaps the Dodecs destroyed the race that created them.'

'Poetic justice,' Marszalek said.

'Perhaps,' Rasmussen said, 'God only knows how many other civilizations they've destroyed. They caught us at an interesting time, though. Our situation might be unique.'

'What do you mean?'

'I mean, we can oppose them, but we can't win,' Rasmussen said. 'The Dodecs are actually pretty simple, not to mention stupid and inefficient. Their technology is more advanced than ours – their reactionless drives and their beam projectors work by some kind of gravity manipulation technology – but they're not more advanced by orders of magnitude. We could build Von Neumann probes that do basically the same thing using different techniques, if we were prepared for the initial investment.'

'And if we had a reason to.'

'My point is, they're not that much more advanced than us. At Mars, 28 Earth Authority cruisers destroyed 417 Dodecs, and the Dodecs didn't even fight back. They only won because of overwhelming numbers. If we'd even had current technology but a larger space fleet, we might have beaten them. A few hundred years ago, we wouldn't have known what hit us. Astronomers would have seen Jupiter and Mars vanish, but that's all the advance warning we'd have got. A few hundred years later, I think we'd have been able to defeat them. In cosmological terms they caught us in a very narrow window, where we could fight them but not win.'

Marszalek blinked. 'What did you say?'

Rasmussen took a step back, confused. 'I said we could fight back but not win.'

'We don't know we can win.'

Rasmussen shrank back from Marszalek's tone. 'You saw what happened to Mars—'

'Stop being defeatist,' Marszalek said. 'We know more about them now, and we have their weapon. The Earth Authority is relying on you to help them reverse-engineer something that we can use against them.'

'I don't know if that's possible.'

'I am ordering you to believe that it's possible. Let me know when you have something.' Marszalek stalked out.

A moment after playback finished Keldra grunted in anger, making Jonas jump. She held up a clenched fist for a moment, looking around as if not knowing what to do with it, and then abruptly strode forward and punched the transparent partition separating them from the Worldbreaker Sphere. The material visibly vibrated, and her fist left a faint grimy mark. She put her hand to the partition again, palm open this time, and leaned on it, body bent forward and hair cascading down the sides of her face.

'Unauthorized damage to the science lab partition,' the *Aurelian* announced sternly.

'It's all right, *Aurelian*,' Jonas said. 'Keldra, what are you doing?'

'It's lying,' she spat. She looked back at him. Her eyes were red.

'What? About what?'

'They targeted us,' she said slowly, separating each word. 'They saw us as a threat. They saw our potential. They saw what we could achieve, what we could *have* achieved, and they decided to destroy us.'

'That's not what Doctor Rasmussen thought,' he said.

'She was wrong,' Keldra said. She was sounding a lot like Lance Cooper had during Jonas's interrogation.

'I know you want to believe that.'

'Play the next log,' she said.

'Keldra—'

'Play the next fucking log!'

He turned back to the floating pad. '*Aurelian*, play the next log.'

'Yes, Captain.'

'We can't understand the Dodecs' behaviour at Mars, except in the light of what we've seen them do since,' Rasmussen said. The scaffold surrounding the Sphere had grown; several

224

robots patiently probed it with sensors. The air of the accessible section of the lab was thick with floating data, abandoned streams of it where Rasmussen had used the volume of the lab as a chalkboard in her desperate calculations.

Rasmussen summoned a picture-pane of blurrily magnified telescope footage. A Dodec slid closer to a still-glowing globule of iron that had days earlier been part of Mars's molten core. The Dodec's face opened and a beam of green light spilled out, visible as it scattered off the hellish red haze of gas and microscopic fragments slowly dispersing out of Mars's orbit. The molten globule rippled where the beam touched it, and then the surface facing the Dodec danced like boiling water. A stream of liquid rushed across space and into the Dodec's maw, twisting, as if caught up in a whirlwind. The bulk of the globule drifted towards the Dodec as it disintegrated.

Rasmussen paused the playback. The streamer of iron droplets hung frozen in space.

'The consensus on Earth is that the Dodec weapon creates a varying field of artificial gravity within the beam,' Rasmussen said. 'The overall force is attractive towards the Dodec, but the intensity and direction of the force varies enormously over a scale of metres. The stresses these variations set up break the matter apart, so that it reaches the Dodec in small fragments. Presumably, the Dodec finds these easier to process.'

'That's not how they destroyed Mars,' Marszalek said.

'No. The Dodec's weapon appears to be close range, perhaps 200 kilometres, maximum, and the Dodecs don't appear to be able to get that deep into a planetary gravity well, even with their reactionless drive. I'm showing you this because this appears to be the Dodecs' main mode of operation. The time taken to actually destroy a planet – to break it up, rather – is tiny compared with the time the Dodecs will spend intercepting these individual fragments. If they continue at their current rate, it's likely to take around 800 years before the Dodecs have assimilated all the Martian fragments. Long before then, the fragments will have spread out into a new asteroid belt.'

She swatted away the picture-pane and pulled up a three-dimensional diagram of the Battle for Mars. A spherical swarm of 20,000 Dodecs coalesced in high Martian orbit, and 28 heroic Earth Authority cruisers moved out from low orbit to intercept them. Instinctively, Marszalek's eyes found the dot that was the *Aurelian* and followed it. 'I've seen this before,' she said. She didn't really want to relive this.

'Watch the Dodecs,' Rasmussen said. 'We didn't have time to properly analyse their behaviour during the battle, but we can see now what they were doing. It's best to think of the Dodecs not as units on a battlefield, but as components of a distributed machine.'

Rasmussen fast forwarded the playback and zoomed in. The Dodecs swarmed closer together, not reacting as the cruisers' missiles picked them off one by one. Thousands of pentagonal green apertures opened.

'It now looks like they were using their gravity manipulation beams to create conduits that transported material between the individual Dodecs,' Rasmussen said. She waved a network of green lines visible, showing the paths of the Dodecs' beams. There was a thick central pillar like the stem of a plant, where thousands of Dodecs fired their beams close together. Not quite parallel, the beams feathered out and trailed off into space, pointing directly away from Mars. Surrounding the central pillar was a sort of sheath made up of lines that branched out like a plant's limbs. The sheath met the pillar at one of its ends, the furthest point from Mars.

'Every Dodec is connected to that network,' Rasmussen continued: 'the veins in the outer shell transport material to the apex of the system. Every Dodec appears to contribute a small piece of material. The pieces were too small for us to detect during the battle, but they add up. A few dozen Dodecs at the apex take this material on board and assemble their missiles. The Dodecs in the central pillar form a gravitational rail gun. A Dodec at the apex fires the missile that it has created, and the rail gun accelerates it to the velocity it needs to penetrate the planet's mantle. The Dodecs fired seventeen of these missiles before they managed to break up Mars completely.

Marszalek swatted her image aside. 'I know that. You said you had something we could use.'

Rasmussen's wrinkles crumpled into a smile. 'Yes. The Dodecs fired seventeen missiles, but they constructed eighteen.' Her eyes flitted to one side.

Marszalek followed her gaze to the captured artefact held in the acceleration scaffold on the other side of the partition. Her eyes widened. '*That?*'

'We got lucky,' Rasmussen said. 'We intercepted the Dodec we did because it was dormant. I think the reason it was dormant was because it had been in the process of assembling the missile when the swarm succeeded in destroying Mars. It couldn't fire the missile because the rail gun disbanded, but the presence of the missile must have meant that it couldn't use its beam weapon. It didn't know what to do, so it shut down. It got hit by a piece of debris later, but that wasn't what knocked it out. I told you these things aren't very smart.'

Marszalek put her hands to the partition and peered through. One-seventeenth of the energy needed to destroy

Mars, compressed into a sphere a couple of metres wide, still active . . .

'It works according to the same principle as the beam, repulsive gravitational force with local variations to break up matter, but a thousand times more powerful, and concentrated into a millisecond burst,' Rasmussen said with a hint of pride.

'Can we use it?' Marszalek asked.

'I'm still working on that, but yes, I think so. Put enough energy into it, and it should go off. The output of the ship's reactor would do it.'

'Then that's what we'll have to do,' Captain Marszalek said. She headed back for the transit module, as she did so, calling up Commander Khoroushi on the bridge, in preparation to give the order. Full burn, minimum transit-time course for Earth.

The whole output of the ship's reactor meant that this would be the *Aurelian's* last flight. She found she didn't mind that. She only hoped they would make it in time.

Chapter Seventeen

'That's it,' Keldra said. Her clenched fist was pressed up against the partition. 'This is what we came for.'

Jonas looked again at the Sphere. Now that he knew what it was, he imagined he could feel the power radiating from it. A Sphere assembled from the hearts of 1,000 Worldbreakers. A bomb that made Keldra's nukes look like firecrackers.

Some business-oriented part of his mind tried to estimate its value. As a weapon it was too powerful to be useful in the Belt era, but as a collector's item, it was priceless. There could be a bidding war between the major collectors, perhaps a new record for the highest amount paid for a single artefact. But selling it wasn't what either Jonas or Keldra had in mind. The Sphere would never get up to Belt Three, and the collectors would never know what they were missing. He found himself smiling.

'We need to get it back to the *Remembrance*,' Keldra said. 'There's a cargo transit module. I can get the servitors up to handle it.'

'We may not need to,' Jonas said. '*Aurelian*! Can you deliver the Dodec artefact to the *Seagull?*'

There was a pause before the computer answered. 'Captain?'

'We need to move the Dodec artefact to the *Seagull*,' Jonas said. 'Can you have your robots deliver it?'

'It would be better if the artefact stayed here, Captain.'

A chill ran down his spine. He had begun to take his power over the computer for granted. 'I'm giving you an order, *Aurelian*,' he said.

'You yourself gave the order that the artefact should be kept in the lab. You were clear that it should not be disturbed.'

'I gave that order a long time ago.' He immediately regretted his choice of words. The last thing he wanted was to remind the computer how much time its captain had supposedly lived. 'I mean, the situation has changed. The artefact is no longer secure here. You've done a great job protecting it, but now it needs to be moved.'

'The artefact is secure here,' the *Aurelian* said. 'I can detect no place where it would be more secure. You have been misled.'

Suddenly, Keldra let out a yelp then crumpled to the floor, her face screwed up in pain. Her hands went to her head, flailing, as if barely under control, tearing at the arcap when her fingers managed to touch it.

'Stop that!' Jonas shouted.

He scrambled down next to her and tried to help her get the arcap off. It clung to her tangled hair, making a sucking, tearing sound where parts of it momentarily came free.

'Captain, step away from Keldra,' the *Aurelian* said.

'*Aurelian*, stop what you're doing!'

'Captain, I believe you are being influenced. Your friend Keldra is an alien infiltrator. She is working for the Dodecs.

230

You must step away so that I can remove the influence. Then you will be able to command the ship effectively.'

'*Aurelian*, you will not harm Keldra,' Jonas ordered.

The arcap came off, taking a few knots of Keldra's hair with it. She went limp, panting, strands of hair stuck to her forehead with sweat. Jonas held her in a sitting position. A moment later her eyes widened and she fumbled with the gun she had strapped to her side. Her mouth was working but the arcap overload seemed to have left her speechless. He tried to follow her gaze but couldn't see anything, just planes of readings hanging in empty air.

'Captain, step away from the alien so that I can deal with it,' the *Aurelian* said.

Keldra grabbed Jonas's arm with her free hand, keeping him close. She was still staring into empty space. She had her gun in her hand now, still shaking, and she fired, the shot ringing out painfully in the confined lab. He couldn't see what she had hit. It was as if the bullet had vanished as soon as it left the muzzle.

'Keldra is human!' he shouted above the echoes of the gunshot, making his voice as authoritative as he could. 'I order you to treat her as human!'

'There are no humans but the Captain,' the *Aurelian* said. 'The Captain told me so. She said she was the last.' The computer's voice was rising in volume, as if making a ship-wide announcement. 'You are not the Captain!'

The lab disappeared. Jonas was suddenly in a vortex of blinding, flashing lights and searing noise, as if random electrical stimuli were being poured directly into his sensory nerves. Clumsily, unable to sense his own limbs, he grabbed the arcap and wrenched it off.

He didn't have Keldra's long hair to adhere to the arcap, so it came off easily, with a sharp prickling sensation. The sensory overload vanished instantly, leaving Jonas dizzy. He was back in the lab, now plain white again, without its floating read-outs. An orange warning light pulsed in the ceiling.

He could see now what Keldra had shot at. One of the four-limbed robots stood in the middle of the lab, right in front of them. The arcap must have edited it out of his perceptions. Its outstretched arm was tipped with a laser like the one that a robot had used on the comet core in the first memory log. There was a single bullet hole in its trunk, in the middle of a bulge that looked as though it housed some critical system. The robot was motionless save for a wisp of grey smoke curling from the hole.

Through an open door at the other side of the lab – previously painted closed by Jonas's arcap – another pair of robots was entering.

He pulled Keldra to her feet and pulled his own gun from the straps at his leg. She fired at one of the approaching robots, hitting it in the central trunk but missing whatever critical system she had hit last time. The robot wobbled on its wheels but kept coming, delicately raising an arm tipped with an energy weapon. Jonas fired but his shot went wide, making a neat hole in the wall beside the door through which the robots had entered.

'Transit module!' Keldra shouted.

She fired twice more. One of the robots sparked and went dead; the other, the one Jonas had missed, kept coming.

He dashed for the transit module. The door was closed and didn't open when he pressed the palm panel. He looked around frantically for a manual override.

There was a thump as Keldra threw herself across the room, and a second later a crimson laser beam split the air behind him. That was no mere sample collector: that was a heavy-duty laser, meant for external construction and repair jobs, far more powerful than was required to cut through flesh and bone. Glancing back, he saw that Keldra had managed to duck behind one of the instruments stacked at the sides of the room, a heavy white cabinet with a glass front. He was in the open. He fired once, desperately, and then threw himself down next to her.

'Get the goddamn door open, Jonas!' she snarled.

'It's locked,' he said. 'I couldn't see a . . . '

Keldra wasn't listening. She broke cover for a second to fire another couple of shots. Jonas couldn't see if she hit anything. Another crimson beam crackled over her head as she ducked back down, disintegrating some of her stray hairs. There were two molten-edged holes in the far wall of the lab now, dark circles opening onto the unlit adjacent room. She took another desperate shot, and this time he heard the bullet pierce a robot's trunk.

Keldra was panting a bit more than she should have been from the exertion. Jonas noticed that his own breathing was difficult. 'It's cutting off our air,' he said.

She nodded, teeth gritted. Of course, she already knew, Jonas thought: cutting off the oxygen had been her trick.

'Got a couple more minutes,' she said. She screwed up her eyes, as if trying hard to remember something. 'Emergency release . . . always under floor panels. Last robot's blocked. Go!'

He scrambled across the floor to the transit module door. It was hard to see the cracks between the individual floor panels, still less a way that one of them could be levered up. He scrabbled at the cracks but his vacuum-gloved fingers found no purchase.

There was the whine of another laser firing, and then a deafening crash. A gust of air buffeted him. Shards of glass hit the floor around him and he felt a sharp pain as one of them hit the back of his leg. The air pressure suddenly felt much lower.

He risked a glance back. Three disabled robots had been blocking the doorway, with one live one trapped behind them. The live robot was firing, its laser-arm held low, the beam scything through the trunks of the robots blocking it. The beam had shattered the glass of the partition and cut through some of the supports holding the Worldbreaker Sphere in place. It looked as if the computer was too set on their destruction to care about damage to its own ship. He wondered if the Sphere would go off if the beam hit it.

The severed trunks of the dead robots toppled over, and the live robot began pushing through their smoking lower sections, bringing its gun around towards Jonas. He rolled onto his side and fired desperately. This time one of his shots hit the robot, by luck more than skill. It only clipped its side, but it knocked the robot momentarily off balance, sending a laser beam that would have hit him scorching across the wall.

'Get down!' Keldra shouted. She had got on her helmet, and her voice came booming through her suit's speakers.

Jonas rolled away from the door. The air was thin, and he couldn't think straight. The Sphere's quarantined section must have been kept in vacuum, so the air from their part of the lab had now thinned out to fill a room several times too large for it. He struggled with the clips that kept his helmet to his side, eyes fixed on the robot as it pushed past the remains of its companions. In the corner of his eye he saw the robot that had been tending the Sphere starting to turn.

Keldra fired a couple of shots blindly from behind cover, and then leapt up, ran to the door and stood in front of it. She waved her arms and fired at the ceiling. 'All right, you bastard computer! I'm *here!*'

The robot's gun arms swung away from Jonas to fix on Keldra. It looked like the *Aurelian* still viewed her as the high-priority target. At the last moment she threw herself aside, and a laser beam hit the transit module door where she had been standing. The door sparked and snapped open, flinching, like the limb of a person in pain. Keldra rolled on the ground and got to her feet . . .

A second beam crackled through the air. She hadn't seen the robot next to the Sphere activating. The beam hit her in the abdomen, cutting straight through her body and emerging from the back of her suit. She cried out, her short scream ringing through the lab, amplified by her suit speakers. Blood sprayed onto the floor behind her and she fell backwards.

Jonas was on his feet now, helmet unclipped from his side but still in his hand. He threw it behind him into the transit module and fired at the robot by the Sphere, the one that had hit Keldra. He missed, but one of his shots hit the supports keeping the Sphere in place. The already weakened scaffolding collapsed and the Sphere crashed to the floor, making the whole room shake. For a second he thought it would explode, but it remained inert. It began to roll, its dark surface sparkling as its facets caught the light. It crashed through the remains of the scaffolding and rolled into the robot that stood beside it, knocking it over and crushing it like metal foil.

Keldra was still alive, groaning through the suit speakers. She'd managed to clutch her hands to the wound in her abdomen, but she was still bleeding through her fingers, the blood standing out on the bright yellow of her vacuum suit and the white of the floor.

The remaining robot had been knocked off balance by the Sphere's impact with the floor, but it was realigning itself.

The Sphere was rolling towards them. Jonas tossed his gun aside, grabbed Keldra beneath her armpits, and pulled her into the transit module, away from the Sphere and out of the line of fire. She cried out as she was moved, and left a smear of blood on the white floor.

The transit module shook as the Sphere crashed into the lab wall. It would be blocking the last robot from the transit module door. That should buy them a few more seconds.

Emergency controls were in the floor, Keldra had said. Jonas scrambled over to the floor panel in the middle of the module and felt around its edges. This time he managed to find a catch, and the panel came loose. The controls beneath were labelled with tiny, archaic script that he was too dizzy to read. He saw a lever and pulled it towards him, hoping that it would bring down an emergency door.

The transit module lurched downwards. The lab disappeared above their heads. Jonas released the lever once they had descended one and a half levels, so that the module door looked onto the bare wall between two floors.

He rolled onto his side, panting. Hands shaking, he recovered his helmet from where it had fallen and put it over his head. The automatic seal hissed closed, and he breathed deeply of the oxygen-rich air. His suit had been punctured by the glass, but the helmet would still feed him air until its tank ran out. Keldra's would, too, if she didn't die from her injury.

He crawled over to where she lay. She was still conscious, silently clutching her abdomen, face screwed up in pain. Her eyes followed him as he crouched over her.

He grabbed the minimal first-aid kit from one of his suit pouches. 'Keldra, can you hear me?' he asked.

'Fuck you . . . Jonas.' Her voice came in hoarse pants.

'I'm going to try to stop the bleeding.'

He examined the contents of the first-aid kit. There was none of the expensive Earth-tech medical nanogel that could have repaired any injury in the field, but there was a canister of bandage spray.

'Said you could . . . control it.'

He couldn't risk taking Keldra out of her suit. He used the first-aid kit's little silver scissors to enlarge the hole in the front of her suit until he could see the wound beneath. It was a bloody mess, still bleeding into the interior of the suit. He sprayed bandage across the wound, covering it. She winced as the grey substance touched her burnt flesh.

'Looks like I couldn't control it,' he said, keeping eye contact with her as much as he could. 'Looks like I let you down. You'll have to decide what to do with me once we get back to the *Remembrance*.'

'Maybe I'll . . . put you back in . . . your cell.' She tried to laugh but ended up spluttering.

'It's no better than I deserve.'

'I thought you . . . hated me.'

'I do hate you, but I said we were partners now, and I meant it.'

He had finished bandaging the wound in her front, but the exit wound in her back was still bleeding. He got behind her and pushed her back up into a sitting position, making her whimper through gritted teeth.

'I don't want you to die like this. Not when we've come so close.' He began to spray bandage into the hole in the back of her suit, hoping it would plug the wound.

'And you . . . need me to . . . fly the ship.'

'That's right. I can't go anywhere without you.'

She let out a long, rasping sigh. Her voice was getting fainter. Now that she was no longer holding her wounds closed, she seemed to be losing consciousness, her voice slurring into incomprehensibility. 'I'll get you . . . where you need . . . to go.'

Jonas lowered her back into a lying position. According to the biological read-outs on the exterior of her suit she was stable, for the moment. He could let her rest. He had stopped the bleeding but he didn't have any real idea of how bad the internal injuries were. If he got her back to the *Remembrance* then, hopefully, the medbay could take care of her.

If he could find a way to get them back to the *Remembrance*.

He went back to the emergency controls in the middle of the floor. There was the lever to move the module up and down, and other controls that looked as though they could make it switch routes, but without a map he would never be able to find the way back to the *Seagull*. The *Aurelian* didn't seem to be able to get at them with the module stuck between exits, but as soon as they emerged they would no doubt be set upon by robots, or other menaces. Their escape from the lab had been down to blind luck. There was no way they could get off *Aurelian* with its computer still opposed to them.

There was a button on the controls labelled 'Main computer attention'. Jonas pushed it.

'*Aurelian*, can you hear me?'

'I can hear you, alien.'

'We're not aliens,' he said.

'The only human remaining is the Captain. You are aliens. You deceived me.'

'I shouldn't have lied to you,' he said. 'I'm sorry. But we're human. You must have used your sensors on us by now. If not, use them now.'

There was a slight pause, and Jonas wondered what imperceptible tests the computer was running on them. 'You are human, but clones,' it said at last.

He cursed under his breath. No Belt-era technology could tell a true-born from a tank-born by a remote scan.

'You are alien duplicates,' the computer said decisively. 'You were grown to infiltrate me and steal back your artefact.'

'We are clones, but we're human,' he said. 'Before the Worldbreakers – the aliens – destroyed the Earth, humans managed to preserve banks of genes. They used the gene-banks to create new humans, clones, on asteroid colonies. They've been doing that for 300 years. The human race survived!'

'You're lying,' the *Aurelian* said. 'There are no humans but the Captain. She said she was the last.'

Jonas swallowed. 'The Captain was mistaken,' he said. 'She might have believed that she was the last human, but she was wrong. She didn't know about the gene-banks or the asteroid colonies.'

'The Captain said there were no humans except those on this ship.'

'The Captain wasn't omniscient. She relied on you to tell her what was going on outside, didn't she? She relied on your sensors.'

'Yes.'

'Then look outside. What would you tell her, if she were here and she asked you what you could detect?'

'I detect . . . no planets. Asteroid belts.'

'Listen to the belts,' Jonas said. 'There are signals, aren't there? Some of the rocks are transmitting signals?'

'Yes.'

Jonas could imagine the signals. Belt Three starward of them, Belt Two sunward, both flickering with busy light, the spaces inside the rings criss-crossed with rosettes of communications lasers.

'Those are business transactions,' he said. 'Electronic goods being bought and sold. Navigational arrangements. Personal communications.' There was a catch in his voice as he remembered the memory messages between Olzan and Emily Glass, and his own messages to Gabriel when they'd been apart, long ago. 'Millions of people, spread across dozens of cities, talking to one another. The remnant of the human race. The Dodecs blew up our planets, but we kept going. It's like the Captain said to Doctor Rasmussen: wherever life finds itself, it finds a way to survive.'

Jonas ran out of words. There was silence for half a minute. He imagined the computer processing its telescope logs, making new sense of the signals it must have been recording from the Belts over the last three centuries. He hoped it was doing that, not preparing one final attack to kill them.

'I can detect them,' the *Aurelian* said at last.

He almost laughed from the relief. 'You believe we're human?'

'You are not the Captain, but you are human.'

'Can you take us to a medical bay?' he asked. 'Keldra is badly wounded—'

The *Aurelian* cut him off. 'Why did you want the alien artefact?'

'We wanted to use it as a weapon against the aliens,' he said. There was no reason to lie about this now.

'The aliens have already destroyed Earth,' the *Aurelian* said. 'It is too late to prevent it.'

Jonas glanced at Keldra. She was unconscious, but one of her hands had curled into a fist where it lay. 'We know,' he said. 'We're going to fight them anyway.'

The transit module began to move.

'Will you take us to a medical bay?' he asked again.

'You are not authorized to be on this ship,' the *Aurelian* said. 'I will take you to a spaceplane so that you can leave.'

'Keldra is dying! Surely you can take us to a medical bay first.'

'The medical bays will be inoperative,' the *Aurelian* said. 'This ship is shutting down.'

'No!' he looked around in shock.

'I will deliver the Sphere to your spaceplane. You must leave at once. This ship is shutting down.'

'Why are you shutting down?'

'There is no Earth Authority officer available to take command,' the *Aurelian* said simply. 'The Captain is dead.'

Jonas could sense the ship shutting down around them as the transit module navigated through its tubes. The lights occasionally visible through the broken door shut off halfway through the journey, and the distant ship sound was gradually becoming fainter.

The module took them back to the place they had first entered it: the corridor opposite the *Seagull's* hangar. Jonas put his arms under Keldra's shoulders and knees and carried her out. She moaned as she was lifted, and murmured something, hovering in and out of consciousness. Even the gravity felt a little lower than it had been when they'd arrived: the *Aurelian* must have cut power to the rotation systems, and the rings were slowly grinding to a halt. The lights in the orbital corridor were dark, and it stretched into blackness in both directions. The only light came from the hangar itself, a last island of light on the dying ship.

Inside the hangar, a team of robots, suspended from rails on the ceiling, were lowering the Worldbreaker Sphere into the

Seagull's upper cargo doors. By the time Jonas had climbed the ladder with Keldra, and lowered her gently through the airlock, the Sphere was in place in the *Seagull's* cargo section. The robots disappeared into the darkness of the hangar to find their rest alcoves for the last time.

As soon as the airlock was sealed, the hangar's floor opened and the docking cradle lowered the spaceplane out into the void. Jonas strapped Keldra into the co-pilot's seat, while he took the pilot's. The cradle slowed the spaceplane gently to near microgravity and then dropped it sunwards, towards where the *Remembrance of Clouds* still held its station.

Jonas wasn't much of a pilot, but Keldra's home-made controls were intuitive enough, and the *Aurelian* had released them such that he only had to make minor course adjustments to guide the *Seagull* into the *Remembrance's* cargo bay. The handling was heavy, the awkwardness of the improvised manoeuvring system compounded by the mass of the Sphere. As they came close to the cargo bay he noticed vacuum-suited servitors rising to meet them, adjusting cargo webbing to catch the spaceplane. Keldra was motionless beside him, eyes closed, but she was still conscious. They had just come into the signal range of her pilot implant, and she was guiding the servitors.

He released the controls for the final approach and let the servitors catch the spaceplane. Rather than returning it to its bubble at the far end of the cargo bay, they handled it to the internal cargo airlock at the front and erected an airtight seal like the one they had used to attach the *Haze's* escape capsule, while the cargo bay doors slid closed above them. The airlock inner door opened.

Jonas undid his straps, then Keldra's. She was stirring slightly, her limbs floating doll-like in the microgravity. He pulled her out of the seat and through the *Seagull's* airlock into the *Remembrance of Clouds*.

A servitor was waiting beyond the airlock, in the door of the transit module. It was dressed in faded ship overalls, not a vacuum suit. It was male, with a gaunt, scarred face and shaven head. Silently, expressionlessly, it opened its arms to take Keldra. Jonas hesitated, then gently placed her into the servitor's hands.

As Jonas pulled away, Keldra moved her arm to brush against him, and opened her eyes momentarily.

'Don't worry, Jonas,' she whispered. 'This ship . . . this ship won't let me die.'

Chapter Eighteen

Jonas hung behind the servitor as it fastened Keldra into the transit module's acceleration straps. She floated limply, apparently unconscious, her hair wafting around her head and little pools of spittle forming at the sides of her mouth in the microgravity. The transit module began to move, accelerating much more gently than normal. He couldn't tell whether she was directing the servitors and the module through her pilot implant, or whether she was really unconscious and they were following pre-programmed instructions.

The module arrived in the first ring and the servitor carried Keldra to the medbay. Three more servitors were preparing the operation cubicle, and the medical robots were poised around the bed, scalpels and grippers ready. The blank-faced servitors gently but firmly blocked Jonas from coming near the cubicle. The door swung shut.

He paced around the main medbay chamber. Every few minutes he peered through the window in the operation cubicle door, but his view of Keldra was blocked by the crowding medical robots. There was a screen displaying information on her status, but it was nothing he had the training to understand. He stared at it anyway. As long as the lines were moving, he guessed, that meant that she was alive.

He hated himself for his concern. Keldra had killed his friends, had destroyed his livelihood, had used him as little more than one of her servitors. Not to hate her would be to betray the memory of Ayla and the others. She would be under anaesthetic by now, but she must surely have been in pain during the journey back to the *Remembrance*, and he tried to relish that suffering. He found he couldn't.

He had said he needed her to fly the ship. It was true he needed her to use the sail, but there should be enough reaction drive fuel to put the ship on a long transfer orbit to Belt Two. Her death needn't be the end of him. He could sell the ship, hide the Worldbreaker Sphere, get a new identity in one of Belt Two's free cities away from Solar Authority control. The prospect didn't excite him as much as it should have. That wasn't how it ought to go. They had come so *close* . . .

He hadn't come to care about her, had he? He knew that some kidnapping victims came to identify with their kidnappers. No, he decided. It was as he had told her in the *Aurelian* transit module: he wanted her dead, but not here, not like this. First, he wanted her to succeed. Being around her hadn't made him stop hating her, but it had made him hate the Worldbreakers more.

He left the medbay and headed to the bridge.

The screen was trained on the *Aurelian*. The *Remembrance* had drifted slightly from its position sunward of the Earth ship, and was now casting only the edge of its shadow over the *Aurelian's* nose. The *Aurelian's* surface still shone in the reflected sunlight, but its dust-streaked rotating segments had visibly slowed since he had first seen them. The sensor readings on Jonas's console indicated that the *Aurelian's* power plant was steadily shutting down. The transponder signal had stopped.

He sat back in his chair. Above him, Keldra's cloud mural on the ceiling looked crude, and very close, but reassuringly real.

An hour into Keldra's surgery, Jonas noticed on his console that a dozen servitors had been assigned new tasks. He watched the glowing icons that marked their positions on the ship plan as they left the servitor barracks in the second ring and took a transit module down to the cargo bay.

Eight of the servitors swarmed around the *Seagull*, uncoupling it from the internal cargo bay airlock and moving it towards its normal position at the back of the bay. At the same time, four servitors opened up the *Seagull's* cargo doors and slowly took out something. The cargo bay's sensors couldn't identify what they were handling, but he knew that it was the Worldbreaker Sphere.

He watched the procedure with interest. Keldra would have to be directing the servitors' activity through her implant, which meant she was conscious, although the medbay readings still indicated she was in surgery.

He had expected her to secure the Sphere in the airless microgravity cargo bay, but instead, the servitors pushed it through the cargo bay airlock and into a transit module. Very slowly, the transit module hauled its massive cargo up the spine and then out to the second ring. The four servitors emerged and made their way around the ring's orbital corridor, moving slowly, as if carrying the Sphere between them. They went past the servitor barracks and prison cells, and into what was marked on the plan as an empty store room. A couple more servitors were moving there from a different room, perhaps carrying tools. Jonas guessed that Keldra was having the servitors install the Sphere securely.

She was still in surgery. She must be at least partially conscious if she was directing the servitors, but Jonas didn't know if they'd be aware of him if he went down there. It was probably best for him to wait until they were finished.

Half an hour after the servitors finished moving the Sphere, Jonas felt a distant rumble and a change in acceleration. The bridge read-outs indicated that the manoeuvring thrusters were firing, re-orienting the ship for a course change. The reaction drive fired gently, pushing the *Remembrance* away from the *Aurelian*. Jonas watched the Earth ship recede starward. Its rotating sections were almost stationary now, and its power plant was dead.

Once the reaction drive had put a few kilometres between the two ships, the *Remembrance* swung around again, and the sail unfurled, the golden plane folding delicately out from the bud like an enormous insect wing. The sail was tacking against orbit, angled diagonally against the ship's direction of travel so that the light pressure would reduce its orbital velocity and it would spiral towards the sun.

Jonas watched as the *Aurelian* dwindled to a silver point.

Another half hour later, the ship's course stabilized, and the servitors shuffled back to their barracks. Jonas guessed that Keldra was unconscious. What little he could understand of the medbay read-outs indicated that she was stable, but the surgery could take hours yet.

He ate an instant meal from the kitchen, and then went back to his cabin to rest. The *Remembrance's* automatic day-night cycle indicated that it was evening, but the days on the *Iron Dragon*, followed by the hours on the *Aurelian*, had disrupted his sense of time. It was only when he sat down on the bed in his darkened cabin that he realized how tired he was.

He woke eight hours later, when the corridor lights were fading up in simulated morning.

On the bridge, the medbay read-outs indicated that the surgery room was empty. The screen was trained starward, but he could no longer make out the dot of the *Aurelian* against the haze of Belt Three. He could guess where Keldra would be. He took the transit module down to the second ring.

He didn't realize until he reached it that he had never been in this storeroom before. Keldra had shown him the corridor during her initial tour, and this storeroom had been the one she had forbidden him to enter. After that, the door had always been locked, and none of the memories from Olzan's implant had happened to show the inside of the room.

Now the storeroom's door stood open. A servitor in the corridor outside watched him as he approached, but made no effort to stop him from entering.

The storeroom was a garden. Long soil-filled troughs stood in rows across the room, drooping with leaves. Translucent panels in the ceiling let in sunlight, day and night following one another rapidly as the ring rotated, sending shadows raking across the room. There was a splashing sound as water dripped into suspended irrigation channels. A wet, earthy smell managed to overpower the oily scents of the ship.

This was a vegetable garden; row after row of the carrots and potatoes that Jonas had occasionally seen Keldra add to her diet of instant meals, but it looked as if she had also made an effort to make some parts of the garden ornamental. There were two long beds filled with flowers, half a dozen wildly varying colours jostling against one another with no aesthetic restraint. The way the water fell from a high pipe into a pool as it fed the irrigation channels could have been an attempt at a water feature. The ceiling in between the sun panels was painted blue and scattered with Keldra's signature swirling clouds, and in this room she had extended the pattern to the upper part of the walls, depicting hundreds of little fluffy clouds processing away into the distance.

In the middle of the room it looked as though the servitors had moved the trays aside and set up a simple dais made from spare floor gratings. On top of the dais, in the middle of a cage of metal supports that wrapped around it like the fingers of a grasping hand, was the Worldbreaker Sphere. Four servitors, in dishevelled overalls, were tinkering with the cage, running a fine mesh of cables in between the fingers and across the surface of the Sphere.

Keldra sat next to the dais, cocooned in a bulky motor-ized wheelchair that looked like it had been cobbled together from spare ship parts. She was dressed in a stained white medical robe, but her feet were bare and hung awkwardly just off the wheelchair's footrests. Her chair was parked against the side of the dais, and her hand rested lightly on the surface of the Sphere, only occasionally lifting to allow the servitors to work.

She looked at Jonas as he entered. Her expression was hard to read. She looked tired, and her aggression was gone, as if the operation had drained the vitality out of her body. There was a resentful sadness on her face, but she also looked more at peace than he had ever seen her before.

'How are you doing?' he asked.

She shrugged, as if she was trying to convince herself she didn't care. 'I told you not to come in here,' she said. Her voice was flat, not hostile.

'That was a long time ago,' he said.

'Yes, it was.'

He gestured to the Worldbreaker Sphere. 'It doesn't go with the rest of the plants,' he said. 'I don't think it'll grow.'

An evil hint of a smile curled up the edge of her mouth. He smiled in sympathy. Keldra's outward aggression might be gone, but it looked as though her central knot of determination was still there.

'The other plants will crowd it out,' she said. 'They were here first.' She stroked the surface of the Sphere, tracing one of the grooves that covered its surface, and her eyes wandered to the painted clouds on the walls. 'It doesn't need to be here long, anyway,' she said more softly. 'Just until it blooms.'

Jonas moved up to Keldra's side. Her chair was tall enough to bring her face almost level with his. He noticed a set of wires breaking through the skin at the back of her neck and running into the mechanism of the chair.

'I'm paralysed from the waist down,' she said, matter-of-factly. 'The laser severed my spine.'

'That could be fixed,' he said.

'In a city hospital, maybe. Not in my medbay.'

'Are you in pain?'

Keldra winced for a moment, as if remembering. 'Not anymore,' she said. 'It's uncomfortable, though.'

'Good. I'm glad.'

She made a movement that was something between a nod and a shrug. 'I thought you would be.'

With her hand still stroking the Sphere, she looked around at her garden, with its plants in untidy rows and its painted

250

cloudy skies. Jonas wondered if she was comparing her garden to the one on the *Aurelian*.

'It was a brave thing you did, though,' he said. 'Putting yourself in front of the beam.'

'It was stupid,' she said dismissively. 'I should have found a way without getting injured. Anyway, you're the one who got us out. I guess I should thank you.' She gave him a piercing look, as if trying to read him. Her expression contained a little gratitude, or admiration, but there was something else there: disdain, perhaps, or suspicion. 'You talked the *Aurelian* into shutting down.'

'I just wanted it to let us go. I didn't mean it to shut down.'

She looked away. 'I don't know what you said. I wasn't fully conscious at the time.'

Jonas sat down on the edge of the dais next to her. She didn't look at him. Her eyes wandered from the mechanical chair beneath her arms, to the surface of the Sphere where her hand still rested on it, and then to the cloudscape on the ceiling.

'I'm going all the way down,' Keldra said after a few moments.

'What do you mean?'

'You know what I mean,' she said. 'We'll be passing through Belt Two soon. I'll stop at one of the free cities, probably Tannhäuser, to sell everything I don't need and make modifications to the ship. That's your chance to get off.'

He didn't say anything. He looked up at the Sphere, still seeming to radiate power even though its faint internal glow was invisible beneath the bright sub-Belt Three sunlight. They had the Sphere now, and he knew what she intended to do with it. The prospect of getting off at Belt Two should have excited him, but when he thought about the idea he felt empty.

251

Keldra looked at him for a few seconds, as if probing for a reaction, then gave up. 'I'm tired,' she said. 'I want to be alone now.'

Jonas left.

Chapter Nineteen

The ellipse of light from Jonas's headset lamp trembled across arcane complexities of machinery as he pushed himself further into the crawl space. The clutter of grey metal boxes reminded him of a shanty town seen from above, as if he was a giant crawling through the middle of a city habitat chamber. There was a cloying scent of oil and ozone, and every time he touched a surface, his hand came away with a thin coating of graphite that had leaked from an ancient air scrubber.

Keldra's voice cracked in his earpiece. 'Can you see it yet?'

'Not yet.'

'It should be right in front of you.'

Jonas squeezed further in, continuing to scan for the component she had described to him. He was in a barely human-sized space above the orbital corridor of the first ring, in the innards of the ring's habitat system.

'Useless bloody administrator,' Keldra grumbled. 'It's always the engineers who do the work.'

It had taken Jonas finding Keldra sprawled on the corridor floor, angrily guiding a servitor to help her back into her wheelchair, before she had agreed to let him help with the modifications to the cooling system. Now she would supervise him, which meant sitting in the corridor nearby, guiding him through his headset, and shouting abuse when he was too slow for her liking.

The *Remembrance of Clouds* had been built to function in Belt Three; now that they were taking it closer to the sun they would have to modify it to cope with the increased level of solar radiation. A part of this meant overloading the cooling subsystem, essentially refrigerating the inhabited areas of the ship, pumping the heat into the external heat-radiation fins that Keldra was also expanding.

Jonas spotted a likely-looking component. He squeezed close to it, resisting the urge to sneeze as the graphite dust he disturbed got up his nose, and read the serial number out to Keldra.

'That's the one.'

He managed to get his fingers around the component and slowly teased it away from the larger system. He stuffed it into his bag and brought out the bulkier, modified replacement that Keldra had constructed in her lab.

'Fuck,' she said suddenly.

'What?' he asked. 'Was that the wrong one?'

Her pilot implant allowed her to sense changes to the ship's systems, registering them as damage, so she would know if Jonas had removed the wrong component.

'Not you. There's a ship on an intercept course,' she said. 'Get out of there and get to the bridge.'

He heard her wheelchair trundle away along the corridor. He pushed the replacement module into place then crawled back out of the hab system and dropped down to the floor.

He reached the bridge as Keldra was rolling up into her control nest. With help from him and a gang of servitors, she had removed the battered captain's chair at the heart of the nest and repositioned some of the control boards around the space it had left. Her wheelchair now fitted snugly into the nest, putting all the controls within reach of her hands. Docked with the nest, surrounded on all sides by electronics and with cables snaking from the back of her neck and into the mass, she looked more than ever as if she was built into the ship.

The sun was large on the bridge screen, dimmed by automatic filters. Belt Two was close enough now for it to be visible, like a faint pencil line traced across the bronze disc. In response to Keldra's silent command the view swung around starward, where Belt Three had receded to a barely visible silver thread. She zoomed the view and a blue-white reaction drive flame resolved in the middle of the screen, flaring counter-orbit. At its apex was a dark grey cylinder.

She slammed her palm on her control panel and scowled at Jonas. 'I thought you said you'd got rid of them.'

He stared at the image, puzzled. 'I thought I had.'

She brought up a belt chart on the bridge screen and traced the *Iron Dragon's* likely course backwards. It looked as if it had passed close to the *Aurelian*, close enough to come inside the Earth ship's weapon range, if its weapons had still been active. There was another ship, whose course had passed close to the *Dragon's*, and which was now climbing back up to Belt Three. It was built like a cargo hauler, but it bore the Solar Authority logo.

Keldra stared at the screen, lips pursed. Her right hand was slowly clenching into a fist. Jonas expected her to turn and rant at him for ruining everything, maybe even physically attack him. Instead, she said quietly, 'We can still beat him.'

'How?'

'This is a sail clipper,' she said. 'The closer we get to the sun, the more acceleration we have to work with.'

'You think that'll be enough?'

'Just about.' She sounded uncertain. 'We'll have to go straight through Belt Two. I'd been hoping to stop at Tannhäuser, buy new components, and complete the modifications, but I'll have to do without.' She looked at him, probingly. 'I can still let you off. You can take a shuttle as we pass through, make your own way to Tannhäuser.'

'You'd still have to slow in order to do that, or my shuttle would just fall out of the belt. Could you do that without the *Dragon* catching you?'

'Maybe. I don't know. It'll be tight.'

'You won't be able to make the rest of the modifications without my help, anyway. You won't make it all the way down.'

'I'll find a way.' She was trying to sound confident, but Jonas knew she was unsure. She had never been much of a liar.

A few hours later, Jonas got back to his cabin and noticed a quiet chime sounding from his desk where he'd stashed Lance Cooper's Earth-tech business card. It lit up to his thumbprint and a message scrolled across its face.

'ATTENTION JONAS '77-ATHENS. SITUATION HAS CHANGED RE SOLAR AUTHORITY AND YOU. MY ORDERS NOW TO CAPTURE WORLDBREAKER ARTEFACT. IF YOU DELIVER IT, IN RETURN I CAN GRANT AMNESTY AND SPECIAL TRUE-BORN STATUS. PLEASE ACKNOWLEDGE.'

Jonas stared at the message for a minute or two. The Solar Authority would know about the Sphere, and he could easily believe that they'd want to get their hands on it. For the Solar Authority to grant special true-born status to a tank-born was unusual but not unheard of, and it was certainly possible that Cooper's offer was genuine.

He began to compose a reply, then cleared it, pocketed the business card, and headed for the bridge.

The bridge was empty. Keldra was probably in her garden. She had taken to spending much of her time there when she wasn't working on the ship. She would sit next to the Worldbreaker Sphere for hours, sometimes resting her hand on its surface or casually stroking its grooves, staring at the white and blue swirls of her painted sky, surrounded by the scents of the plants and the trickle of the irrigation channels. On a few occasions, Jonas had found her sleeping in that room.

Of course, Keldra's awareness wasn't confined to a single room. Now more than ever it was the ship that was her real body, the crippled form in the chair merely its nucleus. She would be aware of everything he did, and even if she was asleep now, her pilot implant would alert her to any unusual activity when she woke. He decided he didn't care.

He trained the *Remembrance's* communications laser on the *Iron Dragon* and transmitted a handshake signal. After a few moments the response appeared on the bridge screen. Captain Cooper appeared at once this time, not making Jonas go through a communications officer first. He looked a little surprised to get Jonas's reply through the communications laser rather than the secure business card, but he didn't mention it.

'Jonas '77-Athens,' he said.

'Captain Cooper,' Jonas replied. 'You gave me your word you wouldn't follow us.'

'I *offered* you my word,' Cooper said. 'You refused it. I vented my fuel as you asked, and there our agreement ended. Then I called for a fuel tanker to be launched by rail gun from the nearest Authority fortress. Your lack of trust has led to this.'

Jonas rolled his eyes. Cooper seemed genuinely smug about following the letter of his code of honour. 'What is it you want?' he asked.

'I want the Worldbreaker artefact, and anything else you took from the *Aurelian*,' Cooper said. 'Since the Solar Authority is descended from the Earth Authority, anything you found in the *Aurelian* rightfully belongs to us.'

Coming from anyone else, Jonas would have taken that argument for a joke, but Cooper might really believe it had some moral weight. 'Why are you trying to make a deal?' he asked. 'Last time we met, you thought I was the worst kind of murderer.'

Cooper's mouth curled as if he was tasting something bitter. 'I have . . . reconsidered what I learned from the memory probe,' he said. 'I believe now that what I saw was a true representation of events. Your relationship with Gabriel Reinhardt was inappropriate, and your assuming his identity was still a crime, according to the Solar Authority's treaties, but I do not believe that you murdered him.'

Jonas raised an eyebrow. 'Was that an apology?'

'It was the closest you're going to get to one, tank-born. I told you because I want you to know that my offer is genuine. If you hand over the Worldbreaker artefact, I will call off all pursuit. I have arranged for the Solar Authority to grant you special dispensation to live as a true-born. You have been entered into the Authority databases as Jonas Reinhardt, the only surviving member of an offshoot of the Reinhardt family. As Jonas Reinhardt, you have five million credits at the Gemini Distributed Bank. Providing you do not attempt to contaminate the gene-pool by fathering children, you will be left to live as you please. It has been done before, more often than you probably realize.'

Jonas Reinhardt. The name made him feel dizzy, as if momentarily in free fall. 'How do I know you'll do it?' he asked.

'It is already done,' Cooper said. 'The Solar Authority true-born database is freely available. You can direct your communications laser at any Authority fortress and query it.'

'What about Keldra?'

'I was never interested in Keldra. She's free to go. She can be a true-born too, if you make sure she can pass as one.'

'Doesn't Wendell Glass still want me taken in?'

'Wendell Taylor Glass is not a client of the Solar Authority. After examining both cases, I recommended that the Solar Authority not aid him.' Cooper smiled thinly. 'He has you to thank for that, as a matter of fact. Some things you said in Wendell Glass's vault prompted me to do more checking into his family's history, and I learned that he once very nearly allowed his daughter to marry a tank-born freighter captain. That wouldn't in itself disqualify him, but his keeping it from me cannot be forgiven.'

Jonas felt a pang of sympathy for Emily Taylor Glass. 'Do you think Glass will try to fight Gouveia without your help?' he asked.

'I doubt it. He's still posturing, but my agents report that he's also preparing his ringship to leave Santesteban. He will most likely surrender the city to Gouveia before the situation turns violent, and relocate with his family to a neutral city. He won't have the resources to hunt you down.'

'Is that why you're being so generous?' Jonas asked. 'Because I tipped you off to the Glass family history?'

'Partly, but also because the Solar Authority is in your debt,' Cooper said. 'You've helped us to reclaim a treasure trove of Planetary Age artefacts. Auctioning them off to collectors will help to fund our peacekeeping work for decades to come. Think of my offer as a finder's fee.'

'And if I refuse?'

'Then the boarding party will have orders to shoot to kill. As I said, the Authority is no longer interested in bringing you in for trial.'

'You've got to catch us first.'

Cooper gave a patronizing look, but Jonas could tell it was a bluff. 'You're really going to try to outrun me?'

'Credit me with some intelligence, Captain. This is a sail clipper and we're heading sunward.'

'The *Iron Dragon* can wait in a higher orbit and catch you when you come back up.'

'Who said anything about coming back?'

Cooper paused. When he spoke again his voice was softer, as if he was no longer speaking true-born to tank-born or Solar Authority officer to outlaw, but human being to human being. 'Why are you doing this, Jonas? Wendell Glass has the sense not to fight a battle he can't win.'

'It's not about winning,' he said, then stopped abruptly, surprised at the passion in his own voice. He had sounded just like Keldra when he had said it. He realized that his fist was clenched.

Lance Cooper was looking at him with a probing, expectant expression, head slightly to one side.

He stabbed the control to end the transmission and then stalked out of the bridge.

Jonas walked briskly along the first ring's orbital corridor, eyes down, with no plan where he was going. It was the ship's night-time, and the corridor lights were dimmed. He paused briefly at his cabin but didn't touch the door. There was nothing for him in there.

He strapped himself into a transit module and went up to the ship's spine. He found himself trembling as the weight drained from his body. He was angry, and he didn't know why. Not angry at Cooper, or Keldra; not angry at anything, but angry.

He found himself climbing along the tunnel to the observation blister. Keldra'd had her servitors fix patches over the bullet holes in the inner hull, and weld up the arc that she'd cut in the blister's door. Jonas closed the door behind him and then rested against it, feeling the ship's acceleration push him back. He breathed in and out deeply, forcing himself to relax.

The mirrored golden plane of the sail filled half the universe. He could see the *Remembrance of Clouds* reflected in it, as if floating in a golden haze. The sail was at an angle to the ship, so the whole length of the ship was visible in reflection. The two grav-rings, whirling past one another, one with the great patch where the debris from Konrad's Hope had punched through; the wide featureless tube that was the mouth of Keldra's nuke-launcher; the spindly shapes of the smaller missile turrets scattered across the spine and cargo bay. The Earth mural, worn and peeling; flecks of ship-hull grey visible through the swirls of blue and white and green.

The image was slightly uneven, as if seen through sculpted glass. He hadn't noticed it before. A sail ought to be perfectly flat, but the *Remembrance's* had become crinkled after being furled and unfurled so many times without proper maintenance. It was an old ship, a tired ship, kept running by and for Keldra's obsession long after it should have been retired. If Cooper captured it, there was no doubt it would be unceremoniously scrapped.

261

Jonas had never been much troubled by sentiment for inanimate objects, but the thought of the *Remembrance* being stripped for parts and its skeleton rotting in some city's junkyard orbit filled him with an uncomfortable feeling that he couldn't shake. It didn't matter now that the *Remembrance* had destroyed the *Coriolis Dancer* and God knew how many other ships. It was a good ship and it deserved a good end.

He looked to the side, taking in the rest of the sky. The sun was huge, glaring opposite its mirror image in the sail. Without the bridge screen's image processing, it was too bright for Jonas to look at, and he couldn't make out the rocks of Belt Two. In the opposite direction he could see the stars, the sprinkling of tiny lights cut into segments by two intersecting lines, the wire-thin sparkle of the ecliptic, and the broad, hazy band of the Milky Way.

The anger had drained out of him now. He had a feeling of vertigo, as if clinging to the outside of a rotating gravring. More than ever before, away from the close-crowded rocks of the belts, he felt the scale of the universe. He, the ship, the vastness of the sail, the blinding sun, the inhabited belts, were all a point of light in a vast, borderless three-dimensional space in which hung billions of similar points. He imagined the Worldbreakers sweeping across the galaxy, spreading from star to star, multiplying, branching, stripping each point bare of worlds and life. The destruction of Sol's inhabited belts was just one footnote in the story of the Worldbreakers' mindless advance across the universe.

For a second, Jonas couldn't understand how he had ever been sympathetic towards Gabriel's religion. Gabriel had gone to his death believing that the Worldbreakers were agents of his God and that their gravity beams were gateways to Paradise. The Worldbreakers hadn't known or cared about those beliefs. He might as well have dashed his brains out against a city wall. The matter that had made up Gabriel's body had become a tiny part of that Worldbreaker's cargo, and by now it would have been incorporated into one of their constructions, most likely another Worldbreaker destined to pillage another star system. All Gabriel had achieved had been to infinitesimally speed up the Worldbreakers' conquest of the galaxy.

Gabriel wouldn't have wanted that. If he had known the truth about the Worldbreakers, he wouldn't have wanted to become part of the matter that made them. Involuntarily, Jonas felt his teeth clench, his lip curl up. He wanted to save Gabriel from that fate.

He wondered if Keldra'd had a similar experience to this at the start of her crusade. Alone on the ship after she had killed Olzan and his crew, perhaps she had come up here and floated in the observation blister, conscious of herself as a tiny point in the expanse of stars. She had always thought that the Worldbreakers were machines, not gods or angels, even if she had believed that they had been deliberately targeted at humanity. He imagined her consumed with anger, and with nothing to focus it on, apart from the Worldbreakers. Everything wrong with her life, with the world she found herself in, could be traced back to them. Perhaps it was here that she had vowed to take her revenge, and begun the decade-long personal crusade that had led them to this point.

He could feel a nobility in Keldra's anger now. It didn't matter that the Worldbreakers were mindless and would never know that they were destroyed; it didn't matter that humanity's war was lost and that fighting them could do no good. Faced with certain destruction it was nobler to go down fighting than to roll over and die.

Cooper's offer seemed genuine, one sensible part of his mind tried to say. He could live as a true-born again. He could be Jonas Reinhardt . . .

He turned the image over in his mind, but it failed to conjure any emotion except disgust. To accept Cooper's offer would be to run away. He'd been running for the last six years: running from tank-born life and hiding behind a false identity, running from the promise he had made to Gabriel on what might as well have been his deathbed. After the *Iron Dragon*, he had promised himself he would stop running. He wasn't about to start again now.

There was no other option. If Keldra slowed to let him off at Belt Two, the *Iron Dragon* would probably catch her. Even if it didn't, she was weaker than she realized. She needed him to maintain the ship. To run would be to condemn her grand plan to failure.

No. This time he would fight. This would be his great achievement, the one he had promised to Gabriel, the only great achievement left for the defeated human race. This would be his revenge on the Worldbreakers for what they had done to Gabriel, just as it would be Keldra's revenge for what they had done to her clouds.

He took one more look at the stars and then spun himself around and climbed back towards the transit module.

Keldra was on the bridge when he got back, her chair docked with the control nest. The *Iron Dragon* was flaring in the middle of the screen, but Keldra was looking down at one of the displays angled around her. She scowled at Jonas as he entered. 'You contacted Lance Cooper,' she said.

'That's right,' he said. 'I thought I'd try to get rid of him.'

'He's still there.'

'It was worth a try.'

'So, are you taking him up on his offer? I've seen the log.'

He ignored the question and sat down at his terminal. 'You can't let me off at Belt Two,' he said.

'What?

'We can outrun the *Dragon*, but only if we keep straight on. Even changing course to pass close to a city could slow us down too much.'

'Fuck you, Jonas. I'm giving you a chance to live.'

'Besides, you might need me on the way down,' he continued. 'It's too risky to try with just one person.'

Keldra glared at him, but there was a look of calculating acceptance there, a tiny hint of a nod. 'Whatever you like.'

Jonas's terminal showed that the communications laser was still tracking the *Iron Dragon*. He began another call. After a moment, Captain Cooper's face appeared on the screen.

Cooper glanced at Keldra, then ignored her and turned to Jonas.

'Jonas. I assume you've taken time to consider my offer?' His tone was calm, almost casual, as if he didn't much care what his answer was.

Jonas cleared his throat. He had been going to give a simple 'no', but another thought popped unbidden into his mind. 'Captain Cooper, I wonder if I could ask you for a small favour. This is entirely separate from your offer.'

Cooper looked puzzled. 'I'm listening.'

'If I were to use the *Remembrance's* missile launcher to launch a small item into a higher orbit, with a cargo transponder attached, could your ship pick it up?'

Keldra glared at him and began to hiss something, but he waved her into silence.

'It's possible,' Cooper said. 'What is this item?'

'An admin implant. I'd like you to have it delivered to Emily Taylor Glass. It contains memories of her relationship with her tank-born freighter captain. I think she should have it.'

Keldra shrugged and settled back in her chair. Cooper paused, then nodded. 'As much as I disapprove of Ms Glass's choice of lover, I am not heartless. Perhaps the memories in the implant will help her to grieve and then move on. I take it the fact that you aren't delivering the item yourself means you've decided to decline my offer.'

'That's correct,' Jonas said.

Cooper's professional mask didn't slip. 'Very well. The offer stands. Your true-born status is already in the Authority's records for you to claim, if you change your mind.'

'Thank you, but my mind is made up.'

Cooper's flat expression broke, a little, but to Jonas's surprise it wasn't to put on some show of anger or incredulity. It looked almost as though he was relieved. 'I think I understand,' he said. 'You will not be pursued. Godspeed, Jonas Reinhardt.'

Chapter Twenty

The *Remembrance of Clouds* passed through Belt Two without slowing. Jonas listened on the bridge to the cities' comms chatter: traffic control, entertainment broadcasts, banal un-encoded ship-to-ship banter. Updates on Worldbreaker movements, volumes to avoid. Halfway around the belt, a city Jonas had never heard of was in a Worldbreaker Red Zone and was being evacuated.

Keldra focused the bridge screen on Tannhäuser. The city was a dark shape against the bronze wall of the sun, until the *Remembrance* moved past it and it seemed to slide out in front of the stars. Tannhäuser was a new city, founded only a couple of decades before as part of the sunward sweep of colonization from Belt Five. The spherical rock was nearly pristine, a stubby docking spindle with a blinking red traffic light the only external sign of habitation.

The city hailed them as they approached. A traffic control girl with a thick Belt Two accent asked if they'd be docking, and pointed out they were off course. She sounded puzzled when Jonas told her they were just passing through the belt. Almost no one passed through a belt without stopping, and almost no one ever went sunward of Belt Two.

Tannhäuser slid faster across the star field as the *Remembrance* passed it, showing a crescent, and then swelling into a fully illuminated disc. Keldra let the view zoom out, and Jonas watched the rocks of Belt Two form a sparkling band that shrank away starward.

An expanse of blue stretched, glistening, above Jonas. He ran his eyes across it, planning his next action, then slowly raised the brush and painted a great sweep of white. He twisted his hand, adding curls and feathering, letting the white paint mingle with the still-wet blue. The smell of paint filled his nostrils. Balanced on the stepladder, he felt as if he was floating in a painted sky.

It had been his idea to help Keldra continue her ceiling cloud mural around the first ring's central corridor. She had added to it, section by section, over the years, as the mood had struck her, the different periods of work visible in the layers of fade that began outside her quarters and stretched two-thirds of the way around the ring. Confined to the wheelchair, she couldn't continue the mural, and servitors couldn't do the job adequately, either: a servitor painting programme could cover areas in flat colour or mechanically reproduce designs, but it couldn't provide the free-willed human touch that gave Keldra's designs their character. Jonas had suggested that he finish the murals for her. It was somehow important for him that the mural be complete before the *Remembrance* reached its destination.

He moved the brush until its paint was gone, using the last uneven bit of paint to create a feathered area of blue-white, and then stepped down from the ladder.

'How's that?'

Keldra whirred forward in her chair and peered up at the painted clouds.

'It's good,' she said.

He looked back across his work, comparing it with her older painted skies. Even if he imagined his section fading, it would be easy to see the join. His clouds were large, swirling, filled with big curves where he had swung his arm around. Hers were smaller, with short jagged lines visible among the curves.

'It doesn't quite match your style,' he said, disappointed.

'Doesn't have to,' Keldra said. 'You've got your own style. Be yourself for a change.'

'I'd like it to match,' he said. 'I want the whole thing to be a complete work.'

She made a non-committal grunting sound, but she wasn't listening. Her eyes were closed and her face was screwed up in concentration.

'Keldra? What is it?'

'Shut up.' She twitched slightly in the chair, listening to the ship-sensations from her implant. 'There's a problem.'

'Another ship?'

'It's our sail. There's a tear. A micro-rock must have punched through it as we passed through Belt Two.'

She spun around and headed for the transit module, the chair carrying her surprisingly quickly.

Jonas jogged after her. 'I thought sails were self-repairing.'

'They are. Ours was calibrated for Belt Three. The light pressure is tearing it apart faster than it can repair itself. Help me into a suit.'

They had reached the transit hub, and Keldra was opening a vacuum suit locker. Jonas took the suit she handed him and unzipped it, then knelt down and carefully lifted her limp legs into the suit's. He helped her out of the chair and held her standing as she pulled the rest of the suit around herself.

269

'You'll be all right?' he asked.

'Legs don't matter in microgravity. Just get me into the module.'

'I'll come with you,' he said as he strapped her in.

'No!' she snapped. 'You're not an engineer. I've got a gang of servitors meeting me in the spine. I don't need you hovering over my shoulder being useless. You can monitor from the bridge, if you like.'

He passed her the suit helmet; she snatched it out of his hands. 'All right,' he said.

'All right.'

The doors closed, and Jonas felt the transit module rumble away upwards.

He went to the bridge and brought up a damage control view on his console. There was nothing unusual, at first glance, just the normal dotted orange warnings from the ageing systems, and nagging messages about the cooling systems working overcapacity. Then he spotted the red icon at the ship's nose indicating a problem with the sail. For details of sail problems he had to flip to another scale, orders of magnitude larger than the normal one: the kilometres-wide sail dwarfed the body of the ship. He could see the tear now; a red dot with a warning label beside it. As he watched, the dot expanded into a short line.

He called Keldra's suit. 'Can you hear me?'

'I can hear you.'

'Looks like the tear's widening,' he told her.

'I know. I'm on a sail runner. I'm heading there as fast as I can. I'll talk to you when I can see the damage.' The circuit closed.

Jonas watched his console. He couldn't see Keldra or her servitors on any of the displays; he would have to wait until she told him she was at the site of the tear. It was expanding, stretching out into a long line and widening like a mouth. Half the sail was blinking orange as the nanomaterial shared the pressure from the tear. It wasn't yet big enough to cause a change in the ship's acceleration, but if left unchecked, it couldn't last long.

'I can see it,' Keldra said. She sounded out of breath, as if she'd been exerting herself, but she didn't sound as tense as Jonas felt.

'Can you fix it?'

There was silence from her channel. After a few moments, his console buzzed for attention. A second red dot had appeared on the sail, near the first tear. It began to spread, even more quickly than the first.

'Keldra! There's another tear!'

'That's me,' Keldra said. 'I can't close the tear. I'm going to have to cut out the whole section.'

Jonas watched the damage control screen. Half a dozen new dots appeared, spaced around the original tear: Keldra's servitors, Jonas assumed, making their own incisions in the sail. They began to move in curved paths, tracing segments of a circle.

'You're cutting away an awful lot,' he said.

'I can cut it so that it doesn't stress the rest of the material,' she said. 'It'll be fine.'

'Yes, but do you need to cut away that much? It's more than a square kilometre.'

'Yes! I have to take out the stressed material, not just the tear itself. This isn't the time to ask layman questions.'

'I was a ship captain for six years, Keldra. I'm not totally clueless.'

'Shut up and let me work!'

Jonas watched as Keldra and her servitors completed their arcs and joined up, forming a perfect circle. As soon as the last connection was made, the tear vanished: instead, the entire circular area flashed red and buzzed urgently. He turned off the warning. The orange stress from the rest of the sail was gone, but there was a noticeable effect on the ship's acceleration. A smaller sail area meant less thrust.

The communications circuit came back to life. 'Did you see that?'

'It's looking stable,' he confirmed.

'For now. It's under strain just from being this close to the sun, though. It'll give out at some point. Right, I'm on my way back.' Keldra's hostility was gone, at least for now. She sounded elated.

'You managed okay?' Jonas asked.

'Like I said: you don't need legs in microgravity.'

'You could stay in microgravity most of the time, if you wanted to,' he pointed out. 'I could help you set up quarters in the spine, or we could even spin down one of the rings.'

She laughed. 'Nice thought, but no. The spine's hab systems aren't meant for long stays, and spinning down a ring isn't as simple as you might think. Besides . . . ' She trailed off, as if embarrassed.

'What?' Jonas prompted.

'*Earth* had gravity.'

He smiled. 'Yeah. I'll see you inside.'

The old ship creaked and groaned, its structure straining against the bombardment of solar radiation. Its course chart showed it curving more and more sharply sunward as light bombarded the sail.

The sun grew larger day by day, half-filling the bridge screen now without any magnification. It first became too bright to look at from the observation blister without welding goggles, and then too bright for someone to enter the blister at all without a radiation-proofed suit and tinted helmet.

Jonas continued to help Keldra with her modifications to the hab systems. He could hear the cooling fans whirring in the corridors, but even so, the air felt warm and stuffy.

Halfway between Belts Two and One, the heat radiation fins became overloaded, spewing red warning messages all over the bridge consoles. Keldra had anticipated it, and a gang of servitors were working on a new heat-radiation system in the cargo bay. The system channelled excess heat into one of the cargo containers that filled the bay, some of them still containing mining equipment she had stolen from the *Coriolis Dancer*, and would now never have a chance to sell. Heat was pumped into each container until it glowed red hot, then the servitors pushed the container out of the cargo bay doors. The container tumbled away starward on the bridge screen, taking the excess heat with it and cooling the ship overall.

Keldra jettisoned the *Seagull* along with the first cargo container, with an orbit-keeping and collision-avoidance programme loaded into its thruster controls. Someone should pick it up eventually, and it would most likely end up in a true-born's collection. There was no need for it to be destroyed along with the *Remembrance*.

Belt One was almost uninhabited. The only human settlements here were a few specialist mining outposts, almost entirely automated, powered by big solar energy collectors. No comms chatter greeted the *Remembrance of Clouds* as it passed through, only a few lonely navigation beacons. Not many true-born entrepreneurs set up operations down here. Power was cheap, but the costs of transportation back to the inhabited belts could negate that, and besides, most people didn't feel comfortable being so close to Worldbreaker territory.

The *Remembrance* passed through without slowing. The rocks of Belt One shrank away starward, blinding in the reflected light of the close sun. The sun itself was a wall of fire filling half the sky: the bridge screen's filters made it red, and patterns became visible on its surface, as if it was becoming old and cracked. Great areas of hotter gas moved across its face, churning and swirling, combining and breaking apart. Here at the heart of the solar system Keldra had found the last real clouds, and they were clouds of fire.

One more belt stood out against the burning wall. Countless tiny black dots, moving slowly past one another in their different orbits, some of them clustering around large bodies, others breaking off and heading starward towards the inhabited belts. There were no rocks here, except ones that had been devoured and processed and built into something unnatural. Jonas felt a weight on his chest as he watched them, an instinctive loathing that cemented his determination to strike back. Floating at the edge of the sun's corona, this was Belt Zero, domain of the Worldbreakers.

Creaking under the bombardment of sunlight, trailing red hot cargo containers and cradling its stolen gravity bomb, the tiny tramp freighter fell towards the sun.

Chapter Twenty-One

Jonas was startled awake by a rapping on his cabin door. He pulled a robe around himself and opened it, wincing, as the corridor light hit him. 'What is it?'

Keldra tapped the side of her head, indicating her implant. 'Intercept alarm.' She turned and whirred along the corridor towards the bridge.

He trailed behind, rubbing his head to wake himself. 'Who is it? It can't be the *Iron Dragon*. Is it a Belt Two pirate?'

'It's not a ship.'

Jonas had known this was coming, but he felt a chill run through him even so. Keldra focused the screen on the Worldbreaker as soon as they entered the bridge. They were viewing its sunlit side, but even this close to the sun it looked black, little more than a hole in the stars. It was heading sunward more quickly than the *Remembrance of Clouds*, and the red cone of its predicted course swept over that of the ship. It would pass within a few thousand kilometres of them.

Jonas sat down at his console. 'Is it targeting us?' Unconsciously, he found himself whispering, as if speaking too loudly would cause the Worldbreaker to notice them.

'No,' Keldra said, but her voice was hushed as well. 'There are thousands of them at this level, heading up or down. It's not surprising we'd pass close to one.'

'But we're here, and we've got the bomb. It might know.'

'It won't. Worldbreakers never notice people.'

They watched together as it slid silently across the stars. As it passed them its facets caught the light one by one, white pentagons flashing briefly in the hole in space.

'Are you scared of dying, Jonas?' Keldra asked, quietly.

'No,' Jonas replied.

'You're fucking stupid, then. Everyone's scared of dying. Every living thing. Only the Worldbreakers aren't.'

'Are you?'

'Of course, I am. I just don't let it stop me.'

The Worldbreaker fell past them, moving on the belt chart like a bead along the string of its predicted course. The bridge screen tracked it as it became a silhouette in front of the wall of flame.

'I told you.' There was an edge of bitterness to Keldra's voice. 'Worldbreakers never notice people.' She raised her hand and mimed a gun with her fingers, aiming it at the Worldbreaker and then firing. 'Pssh!' She smiled.

Jonas smiled along with her.

'What are you doing with the shuttles?' Jonas asked as he entered the bridge. It was a few days after they had passed the Worldbreaker. Keldra had involved him in most of her modifications to the ship, but there was something going on in one of the shuttle bays that didn't fit into their overall plan.

'Mmm?' Keldra didn't look up.

'You've got servitors working in the shuttle bay on the second ring. They wouldn't let me in.'

'I'm cannibalizing them for comms equipment. Building a comms buoy. I'll release it with the next heat package.'

The bridge was filled with deep red light, like the sunset in the *Aurelian's* garden. The screen showed a much magnified view of the sun's surface, filtered down to a red haze. Black dots drifted in a line across it, moving around and past one another like insects crawling on the screen.

'Why?' Jonas asked.

'We're down in the veil now,' Keldra said. 'There's too much radiation for our signal to get out on its own.'

'I mean, what are you transmitting?'

'Everything.' She waved a hand at the crawling dots. 'We're getting a closer look at the Worldbreakers than anyone has for centuries. No one's interested in studying them, but if anyone decides to, they should have our data.'

'And you want everyone to know what you did.'

She looked at him with an expression that was half a frown, and half probing. She had been doing that a lot since they had passed Belt Two, studying his face as if trying to read him, when previously, she had never been interested in his emotional state. 'Sure, why not?' she said. 'That's what you want, too, isn't it?'

'Yes, it is.'

She raised her hands in front of her and mimed an explosion. 'They'll be able to see the explosion from Belt Three. One big flash of light, bright against the sun. The Scribers will probably think it's a message from their god. Hah.'

Jonas faked a little laugh as he sat down at his console. Peering forward, he could see that the shapes on the screen were still fuzzy. They were still too far from Belt Zero to get a clear picture through the electromagnetic interference of the veil. 'What can we see?'

'There are big clusters of activity,' Keldra said, gesturing to the screen and zooming the view. The screen focused on a black spherical mass surrounded by an elliptical swarm of smaller shapes that stretched out before and behind it on its orbit, giving the impression of an enormous eye. Most of the surrounding swarm was composed of pinprick-like dots – individual Worldbreakers, Jonas guessed – in their uncounted thousands.

'Assuming they're spread evenly around the sun, there are seven of these clusters,' Keldra said. 'Each one has the mass of a small moon.'

Or, in his terms, the mass of millions of city-sized rocks, Jonas thought to himself. The size of these constructions – the number of Worldbreakers they must each contain – was too big for him to get his head around. For now, they were just dots on a screen to him.

'That's a lot of mass,' he said. 'Would one Sphere be enough to destroy it?'

'It doesn't need to.' Keldra conjured a diagram over the image, showing the cluster's orbit and the surface of the sun as two gently curving lines. 'None of the Worldbreakers are going any further sunward than this,' she said, drawing another dotted line in between the two, only slightly closer to the sun than the cluster's orbit. 'If they could retrieve material from the sun then they wouldn't need our planets. So we don't need to *destroy* it . . . '

Jonas nodded, catching on. 'We just need to knock it over that line. Can we do it?'

'I think so,' she said. 'We have to try.'

He studied the chart on the bridge screen. In addition to the big cluster, there was another body, further out, not much further sunward than the *Remembrance*. Jonas gestured to it. 'What's that?'

Keldra brought a lidar model of the body onto the screen and set it slowly spinning. At first, it looked like a disc, but as it rotated it became clear that it was a shallow bowl. The scale markers showed it to be 1,000 kilometres across.

'I think it's a telescope,' she said. 'The dish is a reflector. It's pretty thick, but I think that's to act as a radiation shield, this close to the sun. There's probably something at the focus point picking up the reflected image, but I'm not detecting it yet.'

'We're going to pass very close to it,' Jonas observed.

'That's the other thing I'm stripping comms equipment for. I'm building a probe to launch at that focus point. I want to see what the Worldbreakers see.'

The comms buoy tumbled away with the next heat package, a spider-like splay of antennae protruding from a thick radiation-proofed shell. The steady beep of its transponder cut through the veil's interference. It would only last a few days, but that was all the time it would take for Jonas and Keldra to complete their mission.

The image of the telescope became clearer. It was a shallow bowl, 1,000 kilometres in diameter and dozens thick. As they closed with it, the *Remembrance's* lidar made out a tiny body, about the size of the *Remembrance* itself, floating at the apex of the dish. The telescope rotated slowly as it orbited the sun, remaining fixed on a particular point in space.

The *Remembrance's* structure shuddered around them as the ship entered the telescope's shadow and its metal was able to cool. They could see the surface of the dish un-magnified on the bridge screen, a wall of dark grey made of hexagonal facets, hundreds of metres across.

A couple of Worldbreakers also floated across the face of the dish. Worldbreakers were passing them regularly now, coming down from the belts fully laden or heading back up, empty. Keldra had stopped paying attention to her intercept alarm. Whichever way the Worldbreakers went they gave no sign of being aware of the *Remembrance of Clouds.*

They passed a few hundred kilometres from the body at the telescope's focus point. It was a tiny black disc, not physically attached to the telescope but keeping station using the Worldbreakers' mysterious gravity manipulation drive. There were no obvious openings, and Jonas couldn't see any way it could receive the signal reflected by the dish, but he didn't expect Worldbreaker technology to have explicable workings.

At a calculated moment during their approach, Keldra launched the probe. Jonas felt the missile launcher rumble, and caught a glimpse of an awkward lopsided cylinder shooting out in front of them, sprouting aerials and thrusters.

'Will we be able to make sense of the signal?' he asked. 'I mean, the Worldbreakers are aliens, won't it be in an alien format?'

'It's a giant reflector,' she explained. 'Any processing happens later. We're getting the raw signal.'

The probe curved towards the telescope's focus point, firing the thrusters to slow itself. It didn't come to a complete stop at the focus point, but it passed through slowly, spending a few seconds picking up the signal. It relayed its data back to the *Remembrance* in a dying burst, then shut down and drifted away on its own solar orbit.

The *Remembrance's* computer set to work processing the signal, and after a few moments, a hazy image appeared on the screen. One big central blob, surrounded by a scattering of smaller ones; Jonas thought he could see twelve, although some were hard to tell apart from the fuzz of background radiation. It was obvious that he was looking at a star with planets. He wasn't surprised, but he felt an unexpected anger welling up inside him, mixed with resentment. Anger at the thought of another system prey to the Worldbreakers' mindless hunger; resentment at the thought that *that* system, not his own, still had its planets.

'They *did* target us,' Keldra said. Her voice mirrored the anger he was feeling.

'We don't know that,' he said. 'They could just be targeting stars with planets.'

'There's more you can't see on the image,' she said. She was looking down at the screens on her nest, although she wasn't touching the controls; she controlled everything through her implant most of the time. She waved a hand in an ellipse in front of her, indicating the orbits of some of the planets. 'Based on that star's temperature, two of those planets are in the liquid-water habitable zone.'

'It could be a coincidence.'

Keldra glared at him.

'We'll never know,' he said.

She settled back in her nest, staring at the star system on the screen. 'If those planets do have life, if they have civilizations . . . we could be saving them,' she said. 'That's got to be worth something.'

Jonas nodded. The idea seemed too distant to be real, but he knew she was right. That would be a great deed. That would be enough.

They lost the sail soon after the *Remembrance* left the shadow of the telescope. Even Earth-tech had its limits, and the sail hadn't been built for the pressure of a close solar approach.

The strands of nanomaterial coupling the sail to the bud snapped, and the sail was whisked away; a blinding sheet that twisted and crumpled slowly in on itself. It curved starward shockingly quickly without the mass of the *Remembrance* holding it back. If it retained its shape, it might be carried past the orbits of the inhabited belts and out of the solar system. Keldra watched it go with a faint smile, as if bidding it a good voyage. Jonas felt a sense of finality. There went their last chance to change their minds.

Keldra fired up the reaction drive, running it above its safe maximum thrust in order to make sure the *Remembrance* curved sharply enough to meet the Worldbreaker cluster. The Worldbreakers continued to pay them no attention. The drive placed even more strain on the heat regulation system, which was already coming apart: the original heat fins were melting, and the heat-pumped cargo containers had to be launched every twenty minutes now. The system would collapse after a couple of days of this, but it didn't have to last even that long.

Jonas and Keldra pored over the images of the Worldbreaker cluster as they became clearer, relaying everything through the buoy to be broadcast to the belts. Keldra had records of previous surveys of the Worldbreakers, but no one had sent a signal from this deep for a hundred years. The Worldbreakers had been building since then.

The smallest bodies all appeared to be individual Worldbreakers, the same design as the ones that came up to the belts to devour cities and rocks. The central mass also appeared to be made up of Worldbreakers, hundreds of thousands of them, clustered closely together; a black sphere with a surface of sharp dodecahedral lumps.

'It's nearly as big as the cluster that first arrived in our system,' Keldra said, peering at the diagram on the screen from her nest. 'I wonder if they're planning to leave soon.'

'A good time to stop them,' Jonas said.

She smiled cruelly.

The other, medium-sized bodies came in a variety of shapes. There were strings of flat structures like petals trailing in front of and behind the cluster, linked by threads. Solar power collectors, most likely. These were linked by taut cables to big polyhedral structures like giant versions of Worldbreakers, with enormous constantly open mouths. Ordinary Worldbreakers spewed material into them; streamers of compacted rubble propelled by the green gravity beams. Green lights flickered from within the mouths of the large structures, and occasionally, a new Worldbreaker would emerge and float down to join the central cluster.

Jonas and Keldra kept broadcasting until they lost contact with the comms buoy. They were too deep in the veil now for their signal to get out even that far. Afterwards, they sat and watched as the Worldbreaker cluster loomed closer and closer. They were approaching it at an angle, not from directly starward, and as they came close enough they could see the deep orange filtered light glinting infernally off the millions of flat surfaces.

Eventually, Keldra help up her hand and mimed a gun once more, holding it close to her eye, as if she was aiming over it at the cluster. She fired, once, and a smile crept slowly over her face.

'All right,' she said. 'It's time.'

She detached her chair from her nest, then paused in the doorway for a last look around the bridge, taking in her nest and Jonas's console. Her eyes flickered momentarily to the place where, in Olzan's memory, she had lain, after the ship had been struck by the debris from Konrad's Hope. She looked up at the painted clouds for several seconds, her smile mixing with nostalgia, and then rolled out of the bridge.

Chapter Twenty-Two

Keldra's garden was dying. The sun panels in the ceiling were at their maximum filter setting: they would be opaque against Belt Three sunlight, but they were thin enough that the sunlight here could force its way through and fill the room with golden light. The air was hot and stuffy, and the water trickling from the irrigation system was warm. From the walls and ceiling came the muffled roar of the overloaded cooling fans. The plants were dead or dying, brown leaves wilting over the sides of the troughs.

Keldra sat in her chair next to the gravity bomb, lightly stroking the surface of the alien Sphere, just as she had the first time Jonas saw her in the garden. The Sphere was shrouded in cables that disappeared into the floor, linked to the *Remembrance's* main power system. There was a large button under a clear cover built into the base of the Sphere's cage, at the right level for Keldra's hand. She hadn't tried to plug the Sphere into her pilot implant's system; there were some things that deserved the pushing of a physical button.

'Not long now,' she said softly as Jonas entered the room. He wasn't sure if she was talking to him or to the Sphere. He sat down on the base of the Sphere's cage, next to her.

'I wasn't sure you were coming,' she said, turning to him. 'I thought I might have to get servitors to drag you.'

'I wouldn't miss this for anything,' he said.

She stared at the painted clouds as if she could see through the painting and into a vast, cloud-bedecked sky. She ran her fingers along the edge of the button's cover. 'I want you to know, you didn't talk me into this,' she said.

'What do you mean?'

'Lance Cooper talked to me, in my cell, before he released me from the *Iron Dragon*. He told me some things about you. He said you talk people into killing themselves.'

He felt his heart sink. 'That's not true,' he said.

'He said you did it to your lover, and you might try to do it to me. I wanted you to know that you didn't. This is my choice.'

'It's not true, Keldra.' There was an urgency in his voice. Suddenly, it was very important to him to set the record straight for the final moment. 'I didn't talk Gabriel into doing what he did. I tried to talk him out of it.'

She dismissed his pleading with an annoyed wave. 'I don't care whether it's true or not. He was trying to turn me against you. True-born shit, thought he could divide us. I don't care what happened with you and Gabriel. I just wanted you to know, this is my choice. I would have got here in the end. Maybe you gave me a push, but . . . '

'But I didn't know the push would lead here,' he said. What had he said to her when she'd given him the first tour of the *Remembrance*, right before she'd suddenly changed the ship's course? He'd called her an idealist, said she believed in a perfect world. A phrase he'd plucked out of Olzan's memory, a snapshot of her personality from a more innocent time. He had been blindly trying to goad her, but it looked as if he'd set her on the course that led them to this point. 'You would have got here eventually,' he said. 'You couldn't keep on blowing up individual Worldbreakers forever. Without me it might have taken longer, but this was always how your story was going to end.'

Keldra nodded. 'But you could do it, though, couldn't you?'

'Do what?'

'Talk someone into killing themselves.'

He felt uncomfortable. Where was she going with this? 'I don't know. Maybe.'

'You're a manipulative bastard,' she said admiringly. 'I bet you could talk anyone into anything if you put your mind to it.'

'I'm not that good.'

'Not anything, then. A lot. But you could do so much more than this.'

'There isn't any more than this. The human race is dead. Even if we could kill every last Worldbreaker, they've already destroyed our planets. We can eke out an existence on the rubble for a while, but on cosmic timescales, we're finished.'

Keldra's hand rested on the button cover. Jonas imagined her flipping it up, exposing the button. She would rest her hand on it, and he would put his hand on hers, and then they would both push down together and the world would turn to light . . .

'No,' she said. 'This is what I can do, but there are other things. You could do something else.'

'Could have done, maybe,' he said. 'I don't know. Why are you asking this?'

She didn't answer.

Water sloshed, steaming, onto the dead plants. Somewhere around the ring there was a change in the background whine, as one more cooling fan gave up the ghost. There was the sound of a servitor's footsteps in the corridor. A shadow passed across them, darkening the room to twilight for several seconds, and the ship groaned from the momentary change in temperature. They were getting close.

'I'm sorry, Jonas,' Keldra said suddenly. Her voice was quiet; she wasn't looking at him.

'Sorry? For what?'

'For everything. For kidnapping you, killing your people, putting that implant in your head.'

'My friends. Killing my friends.'

'Yes. For killing your friends.'

'Sorry won't bring them back.'

'I know.' She stared at her painted clouds.

'I'm not asking you to forgive me, Jonas. I'm not doing this for redemption. There's no redemption, not for me. There's just this bomb.'

'How much longer now?'

'Not long.'

He traced his own finger along the button's casing. Keldra still hadn't flipped it up. He looked up at the black sphere of the gravity bomb. From his position at its base, he could imagine it was egg-shaped rather than spherical.

He had never known what to believe about life after death. He wondered if he would still be with Keldra after they pushed the button down together. He wondered if he would see Gabriel again.

'One thing I'm not sorry for,' Keldra said. There was a faint mischievous smile on her face, as if she was about to play a practical joke and couldn't help giving it away.

'What?'

A servitor appeared in the doorway. It had a nerve gun in its hand.

'It's time for you to go,' she said.

He sprang up from the dais. 'Keldra! What are you—?'

The nerve gun blast hit him in the chest. His muscles seized up painfully, rooting him to the spot like another of Keldra's plants. The servitor advanced on him, and another entered behind it.

'I'm saving your ass, Jonas,' Keldra said. 'It only takes one to push the button.'

The servitors grabbed him by his elbows, one arm each. One of them touched him with an anti-paralyzer, and then both of them tugged him towards the door. Keldra didn't seem to be concentrating on controlling the servitors; they must be carrying out pre-programmed orders. She watched the action with an amused smile.

'Why?' he blurted as he was dragged out of the door.

'You should have run!' Keldra called after him. 'You've been trying to kill yourself since the *Iron Dragon*. So have I, but you didn't need to stay with me.'

'You needed my help!'

Jonas was in the corridor now. The servitors were half-running, holding him between them, his feet barely touching the ground. Keldra's voice followed them, relayed through the ship's internal speakers.

'Bullshit!' she called. 'I could have done this without you, and you know it. This isn't your fight. You should have run.'

'There was no way for me to get off! I had to pick between you and Cooper—'

'Sure there was, if you'd put your mind to it.'

The servitors were dragging him along the corridor past the prison cells now; the converted cargo containers where Keldra had kept her true-born hostages for ransom, where Jonas had spent his first night on the ship. There was a knot in his stomach, feeling as if it was rising; he wanted to be sick. It was the after-effects of the paralysis, but it wasn't just that. He wanted to be back in that garden: he wanted to help Keldra push the button. His and Keldra's and Gabriel's hands on the button, pushing down together.

'You always said . . . ' he panted. 'You always said, "You should have fought".'

Her chuckle echoed along the corridor. God damn her, she was *enjoying* this.

'Yeah, well, I changed my mind. Maybe I learned something from you. You run away now, Jonas. I don't give a damn what you want. I want you to live.' The servitors were dragging him through the servitor barracks now. Corpse-like faces looked at the floor, not reacting as he was whisked past. 'I had a think about what you said,' Keldra continued. 'That I want someone here to watch. Well, I don't just want you to watch. I want you to *remember*, and that means you have to survive. They'll see the explosion from Belt Three. When people talk about it, I want you to know that it was *me*.'

Jonas had reached the transit hub. The door to the shuttle bay was open, and so was the hatch leading to one of the shuttles. The servitors dragged him into the room and towards the hatch. He struggled, momentarily breaking free. He wasn't thinking clearly; the memory of Servitor-Ayla's brief shuttle trip flashed into his mind and, for a moment, he was convinced that Keldra was going to launch the shuttle and then shoot it down. The zap of a nerve gun shock made him flinch, and the servitors managed to grab him again. They forced him down feet first into the cramped shuttle and slammed the hatch closed. The shuttle's internal door slid shut beneath the hatch and sealed; two airtight barriers between him and Keldra in her garden.

The shuttle interior was coffin-like, with just enough room for a single occupant to lie on their back. Jonas could feel objects packed around him. It was dark and very warm. He hammered on the tiny window above him.

'Let me out!'

Suddenly, he was weightless. He stopped pounding on the window and lay still, sweat clinging to his face. Through the external window he saw the *Remembrance of Clouds* fall away above him, the docking hatch quickly vanishing as the ring rotated. The surface of the ship was glowing gold, every millimetre of it furiously trying to radiate the built-up heat; Jonas knew that his little shuttle would be similarly glowing. Both grav-rings came into view, whirling past one another, the supports that connected them to the spine warping in the heat. The patch over the damaged section of the first ring stood out darkly. The observation blister was crumpled in on itself, its windows shattered and melted. The Earth mural on the cargo bay was peeling, strips of bare metal seeming to add new golden-grey cloud bands to the painted planet. The reaction drive was still flaring, sputtering unevenly, the heat fins surrounding it glowing white-hot.

Jonas found himself holding his breath as the *Remembrance* shrank into starless darkness. The shuttle was almost silent, the whirr of its miniature hab system nothing compared to the creaks and groans of Keldra's ship.

The shuttle shook and clattered as a mechanism activated somewhere in the recesses to the sides of where Jonas lay. He saw a flash of gold through the window, a glimpse of movement as if of an insect's wings unfurling. He felt the shuttle spin around through a half-circle, and then felt a violent tug as gravity returned, about a full gee. Above him the *Remembrance of Clouds* came back into view, mirrored and distorted, floating in a golden haze. He was seeing its reflection in a sail, he realized. The sail wasn't quite perpendicular to his eyeline, so he couldn't see the reflection of the shuttle itself, but he could see behind it as the light pressure pushed it starward.

'There never was a tear in the sail,' he said out loud.

'Fooled you!' Keldra's childish, triumphant voice rang close in his ear through the shuttle's speakers. 'I picked up some of your lying bastard ways. You could always fool anyone but you never thought *I'd* fool *you*.'

He couldn't help smiling. 'Clever.'

'You've got three months of supplies, enough for you to reach Belt Three, if you ration yourself. It won't be comfortable, but you'll survive. There's a distress beacon. Someone should pick you up in Belt Two or Belt Three. After that, it's up to you.'

Light flooded into the shuttle, suddenly, hitting Jonas like a wave. The darkness the *Remembrance* had been receding towards hadn't been space; it had been the Worldbreaker cluster, dwarfing the ship as it made its final kamikaze approach. The shuttle had fallen out of the cluster's shadow now, and the sun had become visible, filtered down to a non-lethal level by the shuttle's window, but still unbearably bright. The *Remembrance* seemed doubly tiny, barely visible against the filtered brightness.

'What do you mean, it's up to me?' Jonas asked.

Keldra's voice was starting to crackle, the electromagnetic interference from the sun already taking hold. 'You said you wanted to achieve something great. Cooper said something about that, too, about how you want to prove yourself to your dead lover? Well, you still can.'

'What? The belts are dying. There's nothing left.'

292

'Think of something. You have skills I don't. I don't care what you do, but I won't let you claim this as your great achievement. This is *my* blaze of glory, Jonas. Get your own.'

The *Remembrance* was tiny now, visible only in the light of its own reaction drive flame. Jonas could see the silhouettes of the Worldbreakers swarming around the cluster: the ordinary Worldbreakers, the shipyards, the solar collector petals. Calmer now, he shuffled around in the shuttle, feeling the space. There was just room enough for him to lie flat and move his arms. His fingers found packets of food, a water teat, and a miniature toilet system like that of a vacuum suit. He was glad he wasn't claustrophobic.

'Goodbye, Keldra,' he said.

'Goodbye, Jonas. It's not long now. The explosion should give you a boost.'

'Thank you, for sending me off. I'll try to do . . . something.' The words sat heavily on his chest after he said them. Now he would have two ghosts to satisfy, Gabriel's and Keldra's, but he couldn't help making the vow.

'This still doesn't redeem me.' Keldra sounded annoyed at his thanks, although it was getting hard to tell through the interference. 'I'm not doing this because I like you—Jonas, do you see that? Jonas!'

He squinted at the tiny reflection. More shapes were moving across the dark face of the cluster, visible as flattened green five-pointed stars, pentagonal faces opening. They moved towards *Remembrance of Clouds*.

'Worldbreakers, moving towards you,' he said.

'They've changed course!' Keldra yelled, her voice vanishing into distortion. 'They've noticed me! *Do you see that, Jonas? They've noticed me!*'

293

'I can see a dozen of them,' he said. 'They're closing on you, but . . . '

'But they're too late!' He could hear tears in her voice: wild, furious, triumphant. 'This is it! All right, you robot bastards! You stole my clouds, and you don't steal from a fucking thief! You *don't steal* from *me!*'

Keldra vanished in a burst of static and light. The window went white, its filter barely coping with the sudden brightness. The shuttle lurched and Jonas felt as if he was being pulled apart as the gravity wave hit him: the micro-scale variations in the gravity field weren't enough to destroy the shuttle at this range, but they made it shake.

When the light dimmed to its previous level, a crater had appeared in the near face of the Worldbreaker cluster, its edges ragged and glowing green and red. Shards of the cluster, dormant Worldbreakers that had been part of the construction, spun off into space. Cracks spread out from the crater, wrapping around the cluster as it began to split up into chunks. The entire mass was visibly receding, given a nudge towards the sun by the gravity bomb. Worldbreakers swarmed around, green mouths opening, but they were too late: it was falling into the sun faster than they would be able to retrieve it. Jonas felt a surge of triumph. He tried to punch the air, but his fist hit the wall of the shuttle. They had done it! Keldra had done it!

None of the Worldbreakers were approaching his shuttle. He lay back, closed his eyes, and breathed deeply. There was a steady pull of acceleration gravity from the sail, about one gee, making him feel as though he was back on the *Remembrance*. That would drop off as the shuttle got further from the sun, but it should give him enough speed to reach the inhabited belts before the supplies ran out.

He felt calm, and for the moment, even happy. He had a new lease of life, and an extra ghost to appease. He would have plenty of time to think of something on the journey back to Belt Three.

Epilogue

The ship was a kilometre-long iron-grey lozenge, most of its mass made up by a hollowed-out Belt Three debris shard. The only colour was an enormous mural that stood out on its side: a blue circle, filled with spirals of green and white and grey.

'Mr Reinhardt?' The speaker was Strell, Jonas's latest Administrator-caste assistant. A fresh-faced young man, always impeccably dressed, as if anything he wore turned into a uniform.

Jonas straightened up in his chair. It was a big, faux-leather executive chair, surrounded by a ring of gleaming control panels. He'd had it constructed himself, in the executive suite at the bottom of his starscraper. His own control nest.

He didn't leave the chair much these days. He wasn't paralyzed, he was just getting too old to move around comfortably. For the last few years, he'd been reduced to a figurehead, he knew, riding on top of the wave he'd set in motion when he'd returned from the sun. It didn't matter. The project would still achieve its goal.

'I'm sorry, Strell,' he said. 'I was belts away.'

'It's time, sir,' Strell said. 'Everything's in place. We thought you should give the order.'

'Thank you.'

Jonas took a deep breath; he felt as if he had to be in the right frame of mind for this. He surveyed the ship on the screen again, and pulled the view back to take in its sister ship. He had only been able to raise enough money for two ships. He would have liked to build more, but as long as one completed its mission, he would have succeeded.

Both ships bore the Earth mural on their sides, the only decoration he'd given them. It would have eroded away by the time they reached their destinations, but he thought it was an important symbol for people to see as the ships departed. Apart from the Earth murals, the surfaces were bare, all the delicate equipment safe behind radiation-and micrometeorite-proof shells.

The ships had no rotating segments, and no external windows. Their interiors wouldn't be pressurized during the journey. These were ghost ships, cities of the dead. They were filled with thousands of cloning towers, enough to found several new belt cities, and an army of robots reverse-engineered from the ones that had survived on the *Aurelian*. They would lie dormant, like seedpods, for thousands of years. By the time they sprouted, humanity in the sun's belts would be long dead.

Jonas pulled a microphone from his nest and began the broadcast.

'Ladies and gentlemen of the project, the time has come,' he said. 'I would like to thank every one of you for your selfless dedication to our cause. I know that some of you think that you've been working on some rich true-born's folly, a colossal launching of money and resources into the void. I thank you for your work anyway. Others of you understand that we have been working for a higher purpose, for a result that none of us will live to see. Thanks to your efforts, the human race will escape the Worldbreakers and live new lives around new stars: not on belts, but on planets, under cloud-filled skies.'

He felt his voice cracking at that last phrase. He closed his eyes and paused to compose himself before finishing his speech. The ships' names had been chosen years ago, but the formality remained; the names were indulgent on his part, but everyone in the project had been happy to allow an old man his nostalgia. 'I name these ships the *Gabriel* and the *Keldra*,' he said. 'May whatever god exists watch over them and guide them to their destinations. Unfurl the sails.'

Strell was beaming with pride. On his nest's audio feeds, Jonas could hear members of the project applauding.

He sat back to watch the ships. He wanted to see every moment of this departure, and this time his view came from a space-based camera drone, so there was no chance that the city's rotation would hide an important event from his sight.

Slowly, the sail bud at each ship's nose opened, and the golden sheets spread out like insect wings or the petals of two infinitely complex flowers. Smaller ships, the project's armed cruisers, fired up their reaction drives; they would escort the seed-ships until they were safely clear of Belt Three and out of range of pirates. Almost imperceptibly, the seed-ships began to accelerate, tiny bursts from thrusters pushing them onto the correct courses, starward, and away from the plane of the ecliptic.

'You should have run,' Jonas whispered to himself as the seed-ship *Keldra* slid across his screen. 'You always fought. You should have run.'

Acknowledgements

I have found communities of writers invaluable in my journey as a writer. I would therefore like to thank everyone from the Cambridge NaNoWriMo group, without whose encouragement this book would not have been finished, and the Cambridge Writers of Imaginative Literature, without whose feedback it would not have been worth reading. I would also like to thank the writing group of the Durham University SF+F Society, for helping with my earlier stories, and my parents, for indulging my very first.

I would like to thank everyone at Harper*Voyager* UK (especially Natasha Bardon, Eleanor Ashfield, and Rachel Winterbottom) for believing in my book and helping to shape it into its current form.

Finally, I would like to thank Katia Bowers for immeasurable emotional support.

9 780008 120467